BURNLEY AND PENDLE ARCHAEOLOGY

PART ONE

Burnley and Pendle Archaeology

Part One

Ice Age to Early Bronze Age

JOHN A CLAYTON

Copyright © John A Clayton

ISBN: 978-0-9570043-3-7

All author and publisher rights reserved. No part of this publication may be reproduced or transmitted in any form by any means, electronic, mechanical, photocopying or otherwise, without the prior written permission of the author or publisher.

Plans, maps, photographic images and diagrams are intended for illustrative purposes only. Neither the author nor the publisher accept any responsibility for mapping information implied within this book: no legal right-of-way over land or water is implied or affirmed within any maps, diagrams or illustrations.

Neither the author nor publisher accept any responsibility for the action or actions of any individual, group or groups acting in consequence of information supplied in this book.

Photographs, maps and plans © the author unless otherwise stated. LiDAR data is copyright to the Environment Agency and cannot be re-used in any form without prior permission.

Spring 2014

www.barrowfordpress.co.uk

British Library Cataloguing in Publication Data.
A catalogue record for this publication is available from the British Library

Acknowledgements

Pendle Borough Council, through their **General Small Grants Fund**, has sponsored the initial print run of this book and this is very much appreciated.

Special thanks are extended to my ever-patient wife, Sylvia.

I am also indebted to the landowners who have kindly allowed access to sites across the Survey area and provided invaluable local knowledge. Not least among these are David Chadwick, the Chadwick family, Roy Foster, Julian Spencer, Sylvia Clayton, Bev Lancaster, Philip Sanderson, Colin Nutter, Ruth Nutter, David Ormerod and Mr. and Mrs. Atkinson.

Stanley Graham B.A. has been generous, as always, in allowing access to his research notes.

Thanks also to Peter Rutkowski whose enthusiasm for the geographical extent of early kingdoms knows no bounds. His input of geographical data is much appreciated.

The help of all the local people who sponsored LiDAR data in order to facilitate the Survey is also much appreciated. This also applies to the Environment Agency for their excellent service and for allowing the reproduction of LiDAR imagery.

Individuals and groups have played their part in gathering evidence across what can be an isolated landscape. Here I must thank Mark Chung for his forays into the wilds of Boulsworth, the *Pendle History Society* and the *Friends Of Wycoller*. Thanks also to Nick Todd for his knowledge of the area around his home on the Castercliffe hillfort and for access to the artefacts he has uncovered there.

The Heritage Trust Northwest (Pendle Heritage Centre) are gratefully acknowledged for allowing access to the Peter Whalley flint assemblage.

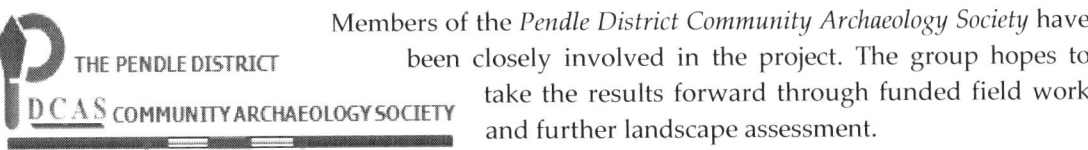

Members of the *Pendle District Community Archaeology Society* have been closely involved in the project. The group hopes to take the results forward through funded field work and further landscape assessment.

Thanks also go out to the numerous people who have been of great help in one capacity or other along the way – if I have not mentioned you by name this does not imply that your input is any less worthy.

John A Clayton
Barrowford
Spring 2014

The English landscape itself, to those who know how to read it aright, is the richest historical record we possess. There are discoveries to be made within it for which no written documents exist, or have ever existed

To write the history of the English landscape requires a combination of documentary research and of fieldwork, of laborious scrambling on foot wherever the trail may lead

The result is a new kind of history which it is hoped will appeal to all those who like to travel intelligently, to get away from the guidebook show-pieces now and then, and to know the reasons behind what they are looking at . . . .
The landscape is full of questions for those who have a sense of the past

W.G.Hoskins

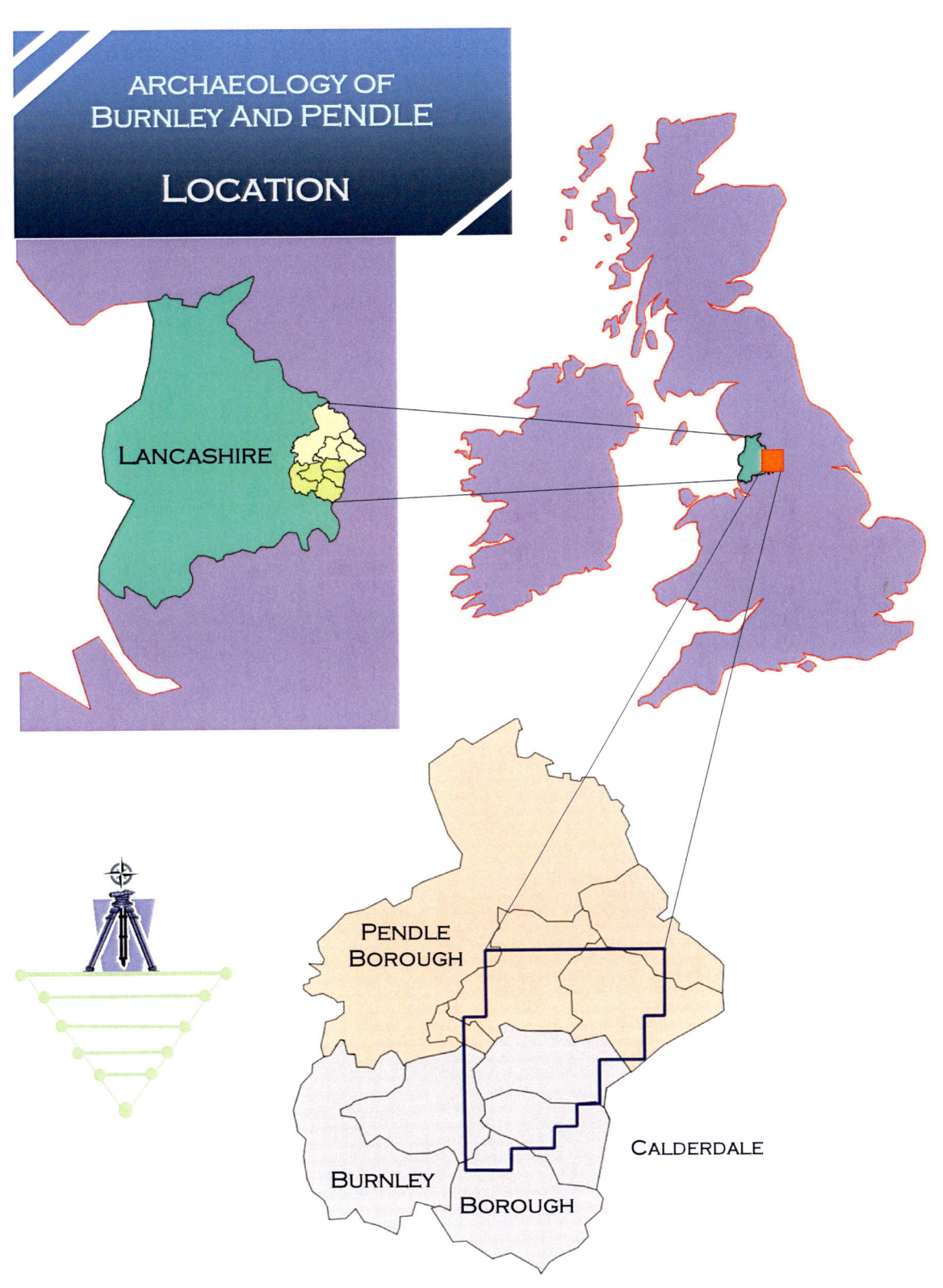

PENDLE HILL
FROM THE PENDLE RIDGEWAY

Contents

Preface		13
Introduction		15
Chapter One	The BNC Survey	23
	LiDAR	24
	Project Location Grid	32
Chapter Two	The Survey in Archaeological Context	33
	Archaeology and History	33
	Social Revolution	40
	Archaeology of Mind	42
	Discussion	46
Chapter Three	Palaeolithic	47
Chapter Four	Mesolithic	51
	Flint Scatter Sites	54
	Regionality	61
	Social Distribution	78
	Territorial Patterns	84
	Discussion	103
Chapter Five	Neolithic and Early Bronze Age	108
	Stone Axes	116
	Later Neolithic	122
	Barrows	124
	Celestial Landscape	162
	Ringworks and Circular Monuments	191
	Discussion	208
Conclusion	Discussion	212
Bibliography		220
Index		222

BOULSWORTH HILL
LOOKING OVER WYCOLLER DENE

PREFACE

The general subject area covered within the following text forms a landscape block within the northern extremity of the district now known as the Southern Pennines. The area covers approximately 180 square kilometres of richly diverse land and this can be roughly divided into two distinct landscapes. From the western slopes of Boulsworth Hill the land takes the form of a series of linear plateaux descending into the surrounding river valleys created by Pendle Water to the north and the River Calder to the south. Interspersed by ridges and rolling hills the plateaux extend beyond the upland peat cover and are generally utilised as Grade III and Grade IV grazing land.

Boulsworth Hill is the name applied to the twelve square kilometres covered by the bulk of the hill while Lad Law is the name given to the highest point of the hill (517 metres at the summit). The Lancashire-Yorkshire county boundary traverses the eastern hillside and from here the landscape of the Yorkshire district of Calderdale takes a different form to the neighbouring area of Lancashire. Western Calderdale forms part of our subject area and the terrain here alternates sharply between tracts of moorland, occupying the 200 metre to 350 metre contour levels, and the uplands proper reaching from 350 metres to over 450 metres.

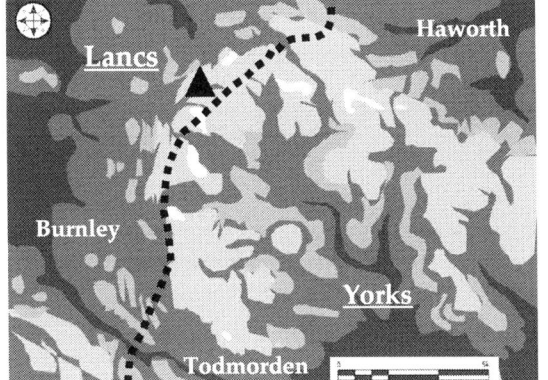

Fig: 1 ▲ *Lad Law* ▪▪▪▪ *County boundary*

Darkest = 100-200m   Lightest = 400m +

Traditionally these combined areas have been something of an archaeological 'no-man's-land.' While the secrets of the long-hidden past of more fortunate districts of Britain have, for generations, been bursting from the soil and filling the pages of archaeology books and magazines the surface of our subject area has hardly been scratched.

There are diverse reasons for the dichotomy of recorded archaeological evidence between our district and other areas of the country. In consequence of ancient human migration from the Continent into good quality grassland, we see a mass of historical data relating to the prehistory of places such as the counties to the north and west of London. In contrast the Burnley and Pendle archaeological record is sparse.

Initially, Palaeolithic and Mesolithic settlers from the Continent travelled into, and across Britain in order to find suitable hunting and foraging grounds. Following a sustained rise in sea levels Britain became isolated from the Continent and the transient visitors became settled across the Isles - the old migration routes became inter-settlement trackways as populations expanded.

The well-drained and level nature of the southern terrain provided a highly suitable base on which the Neolithic and Early Bronze Age people could build their impressive stone and wooden ritual structures: massive engineering projects were carried out and sites such as Silbury Hill and Stonehenge (both Wiltshire) have cast their long cultural shadows into the modern era.

From the end of the last Ice Age a strong trading network existed throughout southern England and this, coupled with good soil, temperate climate and lack of arduous terrain meant that the archaeology of subsequent cultures was steadily laid down.

Winding forward to the modern era it is little wonder that almost two centuries of modernisation have seen the discovery of a large number of ancient sites across the southern wealds, wolds and plains of England. From the latter quarter of the twentieth century, through to today, archaeologists working on the construction of roads and large developments have unearthed a mass of evidence relating to the lives led by our ancient predecessors.

In comparison, Lancashire, and the Pendle/Boulsworth area in particular, have seen little urban development. While the western fringe of the district rapidly expanded from a series of small riverside settlements into the conurbations of Burnley, Nelson and Colne the upland subject of our study survives as a relatively untouched swaithe of marginal dairy and moorland sheep grazing land. No motorway, supermarket or housing development has brought teams of archaeologists onto these moors and for this we must be thankful.

While it may be true that a handful of archaeological surveys have been carried out locally these have taken the form of limited target assessment of water pipeline routes and subsequent watching briefs. However, an archaeological assessment of the prehistory of the whole district is long overdue – not simply to firm up the record but to *create* it where possible.

INTRODUCTION

Born and raised in the shadow of 'Tum Hills,' as the Iron Age hillfort of Castercliffe (on the boundary of Nelson and Colne) is known locally, I have always been fascinated by this enigmatic site. The bulk of the hillfort dominates the Colne and Pendle Water valley and, as a young lad, I distinctly recall its silhouette, shadowy against the brightness of the rising summer sun. It would not be until many years later, however, that I would come to recognise the historical and cultural importance of the Castercliffe site and, indeed, the wider landscape of my neighbourhood.

I was involved in a landscape archaeology project (managed by *Oxford Archaeology North* for the *Pendle History Society - 2010-2011*) covering part of the Pendle Forest district of East Lancashire. It was during this two year survey that I realised the value of aerial LiDAR imaging within archaeological surveys.

During the autumn of 2012 the *Pendle District Landscape Archaeology Society* was busy carrying out an assessment excavation on a water mill site in the Boulsworth area and this rekindled my long-held intention to carry out a cohesive assessment of this ancient landscape. It was decided that the time was right to finally instigate a survey and so the *Burnley, Nelson and Colne Upland Archaeology Survey* came into being in January 2013.

In 2005 Lancashire County Council published an assessment report based on the town of Nelson (*Lancashire Historic Town Survey Programme* - P.14) in which it was stated that: '*Little archaeological work has ever been undertaken in Nelson and no below-ground investigations have ever been carried out.*'

However, this limited archaeological record is not reflected in neighbouring parishes; it is known, for example, that a large cluster of ancient burial monuments exist on the Worsthorne moors. This area of Burnley falls within the south-eastern area of the Survey project and it was clear that the number of *previously* recognised ancient features here diminished in direct proportion to the distance travelled north through the Boulsworth area.

By and large this district, between Boulsworth Hill and the Nelson and Colne urban fringes, was able to boast of the Walton Spire (no surprises here as the four metre menhir stands out like a sore thumb), the Castercliffe hillfort, a couple of lost urn burials at Catlow, a flint knapping 'workshop' on Boulsworth, a possible stone cairn in the northern extremity of Wycoller and a scatter of early stone implements. All-in-all, not a large number of sites for an area of landscape covering one hundred square kilometres.

It is fair to say that Boulsworth is not alone in this lack of record – traditionally Lancashire as a whole has not fared well in the understanding of its ancient past. Thankfully there is hope on the horizon as archaeologists are beginning to address our lack of knowledge of the movement, settlement patterns and culture of Mesolithic and Neolithic populations within the county (see; Barrowclough, D. *Prehistoric Lancashire*. History Press 2008).

Migration and settlement throughout the prehistoric period are key features within any ancient landscape: the inter-relationship between districts, countries and kingdoms shaped the landscape, attitudes to the dead and the correlation between people and their surroundings. Difference in ritualistic practice set communities apart while the need for trade, a fresh gene pool and communal defence saw cohesion in an otherwise competetive environment.

The material framework of these societies has survived in varying degrees and it is the work of the archaeologist, with the aid of supporting sciences, to recognise long-lost societies - to tease-out and tell the story of their cultural practises and their self-perception within a world where 'magic' preceded science.

Modern archaeological methodology has developed to the point where wide-ranging excavation of sites is rarely undertaken as a first principle. There is a general consensus among professionals that the invasive nature of excavation can often lead to the destruction of invaluable evidence. Commonly, this evidence takes the form of stratification and the context provided by biomaterial, ecofacts and artefacts. The removal of volumes of material from a site means that all stratified contextual and associated evidence within the excavated area has been compromised.

In an ideal scenario it would be possible to fully assess any archaeological site by means of non-invasive methods. The advances made in digital and chemical surface techniques promise much for the future of non-invasive methodology but it is fair to say that the profession is not yet at a stage where strategic evidence of excavation has been fully superseded by its technological cousins.

Long before assessment of a site begins it is often the case that all relevant features would have been subjected to a *desktop study*. Here, the resources available to the researcher can be employed to scan the landscape and plot any particular feature that could be of archaeological interest.

DESKTOP STUDY

Common resources:

o   Maps

A primary resource for the location and exploration of sites. Valuable for indicating changes occurring over time. Can be used to fix a site within a context of geography and topography. Specific land-use maps can indicate early boundaries and field names show land use

o   Historical Documents

Useful where a site has been previously assessed and recorded. Early sites are unlikely to appear in the written record but those dating from the latter part of the Medieval period onwards often benefit from an increase in written land-based records.

o   Legal Documents

Tax records – economic records – land-exchange deeds – wills - pictorial records – written accounts – archaeological records. Repositories for these are commonly the County Record Offices, libraries, Council Planning Offices, Sites and Monuments Records, Heritage Environment Records and National Monuments Records.

o   Aerial Photography

Satellite technology has transformed this valuable resource both in quality of image, accessibility and cost. Air images are widely available in many formats including satellite data, sub-metre LiDAR technology and infra-red sensing.

Surface Survey Technology

Useful in the provision of information relating to the background and location of sites. Allows for a specific and structured methodology in the search for archaeological evidence. Techniques include:

- Field walking

Useful in finding traces of unknown sites and for consolidation of artefact patterns across a known site.

- Geographic Information Systems (GIS)

These are powerful databases capable of storing large amounts of information relative to a particular site or sites or extended geographical areas on a global scale. Can include information on geology, demography, topography, vegetation, water systems, GPS and archaeological information. Existing site plans can be accurately added to maps and overlaid with new information.

- Geochemical and Botanical Prospecting

Chemical soil-sampling can pin-point areas of former human and animal activity through study of tiny mollusca and rodent bones. Palynology provides information relating to pollen diagrams to inform the study of environmental change. Often a combination of these sciences can help to pinpoint archaeological features such as burial mounds within a specific environment.

- Geophysics

Depending on ground structure, and the type of site under investigation, geophysical equipment can allow for the detection of magnetic and electrical anomalies in order to build an accurate picture of a site without the need for excavation.

- Auger Sampling

Provides immediate evidence of soil strata beneath a site along with insect, pollen, snail and grain samples at specific depths.

SURVEY AREA - DESCRIPTION

The Burnley, Nelson and Colne Upland Survey takes the form of a desk and field based survey with particular emphasis on the data supplied by LiDAR, satellite and standard aerial imaging. Initially the geographic limits of the Survey were set in accordance with an eight kilometre strip stretching from the natural landscape boundaries formed by Wycoller Dene in the north and the Cliviger Gorge in the south - the edge of the Burnley, Nelson and Colne urban conurbation set the western limit. A line roughly along the ridge of Boulsworth Hill separated the Survey from neighbouring Calderdale as this corresponds with the limit of local one metre LiDAR availability.

As the Survey progressed, however, it became clear that the archaeology within the western district of Calderdale formed an integral part of the initial Survey. With this in mind it was decided that this area should be included as an extension - the main problem being that only two metre and five metre resolution LiDAR images are currently available for this district. Nevertheless, the data from these has proved very useful. For the sake of clarity throughout the following text the initial BNC Survey area will be referred to as the *One Metre Survey* and the Calderdale area will be the *Two Metre Survey*.

The rural landscape within the northern half of the One Metre Survey rises from the periphery of Nelson and Cone and then sweeps towards the rugged moorland plain forming the western base of Boulsworth Hill. This plain runs from its northern head at Brink Ends Moor, above the hamlet of Wycoller, and follows south as a glacial scour before plunging into the Thursden Valley. The Boulsworth plain acts as a buffer between the green farmstead enclosures to the south of Wycoller, Winewall, Trawden, Colne and Nelson and the bleak western face of Boulsworth Hill. An impenetrable blanket of peat across the valley and onto the hill ensured that the Medieval farming expansion seen across the lowlands never encroached beyond the eastern edge of the plain.

The lower Boulsworth plain, spreading around the Lancashire hill and into neighbouring Calderdale, provides extensive areas of semi-natural habitats with vegetation dominated by purple moor-grass, mat-grass and cotton-grass. The area dominated by the bulk of the hill supports true upland habitats including peat bogs and upland heath which combine to provide an environment in which bird species such as merlin, grouse, twite, short-eared owl and golden plover flourish.

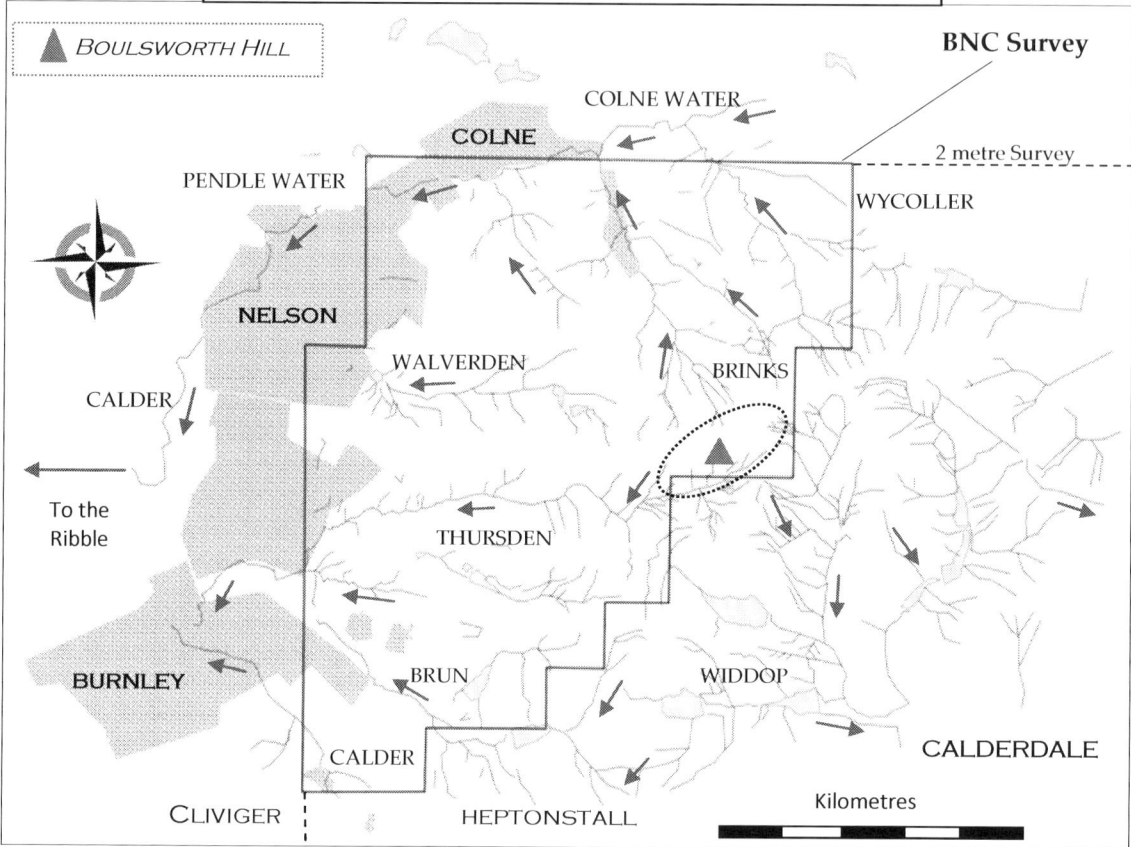

Fig.2 THE BOULSWORTH RIVER DRAINAGE SYSTEM

The Boulsworth plateau is cut by deep cloughs formed by the run-off of numerous moorland streams. Deep Clough and Turnhole Clough drain the Brink Ends Moor into Wycoller Beck and, while this water is ambling through Wycoller, Turnhole Beck tumbles down from the height of Boulsworth Hill. The two waterways are united within Colne Water which becomes Pendle Water at Barrowford. Here, at Reedyford, Walverden Water ends its journey from Deerstone Moor on the Boulsworth plain and joins Pendle Water which soon becomes the Calder.

In the meantime the southern and western Boulsworth moors drain into the river Don which becomes Thursden Water and then joins Swinden Water and the river Brun near Heasandford. The line of the River Calder skirts the southern edge of the Survey areas where it forms a deep valley through Hebden Bridge, Todmorden and Cliviger. The river then flows through Burnley where its joined by the Brun on the final leg of its journey to the River Ribble and the Irish Sea to the west of Preston.

Fig: P3 The north-western Survey area of Wycoller looking across Parsons Leap to Dove Stones Moor. Deep cloughs drain the northern Boulsworth ridge into Wycoller Dene

The post-Conquest Norman overlords established hunting forests within East Lancashire: somewhere around the end of the eleventh century Pendle Forest and Trawden Forest were the designated as hunting 'chases.' Approximately one third of the One Metre Survey is covered by the historical extent of Trawden Forest while Pendle Forest lies to the west, divided from the Survey by the boundary of Pendle Water. The early Norman hunting forests of Pendle and Trawden were replaced around the thirteenth/fourteenth century by the vaccary system when a number of stock breeding farms were created by the overlords. This was the period in which many of the field patterns we see today were introduced. The deer from the old forests were confined to enclosed parklands and the Boulsworth moors. This could possibly be the reason why a number of sites around the hill are known as Deerstones.

Modern agriculture within the survey district is largely confined to small scale dairy farming on the edges of the conurbations and stretching out to the moorland periphery. Recently a herd of Belted Galloway cattle was introduced onto Deerstone Moor and Will Moor within a Boulsworth moorland management scheme. The upper hill slopes are mainly grazed by sheep. Established farmland forms small field patterns enclosed by sandstone and local gritstone walling with occasional runs of post-and-wire fencing. Many local farms historically held common grazing rights over the moorland areas but this number dwindled following Parliamentary enclosure in the earlier nineteenth century – in fact the Boulsworth moorland was the last area within the wider district to be enclosed. The grazing rights are now largely exercised by a handful of farmers.

The Boulsworth valley and hill now form part of a *Special Protection Area* of around 21,000 hectares known as the *South Pennine Moors Phase Two*. Lad Law, the summit area of the hill, rises to 517 m (1,696 ft) at which point it forms a 23 hectare level plateau. Boulsworth is the highest hill within the South Pennine district (the only one to rise above 500m) and shares a formation of millstone grit with its geological parent, Kinder Scout in Derbyshire.

The name of Boulsworth possibly relates to the Old English *bǣl* (beacon) and *worth* (*area on the periphery of established agriculture*). There is a school of thought that the name given to the highest part of the hill, Lad Law, has its root in the Celtic word *Lladd* (slaughter): *Law* is the modern version of the Old English term for *hill* and invoking Druidical connotations it has been said that *Lad Law* means *Hill of Slaughter*. This is unlikely, however, as the Old English word *Lǽd* can mean *boundary*, *track* or *passage* – as will be seen later, Boulsworth possibly marks an ancient territorial boundary and also sits on a series of formerly important early routeways.

Given the number of tracks that once criss-crossed the hill it is perhaps surprising that there was no public access to the hill until the *Countryside and Rights of Way Act* was passed in the year 2000. Access is now possible from the Lancashire and Calderdale sides of the hill.

The BNC One Metre Survey can easily be divided up into its component pattern of small moorland areas – few of which tend to stretch to an area exceeding one square kilometre. Listed from north to south the moors are: *Herders Common: Coombe Hill: Fence Moor: Flake Hill Moor: Dove Stones Moor: Brink Ends Moor: Stack Hill Moor: Brown Hill Moor: Pot Brinks Moor: Broad Head Moor: Bedding Hill Moor: Boulsworth Moor: Will Moor: Red Spar Moor: Widdop Moor: Extwistle Moor: Hameldon Moor: Worsthorne Moor.*

Here we see a large group of moorland sub-districts which serves as an illustration of how the land of the Boulsworth district was initially created. In consequence of a number of local farmers holding common grazing rights over the hill a patchwork of small areas developed to serve each landowner. This contrasts sharply with other moorland areas of Britain where a single landowner might have sole ownership of many thousands of acres.

The BNC Survey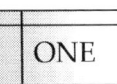

Aims

The basic BNC Survey project remit was to obtain an overview of landscape archaeological features within the sixty three square kilometres of the Survey. One and two metre resolution aerial LiDAR images for the Survey area were obtained and these, along with other forms of aerial imagery and historical records, were employed to record apparent archaeological features. The resulting data were logged and mapped through the facility of GIS and stored in GIS database form for future reference and submission to interested parties (the Lancashire HER project etc.).

The analysis of the archaeological resource involved the quantitative and qualitative evaluation of recorded sites and monuments, followed by the analysis of their location and distribution, highlighting significant patterns or groups.

As we have seen, a second district was appended to the initial Survey - this is the area of Calderdale covered by two metre resolution LiDAR. This Survey extension is vital in the assessment of the archaeological development of the Boulsworth (One Metre) Survey but the lower LiDAR data resolution means that it is not possible to produce accurate landscape archaeological records for this area.

This, then, covers the intent of the Survey in as much as the intention is to provide as much evidence for surviving prehistoric landscape archaeology within the Boulsworth district as possible within the constraints of a non-invasive survey. Although the Survey project is heavily plan-orientated the author, and members of the *Pendle District Landscape Archaeology Society*, have been involved in a great deal of fieldwork to assess possible sites through liaison with landowners, limited GPS site survey and field walking.

The following text aims to place the BNC Survey results within a wider archaeological context - it is hoped to publish all of the detailed Survey maps separately in the near future. The hoped-for outcome, following eighteen months of constant surveying, mapping and recording is that the published Survey results will provide a new insight into the long-neglected ancient history of an ecological and ethnographically stunning landscape. It is further hoped that the project will facilitate the process of local archaeological discovery through interested local public groups and individuals.

Project Method

Aerial Imaging - LiDAR

The BNC Survey was designed to interpret the information provided in aerial LiDAR and standard aerial imaging. A large percentage of Britain has been overflown by commercial enterprise in order to obtain LiDAR (*Light Detection and Ranging*) data at varying resolutions. Basically the finer the resolution the more useful the LiDAR information becomes for archaeological purposes. Sub-metre resolution is available (down to fifteen centimetres) in certain areas of the country and this allows for a far more detailed assessment of landscape features (ditches/banks etc.) than would a resolution of, say, five metres.

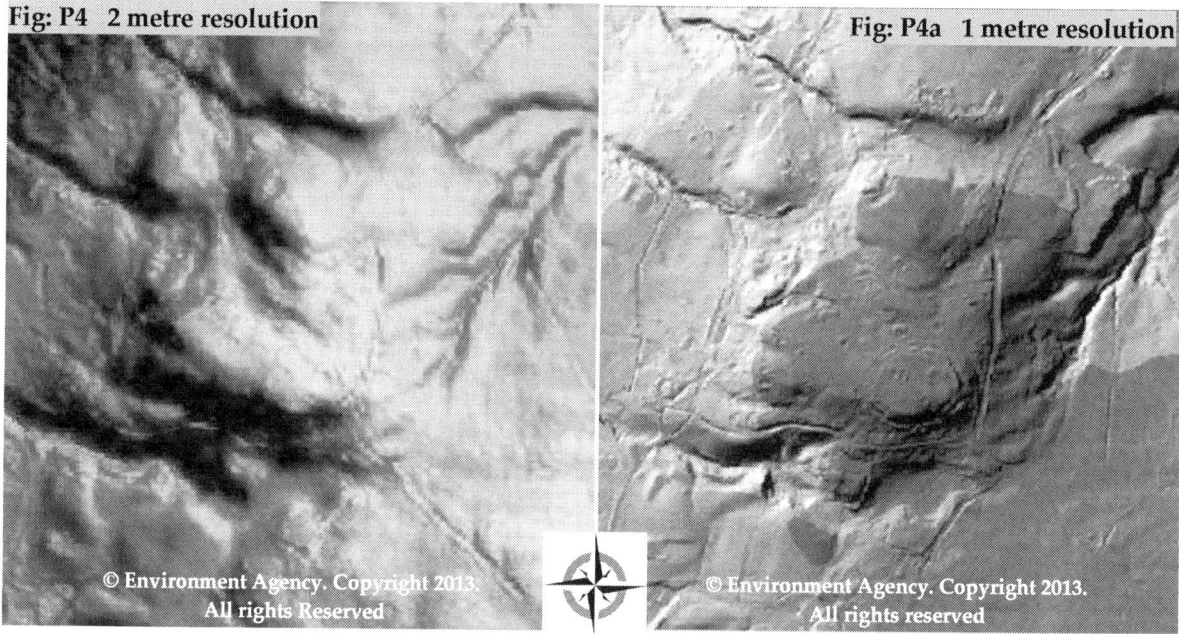

Fig: P4 & Fig: P4a - Comparison of LiDAR data: these images of the Iron Age hillfort at Castercliffe (Nelson/Colne) illustrates the benefits of both two metre resolution (left) and one metre resolution (right).

The two metre surface data accentuates height contrast between hills and valleys and, over a wide area, this can be used to plot glacial erosion patterns to illustrate features such as ridgeways and river systems. The one metre resolution is the preferred data for the BNC Survey as this is the finest resolution available for the survey area and allows for assessment of maximum available detail within the subject landscape

Aerial photography was pioneered in the early twentieth century by O.G.S Crawford and its usefulness within archaeological applications was quickly recognised. However, there are distinct weaknesses within standard aerial photography. The extent to which archaeological features, such as banks and ditches, become visible is dependant very much on external circumstances – the weather, season and time of day all play a significant role in the determination of the quality of images. Under certain light conditions archaeological features can show up in bold relief while a photograph of the same terrain, taken hours earlier or later, might show nothing whatsoever. Further, standard aerial imaging is unable to penetrate, or 'see through' dense woodland foliage but this shortcoming has thankfully been addressed by the advent of laser imaging.

LiDAR data is captured in much the same way as traditional aerial images whereby small aircraft overfly the country in accordance with a set grid system. The difference between the two technologies is that LiDAR generates laser energy to sense the terrain. The laser reflects from the earth's surface in a 'first return' and thus forms a digital 3D image of the ground surface. Where tree cover presents a barrier then a 'second return' is taken and the results are collected at a predetermined height in a *point cloud*. The laser reflection reacts according to the positive and negative height features on the ground: the light reaches the point cloud more quickly from a hill than a valley and the difference in time taken for the light to reach the point cloud is translated into LiDAR data. This can then be manipulated to form digital mapping information (i.e. ASCII files) and images (jpg/tiff etc.).

The resultant image can be manipulated by combining a number of light source angles in order to achieve a single full-relief image. Apparent features can then be assessed and recorded with an awareness of the caveat that some features will prove to be of natural origin while others will be modern and of limited archaeological interest within a prehistorc context. However, the technique is capable of detecting a variety of previously unknown features, such as ancient earthworks and habitation sites, burial mounds, roads and agricultural enclosures.

The LiDAR images are supplied in the basic chromatic set of red, green and blue (RGB) which allows for the manipulation of the image in GIS software by adjustment of colour levels. This provides for enhancement of physical features such as large shallow depressions and low embankments that would not be apparent on the basic LiDAR imagery.

The use of light spectrum layers is also employed in satellite data where military technology is becoming increasingly available to the archaeologist. Global geographic information can now be accessed from the latest satellites, such as Quickbird, and this allows for assessment of the earth's surface at levels ranging from sub-metre to a Continental scale.

Using different spectrum analysis, satellite imaging can be obtained for assessment of various ground elements such as forest and water cover. The near-infrared spectrum is particularly useful for the location of archaeological features in arid areas of the world. An example of this is where a number of lost pyramids and settlements have recently been discovered in Egypt. LiDAR imaging for the UK can be obtained in near-infrared but, given our ground conditions, this is of limited value for archaeological purposes – unfortunately the cost of high resolution satellite imagery to the public is (at present) prohibitive.

Block pixel satellite imagery is readily available online in the form of *raster* data – this is updated on an hourly basis and can be easily converted within GIS programmes to illustrate events (such as wide-scale flooding) across areas covering thousands of miles.

The primary image data employed in the BNC Survey is Digital Surface and Digital Terrain Model LiDAR at a resolution of one metre and two metre and an extent of one square kilometre. However, as is the case with all aerial imaging, LiDAR does have its limitations. It cannot show the crop and soil marks created in fields by the effects of buried wall and ditch features: this is unfortunate as crop and soil marks are among the most valuable indications of hidden archaeology within the landscape.

To address this situation the LiDAR images are used in tandem with the wealth of traditional aerial images available for most areas – these range in date from the earlier twentieth century to the present day. Earlier photographs tend to be of poorer quality but this is compensated for by their historical value.

The standard aerial image is traditionally taken from cameras mounted on light aircraft: the aircraft overflies the area to be surveyed according to a rigid grid pattern of flight lines each of which overlaps by 60%. This allows for adjacent images to be viewed through a stereoscope to enable 3D viewing. By flying at a constant height, and angling the camera straight down from the aircraft, a vertical set of images are obtained at a fixed scale and a constant 180º angle at the centre of each frame.

Where features can be identified from vertical images, or when a known site is to be surveyed from the air, oblique aerial photographs often provide a new perspective. Oblique images are commonly taken from light aircraft by archaeologists using a hand-held camera. Because they are taken at a sub-obtuse angle the images contain inherent distortion due to the curvature of the earth's surface - this means that orthorectification is necessary before the photographs can be used in mapping procedures.

Online sources of aerial imaging include Google Earth, where vertical and pseudo-oblique angles are available, and Microsoft Bing. These are an excellent free resource for quick evaluation of the landscape – Google Earth also includes a handy feature for creating drawings and transforming them into GIS mapping information. The main drawback with most free resource imaging is that the resolution is less than that preferred by the professional archaeologist.

Lancashire County Council have provided an excellent free mapping and imaging service for the county in their *Maps and Related Information Online* programme (MARIO). Through this GIS based system can be found modern interactive maps of the county ranging from 1:1,000,000 down to street level and aerial photographs dating from the 1940s, the 1960s and present day.

Private sources of local air imagery are more common than might be imagined: amateur and professional historians and archaeologists alike often amass individual collections. Some of the aerial images used within this book belong to the author and are extracted from a series of A3 photographs taken from a flyover of the Pendle and Burnley districts commissioned in the late 1980s.

Institutions, such as universities, hold historic aerial archives – these can be difficult to locate but County Record Offices can usually supply details of these.

Alongside the use of one and two metre LiDAR data all of the above aerial resources have been consulted to inform the BNC Survey.

LiDAR data was obtained from the Environment Agency in image rectified format. A map covering the whole sixty three square kilometres of the One Metre Survey area was created in a GIS programme in order to create a ground for vector images. Layers were created to show field boundaries (walls, ditches and banks) as they exist today and, as far as can be found in early maps and aerial imaging, as they were around 250 years previously. Wall lines are represented by a single grey line in the ground maps - no differential is shown between extrapolated field boundaries and extant boundaries as this would tend to over-complicate the map visual.

INTERPRETATION

Today many archaeological projects take the form of desk-based surveys where the surveyor consults aerial photographs and historical records in order to provide an overview of the archaeological potential of a given area. This is a relatively quick and inexpensive method of appraisal and is commonly used in the pre-development stages of building construction and road building.

There are limitations within a desk-based survey, the obvious one being that the surveyor often does not actually visit the survey area. To a degree this does not apply to the BNC Survey; time constraints have prevented site visits to *all* of the apparent features but, as the operatives are based within the Survey area, a number of the sites have been the subject of a preliminary ground assessment. Further, local experience and knowledge of the survey site allows for a certain level of informed interpretation not available to the remote surveyor.

Air photographs provide an overview of the rich history locked within our landscape while the evolution of land-use can be illustrated by a comparison of air imagery, early maps and historical documents. Many subtle archaeological influences can be detected in the images by an experienced surveyor but most people are capable of picking out the basic information, especially with a little practice.

It is commonly known that clusters of nettles can indicate the sub-surface presence of a lost building, or the dumped remains of a building, and this is reflected in the crop, grass and vegetation marks apparent in many air images. Unfortunately, the clay soils and ubiquitous grasslands of our survey district do not provide ideal conditions for the clear crop marks seen in arable landscapes. A filled ditch can provide increased root efficiency in cereal crops, thus allowing the crop above the ditch to grow greener and show as a linear crop mark - unfortunately the grassy clay soils of the BNC Survey rarely provide clear indication of this.

Another caveat relating to the district covered by the Survey is that a large percentage of the agricultural land, and a surprising amount of moorland, has been subject to plough action at some time or another. Constant ploughing has the effect of levelling the ground which means that positive features, such as banks and mounds, are flattened while negative ditch and hollow features are filled in.

Where the air photography captures the exact time when grass lands have been newly mown, or a field recently harrowed and replanted, then soil marks can show lost features as dark patches. Fields untreated by pesticides or commercial fertiliser tend to revert to native flower cover (especially buttercups in grass) and the flower concentration can indicate sub-ground features when viewed from a reasonable height.

In most localities the optimum time to take air photographs is during a period of drought when grass and crop cover is limited. Grass becomes straw coloured and shows indications of buried features not normally apparent.

Where database information is relevant to the Survey area (*Sites and Monument Records* etc.) it has been necessary to build files of coordinates in order for these to be converted into the Survey GIS. Further to this, the period of finds, monuments etc. have been isolated into data sub-groups and this involved the entry of thousands of coordinates. The entry of data has been a very time consuming project and I am grateful to local historian Peter Rutkowski for his help in this somewhat onerous task.

Each one kilometre square LiDAR grid tile was georeferenced to the Survey ground map and any apparent archaeological features were drawn according to type. All available air images were then scanned and, where these provided new evidence, or confirmed the LiDAR evidence, then these were also georeferenced into the ground map in order for any features to be drawn in.

Certain features on LiDAR and air images are difficult to decipher accurately – in particular, field drains and drainage ditches can easily be mistaken for early settlement and field boundaries. Similarly, where soil discoloration and crop marks indicate circular or sharp-edged linear features, care must be taken in assigning these to archaeological origin. Under certain soil conditions vegetation can form regular geometric patterns and these are difficult to distinguish from the vestiges of earlier occupation.

Rarely is any degree of certainty implied within the Survey results – rather, the information is intended to provide a guide to the possibilities of archaeological presence within the Burnley, Nelson, Colne and west Calderdale upland districts. An exception to this is where known sites (as per the *Sites and Monuments Records* etc.) are indicated – in this case the sites will be illustrated along with the relevant providence.

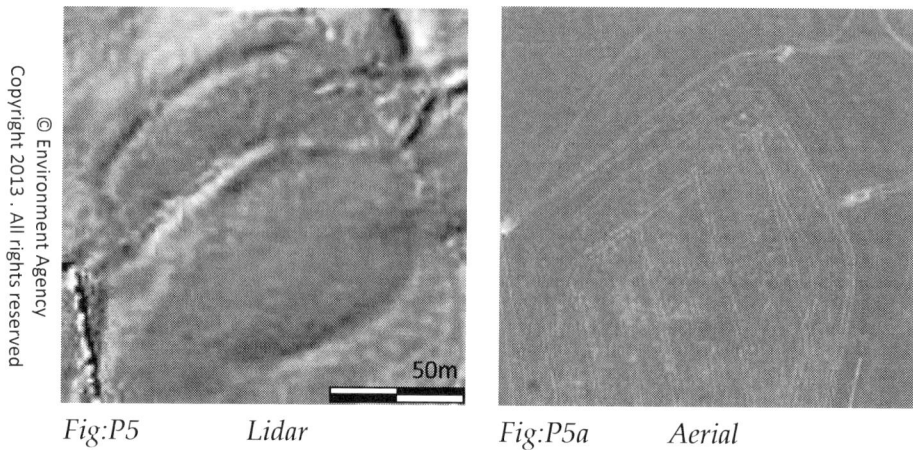

Fig:P5   Lidar   Fig:P5a   Aerial

The images in *Fig:P5* and *Fig:P5a* serve to illustrate the value of LiDAR in highlighting positive and negative features, such as banks and ditches. The LiDAR image (*P5*) is a 150 metre square extract from a one square kilometre tile showing what appears to be an ancient ditched enclosure (possibly a Bronze Age settlement or stock enclosure) on the outskirts of the Nelson urban district.

The ditch has been confirmed on the ground as extending to an original width of some seven metres. There is little indication within the aerial image (right) of the existence of this feature (the lines in this clip were created by tractor activity) – lack of evidence for this feature also applies to the numerous other standard aerial images of this site.

The difficulties in the assessment of aerial data, then, are fully acknowledged within the Survey and this should be accounted for when assuming the existence of features within the landscape. That said, a careful and painstaking analysis of the available data has been carried out by experienced operators and we are confident that the Survey will provide a level of archaeological indication within the Survey district that has never before been attempted or accomplished.

Evidence from artefacts and prehistoric burial customs has shown that the area around Worsthorne and Widdop, a tract of moorland to the south of Boulsworth Hill, appears to have been visited and occupied during much of the post-Ice Age period. This continuity of occupation has possibly extended through to the present day but, to date, has not been particularly evident to the north of Boulsworth Hill where, as we have seen, only sporadic archaeological research has been carried out.

The Lancashire/Yorkshire border follows a route dividing the bulk of the Lancashire section of Boulsworth from its Calderdale neighbour. Only a few hundred metres separate the two valleys but the cultural difference seems to be marked. While Calderdale can boast many carved stone monuments scattered over a wide area, Boulsworth appears to have only two or three examples and these are uncorroborated.

What, then, was the reason (if any) for an apparent difference in culture between the people of Yorkshire Calderdale, the Burnley moors and the uplands of Nelson and Colne? Was it simply that the latter had no population to speak of or were the areas populated in the Mesolithic, Neolithic, Bronze and Iron Ages by people who originated in very different geographic locations? Is it possible that among one community the practice of carving earthbound rocks and boulders with cup-and-ring motiffes was the done thing while their neighbours looked on and sniggered at such strange behaviour?

The archaeological evidence we have to date suggests that our Survey covers an area with undoubted potential for new discoveries (and, therefore, possible answers to the above questions) while the neighbouring district of Pendle, north of Pendle Water, is contrastingly devoid of prehistoric burials, encampments and stone monuments. Is this because the two districts were occupied by people of a different culture - or was the Pendle district somehow unnatractive to early settlers?

How did our location within the Pennines dictate the lives of the people who passed through our area, or the people who decided to put down roots here? How did we relate to the extended districts throughout the north of England, or, indeed, Britain? Research into our past raises many such ethnographic questions and they are not easily answered - to many people, however, this is part of the attraction of archaeology.

Prehistory does not often reveal itself to those who do not make the effort to find the symbology of peoples that we can never truly understand. However, we can at the very least hope to offer a degree of truth when we strive to tell an ancient story. This, then, is the basis on which the results of the Burnley, Nelson and Colne Upland Archaeology Survey are observed.

32

The BNC Project Grid

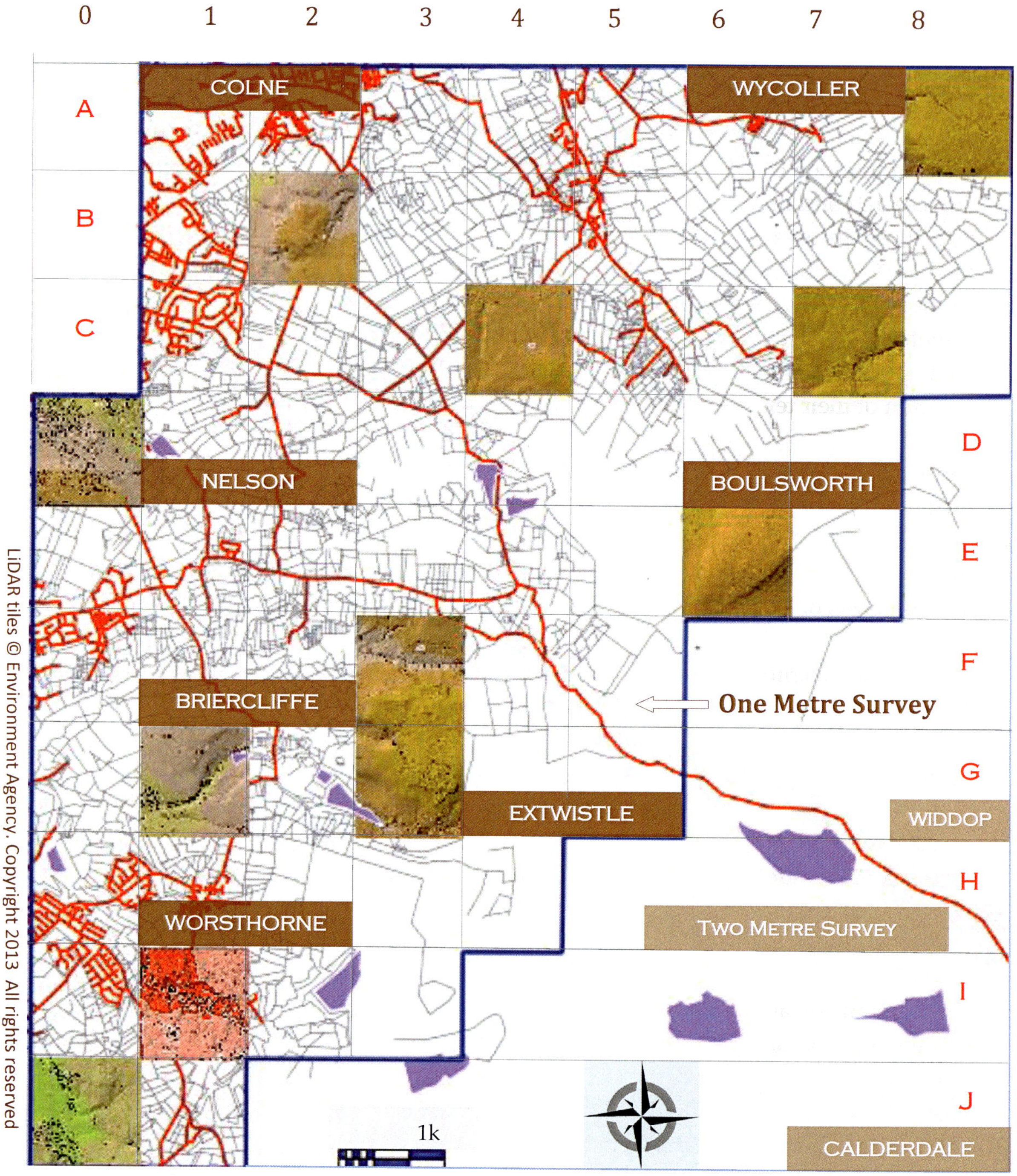

Fig.G5 **CRS WGS84 EPSG 4326**

LiDAR tiles © Environment Agency. Copyright 2013 All rights reserved

The Survey in Archaeological Context

TWO

Archaeology and History

It is fair to say that archaeology and history are two sides of the same coin – it is often the case that one cannot reach its full potential without the other. To a certain extent the research and recording of history was the first of the two disciplines to have been formalised; the studies and observations carried out by Classic scholars paved the way for all future writers of history. From ancient Greece to the Norman invasion of Britain we see that historians were busy documenting the religious, political and military machinations of their particular culture. Furthermore, these scholars also recorded other societies through events that had impacted upon their own culture by means of invasion of their territory or through technological influence.

During the seventeenth and eighteenth centuries a burgeoning interest in British history found a wide audience. Beneath the penumbra of antiquarianism a generic mix of disciplines came to the fore; this led to the embryonic formation of a mutual recognition between the archaeologist and the historian that would eventually lead to the symbiosis of the disciplines that we see today.

There was recognition of the necessity for specialised ideas. The study of artefacts, creation of museums, repository of manuscripts; teaching of the subjects within schools of history and field archaeology were all to play an invaluable part in the expansion of knowledge and skills.

Archaeology, in its basic form, is the study of humanity through the recovery and assessment of identifiable evidence relating to the linear time period between yesterday and the quantifiable limit of human existence. This evidence takes the form of a variety of physical elements - chiefly artefacts (material) and ecofacts (biological). Other means of archaeological assessment are the study of changes within the environment of an archaeological site where human deposition within a particular section of the landscape might differ from the reasonably expected natural state.

History, on the other hand, relies very much on the written aspect of human society and this, by default, is limited through time to the advent of the written record and, arguably, a representation of societies through artistic mediums such as early cave paintings.

The symbiosis of history and archaeology is at its most valuable where the one can test and prove the other. In some cases archaeological sites can be found through the historical records. Where a land record/tax record/map might indicate the existence of (say) a building – and there is no extant physical evidence of that building – archaeology can be employed to uncover traces of the lost feature.

Historical records can provide the approximate location of the building and the archaeology can uncover its exact position. An assessment of the site, using all the tools available to modern archaeology, often provides evidence of its occupation. For example, where historical record might suggest a former use (domestic/industrial/military etc.) then the archaeology is capable of confirming (or disproving) the record. Perhaps direct evidence of a person who lived or worked in the building can be found and dated, through scientific methods, to a narrow date-bracket. This would allow the historian to return to the records and provide a story for that person – and so we see the value of the interaction between archaeology and history.

To the modern eye the early pioneers of historiography were not the ideal conduits through which a fair and broad account of their particular subject or area could be left to posterity. Because these writers were largely from an extremely narrow social background we have to take care in the assessment of the historical content. Philippa Levine shows that the early antiquarian can be said to have belonged to an elite whose numbers were made up of the clergy and the gentry (Levine, P. *The Amateur and the Professional - Antiquarians, Historians and Archaeologists 1838-1886* Cambridge University Press 1986). Levine also shows that a study of nineteenth century history writers illustrates that they were overwhelmingly male and middle class. Very few members of the elite were from a non-Anglian background.

As a consequence of the socially confined nature of early writers our literary historical heritage is heavily biased toward the socio-economic domain of the ruling elite, male professionals, merchants and the landed classes. Things did at least begin to change in the nineteenth century when the former elitist groupings of antiquarianism slowly evolved into a fairer representation of society (albeit still with the general exclusion of women). The professional oligarchy began to give way to a more disparate grouping of, amongst others, merchants, soldiers and traders.

From the fifteenth century we see an emergence of a more standardised approach to historical research and this advancement within the subject carried through to the modern day. An acceptance of the humanist approach, and the nineteenth century devolvement of history from antiquarianism, played no small part in the development of modern history. Of equal importance here was the combination of specialised skills: archaeology, place-name study, topography and cartography all gelled in an invaluable contribution towards the search for our past.

Of these specialities the discipline of archaeology has provided the clearest interpretation of the development of global humanity. However, the archaeologist must always question the bias of any historical source material relating to an archaeological assessment or survey. It would be easy to assume that, in general, the earlier the source the more likely it is to have been skewed in favour of the patron, or patrons, to whom the author was directly answerable. However, true as this might be, we also have to recognise the inherent bias within the modern media and within some publications dedicated to the advancement of specific sections of the scientific corpus. That said, modern archaeology is able to employ a plethora of scientific techniques to reinforce comparative studies of artefacts and ecofacts and this allows for the questioning and reassessment (where necessary) of the historical record

To understand the origins of the prehistoric people within our own environment it is useful to look at the evidence resulting from the work being carried out by palaeoanthropologists and specialists from other disciplines (climate change, palynology etc.) in order to form as accurate a view of the origins of our species as possible:

- 8 to 5 million years ago a split occurred within our common ancestral species

- 4 million years ago Australopithecus (hominid) evolved in East Africa

- 2.6 million years ago – the world's oldest stone tools dating to this period have been found at Gona in Ethiopia although cut marks have been found on bones in Ethiopia dating to 3.4 million years ago

- 1.8 to 1.3 million years ago Homo erectus appeared

- 800,000 to 700,000 years ago saw the appearance of Homo heidelbergensis of the genus Homo which may be the direct ancestor of both Homo neanderthalensis in Europe and Homo sapiens. Early human settlement in Britain has now been dated to 800,000 at Pakefield and 500,000 at Happisburgh (both Norfolk)

- 120,000 years ago – the first modern symbolic behaviour was recorded in sea shells from north Africa

- 30,000 to 40,000 years ago - European art in the Upper Palaeolithic – bone and ivory carvings and musical instruments found in caves in France and Germany include the earliest known human figurine. Creswell Crag caves, on the border of Derbyshire and Nottinghamshire, have the earliest known artistic depictions of animals in Britain.

The *Single Origins Theory* now has a consensus within relevant scientific communities. Some 200,000 to 150,000 years ago the first fossils of Homo sapiens were found in Ethiopia: however, these fall within the outer limits of homo sapien time development and, although classed as Homo sapiens these fossils may not be on direct lineage of modern humans.

Neanderthals and modern humans shared a common ancestor around 800,000 years ago and they co-existed and interbred for a period of some 300,000 years in Africa: for some reason this came to a relatively abrupt halt around 400,000 years ago. The Neanderthals went on to evolve in West Eurasia while humans continued to evolve in Africa. The lineage of modern humans appears to date to around 190,000 to 130,000 years ago.

From the archaeological record it appears that between 160,000 and 170,000 years ago modern humans in Africa were studying planetary movement in order to accurately predict the phases of the lunar month. Before this time it does not appear that people operated any systematic harvesting of coastal shellfish resources. Foraging in the high tidal periods was a dangerous occupation but it was realised that the juxtaposition of the moon and sun affected the tidal phases. At certain times within the lunar month shellfish breeding activity was at its most prolific: further, the majority of the crop lay some distance from the shore. By knowing exactly when the spring tides, and the low neap tides, were due to occur a very valuable source of protein could be gathered safely and predictably.

It is probable that lunar prediction took the form of simple markers in the landscape: wooden posts or standing stones would be erected in a specific geometric association in order to track movement of the planets. This was the first use of the predictive 'observatory engine' that would culminate in the Stonehenge monument. It is very possible, therefore, that migrants from Africa took their knowledge of the cosmos with them when they began to move into Eurasia.

There is another theory (Dawkins, R. *The Selfish Gene* Harper Collins 1978) that the increase in protein and nutrients supplied by the new shellfish harvesting method allowed the brain capacity of modern humans to expand. The increase in cognisance that this created led to a significant advance in tool technology.

By around 71,000 years ago Africans had mastered the technique of manufacturing microlith blades from a local soft-stone called silcrete. In its raw state this material is useless as a tool or weapon making medium – however, it was realised that heating the stone in kilns to an exact temperature over a controlled period of time (around 24 hours) silcrete hardened to a flint-like brittleness. Making microlith blades from the hardened material allowed for projectile weapons (spears and arrows) to be made and, in turn, this allowed for the organisation of groups of hunters and warriors. This microlith technology became common in Europe 20,000 years ago and it is thought that it gave a decisive advantage to Homo sapiens over the Neanderthal population which resulted in their eventual demise.

A long dry spell resulted in the growth of the Sahara Desert across North Africa and this forced the population into the more temperate southern coastal regions. The advancement in communal lifestyle, especially in hunting and fighting, saw the movement of groups over ever-wider areas of the landscape. Eventually, around 60,000 years ago, population expansion, climate change and decreasing hunting grounds, caused an exodus of groups from Africa. Travelling through the Sinai Desert modern humans from the African continent spread out westward and eventually gave rise to all those of Eurasian extraction.

To what exact degree the Homo sapien migrants into Europe interacted with the established Neanderthal population is unclear; what is known is that the immigrants bred with the Neanderthals. Eventually the Neanderthal sub-species became extinct but the genetic pool lives on in the modern population – most of us carry between 1% to 3% of Neanderthal genes.

And so the spread of the modern human population continued across the face of the earth – by 25,000 years ago Palaeolithic people were living in Britain according to the evidence of modern human bones found in the Goat Cave on the Welsh Gower Peninsula. Britain was firmly in the grip of the last Ice Age by about 22,000 years ago and it is thought that man survived across Europe in small scattered communities living in micro-climatic pockets. Traditionally it has been thought that at the end of this glacial period (12,000 to 10,000 years ago) there was a revolution in agricultural practice across the 'fertile crescent' of the Near East and that this eventually spread into Europe.

However, Professor Bill Finlayson (*British Research in the Levant Project*) suggests that the acceptance of a spread of Neolithic farmers from a small core zone is no longer tenable. A synchronistic advancement in agriculture across South-west Asia shows that ceremonial and symbolic architecture has far earlier roots than previously imagined. The roots of this innovation appear as early as 20,000 years ago at an archaeological site known as Ohalo II, on the shores of the Sea of Galilee.

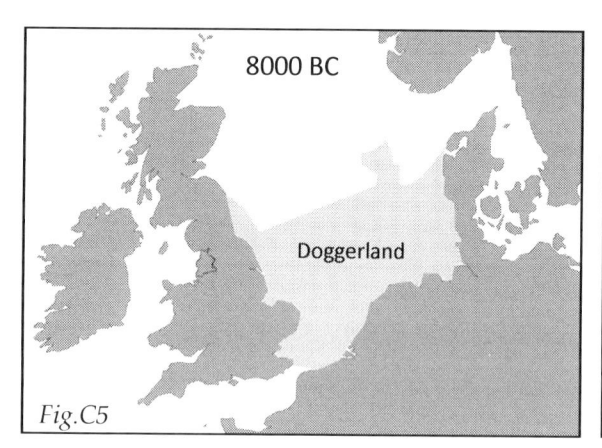

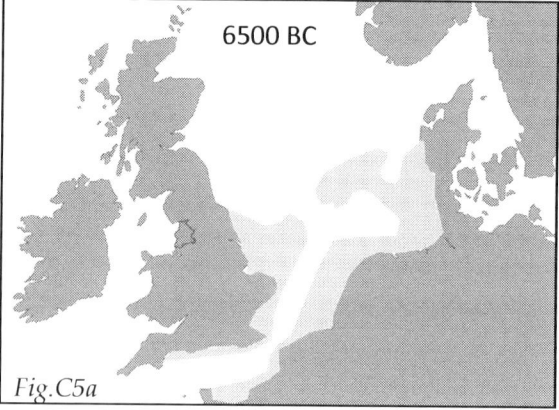

Fig.C5 — 8000 BC — Doggerland

Fig.C5a — 6500 BC

Rising sea levels following the last Ice Age caused the separation of Britain from the continent

Rising sea levels finally separated Britain from the continent between 5,500 BC and 6,500 BC but before this the land bridge can be seen to have been a country in its own right *(Doggerland - Fig: C5)*. Wooded areas and lakes here provided an ideal hunting environment for the Palaeolithic and Mesolithic inhabitants of Europe and they crossed to-and-fro into the British Isles on a regular basis. Even when the sea had covered the land bridge it was still possible to cross the shallow English Channel with relative ease. By around 5,500 BC Britain had finally become an island and the former inter-migration of Europeans changed in favour of an indigenous population.

The Ice Age culture of the Lower Palaeolithic period evolved and the people of the new Mesolithic continued to follow a largely nomadic existence – there were, however, settled sites within the Mesolithic world as evidence at Starr Carr (East Yorkshire) shows a relatively extended occupation throughout much of this period.

The Mesolithic slowly gave way to the Neolithic and it is commonly taken that this is the period in which the foundations of society as we know it were put down. In reality there is no defined cut-off period at the termination of each prehistoric period. Periodic dates are used by archaeologists and historians purely as a datum on which to hang a convenient theory or to quickly communicate a general period. Each subsequent culture - Palaeolithic, Mesolithic, Neolithic, Bronze Age, Iron Age, Roman Iron Age – was born of its predecessor, inherited the mindset of its ancestors and then evolved within its own particular social environment.

Although each period is quantified by a typology of tools, pottery, materials and burial practice, a long transitional period existed where, for instance, Neolithic people were following a Mesolithic lifestyle and metal age people still used the flint tools of their 'stone-age' forebears. The real differences between the ages can be seen over the longer term where archaeological evidence provides an insight into agriculture and the ritual practice of death and devotion. The following table provides a working timeline for British history. Archaeologists further divide each period according to contemporary qualifiers such as tool type, burial type and pottery type.

PALAEOLITHIC	To 8500 BC	Old Stone Age	Hunters	Microlith tools
MESOLITHIC	8500 to 4000 BC	Middle Stone Age	Hunter gatherers	Microlith tools
NEOLITHIC	4000 to 2000 BC	New Stone Age	Early farmers	Stone monuments
BRONZE AGE	2000 to 750 BC	Metal workers	Farmers	Burial monuments
BRITISH IRON AGE	700 BC to 43AD	'Celtic' age	Farmers	Hillforts
ROMAN IRON AGE	43AD to 410AD		Military Occupation	
DARK AGES	450 to 1066 AD	Saxons Scandinavians	Early Medieval	
LATE MEDIEVAL	1066 to 1500 AD			
TUDOR	1500 to 1603 AD			
EARLY MODERN	1603 to 1750 AD			

It is worth noting that these periods are not universal in that the beginning and end of each timeline differs between countries.

Social 'Revolution'

Since the epoch of our evolution in Africa humanity has followed the basic dependant instinct of group function. Initially small family groups would wander the landscape, only interacting with other groups by coincidental meeting or occasional predetermined gathering. The social binding here was the cement of close family ties and this lifestyle abided for a long period. It was not until an increase in population coincided with a reduction in available hunting grounds (through climatic effect) that the tradition of scattered family groups began to change.

The exodus of people from Africa around 60,000 years ago meant that families were channelled along defined routes into new lands. Migrant groups were spatially compromised and over time it became necessary for small groups to combine within a new era of social interdependence. As the new wave of migration slowly pushed into Eurasia nomadic groups consolidated within larger loosely defined cultures. In turn, the post-Ice Age occupation of the British Isles reflected what had now become a spatial shift in cultures, rather than isolated tiny pockets of humanity with no consequence within the landscape.

Wherever the migratory peoples settled in any numbers we see a commonality in the evolved systems of social manipulation. Anatomically modern people developed a unique capacity for symbolic and spiritual thought – they were able to define the boundaries of existence, the individual, the group and the cosmos (Fagan, B. *From Black Land to Fifth Sun* Addison Wesley 1998). Cave art tells us that humans were combining the spiritual and physical worlds at least 30,000 years ago.

Between 20,000 and 10,000 years ago farming societies in Western Asia possessed knowledge of cosmology, and a related belief system, that would be shared across the ancient world. A common principle was that human life existed in the centre of a multi-layered cosmos; the ancestors inhabited the upper layer of the supernatural realms of the heavens and the underworld below. Genesis describes the creation of this universe as a world *without form* (Fagan 1998).

Another shared belief was that the heavens were supported on a vertical axis that linked all the layers of the cosmos. This axis, often symbolised in the form of a tree or 'world pillar', joined the spiritual and living worlds at a sacred centre. The supernatural inhabitants of the otherworlds could be contacted through certain places on the surface of the earth (springs, caves, bodies of water and mountain peaks) or in the heavens where the stars pivoted around the head of the pillar (evidence for this in the Survey area will be covered later). The building of the Egyptian pyramids can be seen as an attempt to create sacred mountains linking the realm of the sun to the world of the living. It was also commonly believed that all the realms of the cosmos were connected as a single entity with no defining boundaries. Landscapes of the earth also existed within the mind and features such as tree groves, springs, mountains and cardinal direction were spiritual entities and, as such, were embedded within the psyche of a community.

Certain people who were thought to possess heightened supernatural powers took the adoption of the external world into the mind a step further. These shamans, or spirit mediums, passed easily into a state of altered consciousness and were able to travel within the spirit worlds. These men and women mediated between the living and the spirits and ancestors. The knowledge of the ancestors in particular was often sought as they were considered to be the guardians of the living and the physical world. When the shaman returned from the spirit world he or she would paint images of the things they had witnessed; there were often scenes of animals and gods and also visions of lines of dots and wavy lines. It is interesting to note that these patterns are commonly found on rock carvings within many parts of Britain.

The experienced shaman was a highly skilled person with the ability to manipulate political activity within the community through wisdom of 'the whole.' He or she was able to keep the cosmos in balance, to influence future events, to cure the sick, to bring rain and to cause or prevent wars.

It was also widely believed that the quality of life was dictated by the nature of the seasons. Study of the cosmos identified the correlation between the movement of the heavenly bodies and the life-sustaining cycle of sowing, growth and harvest. This was expanded to a point where the fundamental life force was governed by the cycle of fertility, life and death. To consolidate this vital perception the spiritual elite engendered a system of ritual and myth: music, dance and poetry were performed in sacred surroundings and the world order was indelibly impressed on the minds of each successive generation. This was the way the people had been subliminally instructed to see their world - they did not question it or wish to change it.

The tribal chieftain and the shaman were omnipotent within structured society. They ensured that the wheels of the universe were well oiled and that the world turned as it was expected to do by the populace. A series of ritual services throughout the year were held in order to maximise the harvest or to coax the sun to return from the underworld in midwinter. In this way everyone was afforded a place in the community and each was dependant on the other – to deviate from this accepted norm was to upset the universal balance and bring down certain death on the individual and devastating consequences on the community as a whole.

So we see that the people who settled within the British Isles following the last Ice Age were the recipients of an evolved belief system whose epoch can be seen around 170,000 years ago in Africa. The necessity of ordering time through the study of lunar cycles created a new awareness of the cosmos and this gradually expanded as the African population spread across Europe and Western Asia. Over a very long period the consequence of settled agriculture allowed for the adaptation of a core belief system and inter-regional exchange created a degree of universal commonality. The builders of the successive phases at Stonehenge, and those who buried their dead in mounds on the Burnley moors, were unknowingly practising a folk-magic handed down to them from beyond the depths of perceptible time.

The 'Archaeology of Mind'

From 4,300 BC the new Neolithic culture created monumental construction projects across Western Europe; the introduction of ritual and religious practice relating to the veneration of the dead was adopted in southern Britain around 4,000 BC and spread steadily northward. Although cultivation of the land, and animal herding, were not exactly new forms of lifestyle to the Early Neolithic people it appears that Britain began to adopt the intensive agricultural practises from the East and this gradually led to the end of their traditional nomadic lifestyle in favour of settlement. By the beginning of the Bronze Age the whole of the British Isles had adopted *settled* agriculture in one form or another.

Traditionally it has been taken that the new patterns of farming introduced a form of *'Neolithic Revolution'* but this should read *European Neolithic Revolution* given that the revolution had taken 16,000 years to gain a foothold in Britain. Once the concept of remaining in one location over successive seasons and years had been adopted a number of related factors came into play. The skeletal communal infrastructure that defines our modern lifestyle began to appear when the Neolithic people created inter-settlement communication: paths and trackways were necessary for people to commute between their settlement and fields. Settlement boundaries were fixed as were field boundaries and this embryonic concept of land ownership remains today.

The old hunting skills were gradually replaced by the skills of the specialist craftspeople required to create and maintain a settled community. Wood and stone workers erected dwellings, fences and storage buildings while others developed skills in stock management and improvement. Grain types were improved to allow for an increase in quality and yield: tool makers made implements more suitable to the new farming methods - and so technology advanced. In some districts the recovery of minerals and materials (such as flint) was carried out on an industrial scale by skilled miners and other specialists were then required to transport the raw material or exchange the implements/utensils/jewellery etc. created from the mined materials by other artisans. Surveyors were also required to quantify and stake out the lands occupied by a community and to settle boundary disputes with neighbouring settlements.

Hunting was still practiced but only on a more localised scale – movement across the landscape, and freedom to kill animals, became more restricted as the land was becoming increasing owned by a rising population. An educated priesthood helped to adapt the mindset of the old ways towards a new way of dealing with the religious and ritual requirements of a farming age. The traditional concepts of looking skyward within a *cult of the cosmos* changed and the spiritual focus became more earth-centric.

The seasons and the climate were now all-important and religion was increasingly concentrated within the landscape. It is possible that the changes in ritual practice that took place over the millennia of British pre-history were in direct relation to the degree of settlement and communal expansion. An expanding regional population would need to be controlled and this would be done through the efforts of an elite who recognised the value of creating a cohesive mindset of 'belonging'. By engendering, confirming and maintaining a common loyalty the leaders within a community ensured that the people of their settlement functioned within the social parameters expected of them.

Architecture was a powerful form of communication to keep the messages of ritual in people's minds. Burial mounds, earthworks, pyramids, temples, menhiric structures and massive earthwork cursors were all highly impressive feats of landscape engineering designed to propound a continuing system of social engineering.

The abiding problem that archaeology has had when it comes to the assessment of cultural belief and practice is the difficulty of placing strange or previously unknown objects within a viable context. Traditionally any artefacts that could not be related to the known were labelled with the generic term of 'ritual' and consigned to a dusty museum shelf.

Around the middle of the twentieth century archaeologists began to question this approach and took their research beyond the material level of ecology and technology. A new scientific methodology for the scientific study of human consciousness was born and became known as the *archaeology of mind*. This methodology is a marriage of cultural systems, theory, settlement archaeology, environmental reconstruction, contextual archaeology and the decipherment of written records (Fagan 1998):

- **Cultural systems theory** assumes human consciousness, cosmology and religious belief touched all aspects of existence and cultural activity

- **Settlement archaeology** is generally a post-War method of shifting focus from single sites to entire regions and landscapes. Entire hierarchies of settlement from ceremonial centres to tiny hamlets. Geographic Information Systems (GIS) has transformed settlement archaeology through large database of archaeological and geographical information which allows for understanding of a myriad of relationships tying art, buildings and individual artefacts to an entire culture or community.

- **Environmental reconstruction** is the close relationship between the way people perceived and exploited their environments and their world view - it makes environmental reconstruction a vital part of the study of the intangible.

  Stone Age man (the hunter-gatherer) was part of the animal kingdom in that he left little imprint on the environment. Farmers drastically modified their environments. Palynology identifies pollen grains from bogs, marshes and Insects can provide archaeological evidence for the use of structures and sites.

- **Contextual archaeology** - artefacts, architecture and art are set in the precise context of time and space and are the ultimate foundations of the archaeology of mind. Stratigraphic observations provide one element of archaeological context. The law of association deals with spatial relationships where finds within a single layer are associated. This is vital to the study of sacred places. Spectographic analysis, and other methods, identify trace elements in artefacts such as glass, volcanic glass and metal objects. This can then identify trade routes and connections between major ceremonial sites.

In oral societies their architecture and art communicated powerful messages. Ethnographic analogy is the comparison between living and ancient peoples - this can be controversial. Direct historical method works backwards and is useful with certain societies displaying a strong contemporary link with their past (such as Pueblo Indians). Ethnographic analogy can provide a broad insight into how people viewed their world as it appears in the material archaeological record.

o **Decipherment of written records** - written record is apparent in such things as decipherment of Egyptian and Myan scripts. Astronomical glyphs provide a mass of cosmological information but general records tend to be biased toward the ruler and the communal point of view as opposed to the view of the individual.

The vast majority of people who have inhabited these islands from the last Ice Age are not visible within the archaeological record and this means that the gaps between the surviving burial evidence must, by and large, remain a mystery. However, the modern archaeological approach has furnished ample evidence to formulate a working hypothesis for what is sometimes called the 'otherness' of our ancestors.

It is certain that early societies all disposed of their dead in some way or other. Modern taboos surrounding the dead are so deeply rooted that it is difficult for the modern mind to relate to the funerary practices of other cultures. We have tangible evidence for the way in which successive cultures within Britain disposed of their dead. The earthen barrows and stone tombs of the Neolithic and Bronze Age people have survived in some numbers across the land and it is certain that many more have yet to be found.

There is an obvious difference between the attitudes of a community who treated the bones of their ancestors as if they were still playing a part in society and the community that cremated their dead and buried them in the ground in small pottery urns.

Burial practice allows archaeologists to create a virtual section through time where the context of burial pattern is used to date a specific culture. Burials, then, are a major resource within the archaeological record. However, knowing how communities buried their dead does not mean that we know why they practiced a particular method. Were methods of disposal of the dead influenced purely by religious belief or were they simply a pragmatic necessity – or perhaps a mixture of both?

Discussion

By and large the archaeology of the BNC Survey covers the 10,000 year period stretching from the last Ice Age to the Roman Conquest. Study of this period can be defined by the landscapes of post-glacial hunter-gatherers and foragers, early farmers, ceremonial monuments, later farmers (field systems and land boundaries) and settlement (enclosure and fortification).

Primarily the Survey is concerned with the archaeology of a Pennine landscape and the people who functioned within it. Can the evidence locked within the landscape provide us with information about long-past socio-political organisation or the exercise of power in the land? To be fair, these are big questions to ask of a largely desk-based study but it is hoped that a sense of the regionality of our ancient forebears can be gleaned from the Survey in order to set the parameters of possible regionality.

Over the past few decades the archaeology of prehistory has shifted from reliance on an approach where a *march-past of cultures* was created by the dating and grouping of artefactual evidence. More recently the science of accurate dating, and a shift in political approach, has led to a pragmatic reassessment of world prehistory. The *otherness* or *strangeness* of our predecessors is adopted by some as a method of separating the socio-political attitudes of those who inhabited our landscape within the long period of pre-textual human existence.

Differences between the sub-groups within each broad cultural period are being increasingly recognised. In some cases only a subtle nuance in burial practice can separate the occupants of a particular landscape while evidence for very different ritual practice between communities can indicate migration patterns and a geographic cultural origin. The beliefs and practises of Middle Bronze Age folk along the West Lancashire coast, for example, have been shown through archaeology to contrast with contemporary societies within the Lancashire Pennine uplands. The land to the east of the Pennines was also populated by people of a different background to their Pennine neighbours - and had done so since the Mesolithic period at least.

This is not to say that the north of England was beset by the tensions of non-compatibility. Up to the onset of the Late Bronze Age it appears that a relatively stable socio-political climate meant that communities, tribes and kingdoms lived relatively peaceably. Sophisticated trade routes knitted together the settlements and economic necessity consolidated an inter-communal political tolerance.

Palaeolithic
2.5 million years BC to 8,500 BC

THREE

47

The Palaeolithic (*Old Stone Age*) began around 2.5 million years ago and, during this long period, a large number of climatic episodes jostled with repeated glacial intervals lasting thousands of years. The final Ice Age of the Palaeolithic (*the Devensian*) ended around 10,000 years ago (slightly later in northern Britain) although, strictly speaking, we are still officially in an Ice Age remission known as the Holocene.

In the Middle Palaeolithic, around 200,000 years ago, human tool making technology advanced through the new *prepared-core* technique. This allowed for the manufacture of controlled and consistent flint flakes thus allowing humans to create the earliest composite hunting tools in the form of spears. Carefully prepared sharp pointed flakes were hafted onto wooden shafts; this method was the pre-cursor of the microlith tools that, as we have seen, emerged in Africa some 70,000 years ago.

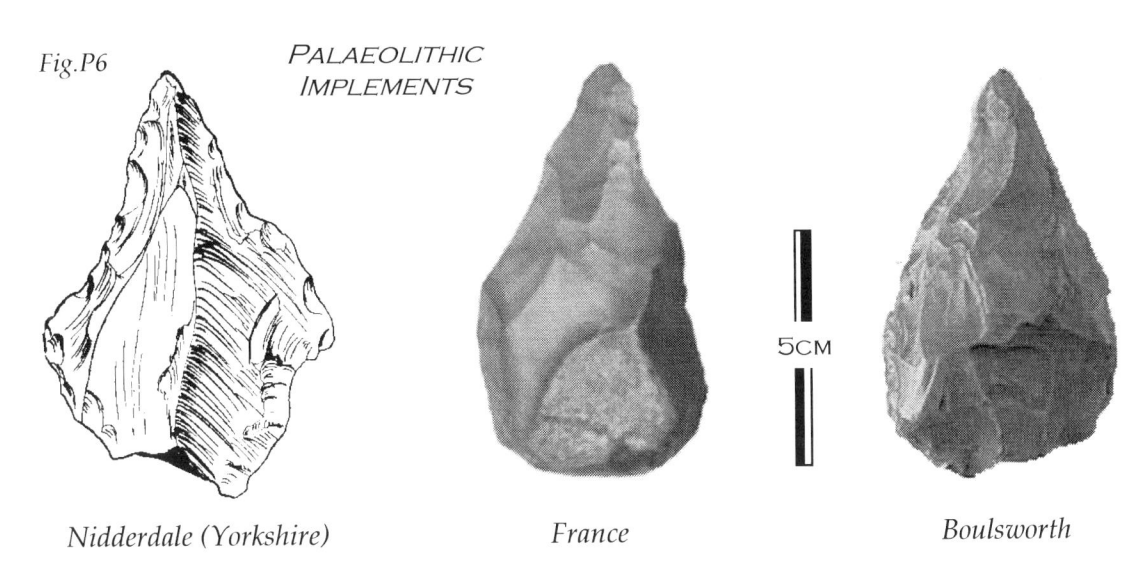

Fig.P6

PALAEOLITHIC IMPLEMENTS

5CM

Nidderdale (Yorkshire)   France   Boulsworth

The Palaeolithic flint 'hand axes' (above left and centre) are of the Mousterian period (Middle Palaeolithic) and date to around 100,000 years ago. The tool (right) was found on Boulsworth Hill sometime around 1905 by local historian, Peter Whalley. This implement displays the same Levallois technique of applying sharp points to implements as the accepted Palaeolithic tools (left and centre) and it is fair, therefore, to assign the Boulsworth tool to the same period

During the Upper Palaeolithic, sometime between 29,000 and 22,000 years ago, hunting techniques advanced with the introduction of nets, bows and arrows and the spear-thrower. Dogs were being used for hunting and the possession of a calendar based on the lunar cycle would allow for the migration of game animals to be predicted.

The Late Upper Palaeolithic covered the period 11,000 BC to 8,000 BC and this was a general period of warming where the ice sheets of the Devensian glacial event began to recede. This period of climate change saw a defined change in the landscape and, consequently, the lifestyle of the people who ranged the Continent and the British Isles.

Fig: 7 - The ice-fields across Britain at the height of the Devensian glacial period

In the interglacial period before the Devensian our part of the world experienced a climate similar to that of Africa. Victoria Cave, on the outskirts of Settle (Yorkshire), was the home of *H. crocuta spelaea*, a large species of the African spotted hyena. Mingled with their dung and their bones were the teeth, and the gnawed and split bones of the hippopotamus, the straight-tusked elephant and woolly rhinoceros. This latter species signals the beginning of the Devensian glacial period; in the higher parts of the cave floor section were the bones of the brown bear, the grizzly bear, the fox, the urus and the red deer.

In a rock fissure at Ray Gill quarry, Lothersdale, a short distance to the north of the Boulsworth area, were found the bones of hyena, straight-tusked elephant, slender-nosed rhinoceros and the molar tooth of a lion (Kendrick, T. ed. *The Archaeology of Yorkshire* 1932).

The Ice Age lasted for thousands of years during which period vast swathes of the Lancashire landscape were covered with thick deposits of boulder clay, intermingled with beds of sand and gravel.

Artefacts from the Late Upper Palaeolithic in Lancashire are scarce – a handful of flint blades have been recovered from the coastal region between Warton and the Lune. The most valuable evidence to have been found is the skeleton of a male elk at High Furlong, Poulton-Le-Fylde near Blackpool (Barrowclough 2008). The animal was discovered in shallow water deposits and a barbed arrowhead found within the skeleton suggests that it died from wounds inflicted by a hunter. The elk also displayed numerous other wounds from earlier contact with hunters; having escaped carrying severe injuries it appears to have had the misfortune to drown in a shallow lake. The skeleton has been dated to between 13,400 BC and 11,700 BC

If the Boulsworth hand axe in *Fig:P6* can indeed be assigned to the Middle Palaeolithic then it is very rare evidence for human occupation within the period. However, many upland finds of early stone implements do not reflect the exact location in which the tools or weapons were lost. Glacial movement ground and scoured the land surface and carried objects over large distances. It is possible, therefore, that the Boulsworth axe originated to the north and east from where it could have been transported before being deposited by the melting ice on the slopes of Boulsworth Hill. That said, it is also possible that the implement was lost on the hill at a location above the glacial surface. The ice extended to a depth of around 365 metres in the East Lancashire and the 'shelving' effect of this can be seen on the higher hills of Pendle Hill, Boulsworth Hill and Hameldon Hill.

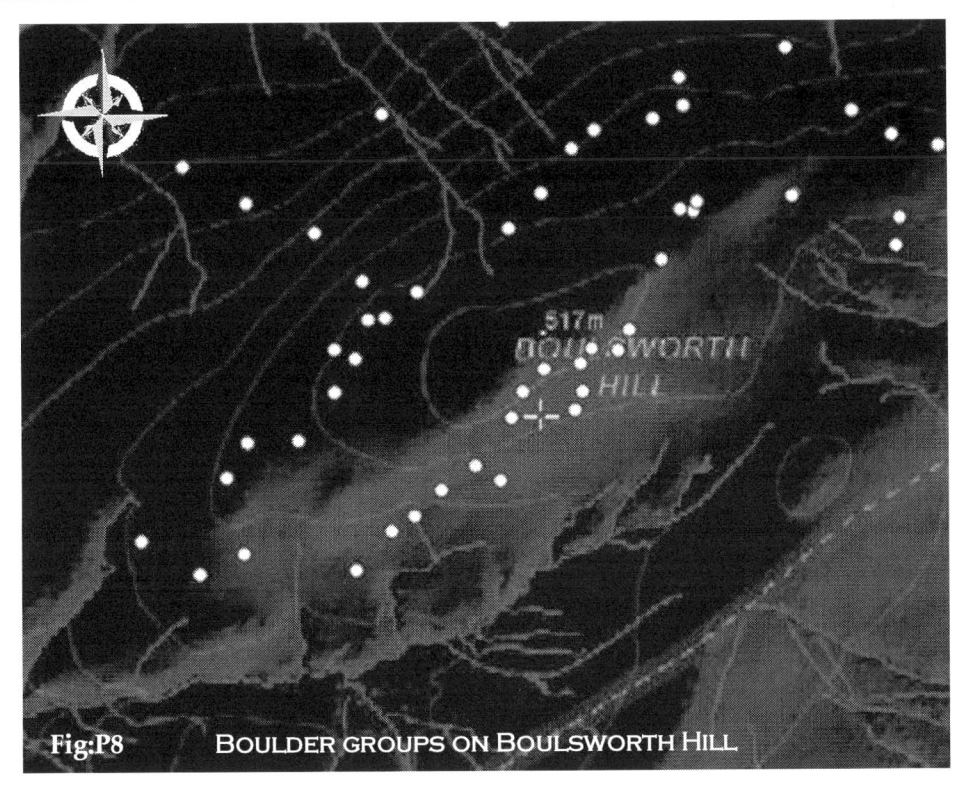

Fig:P8   BOULDER GROUPS ON BOULSWORTH HILL

Fig.8a

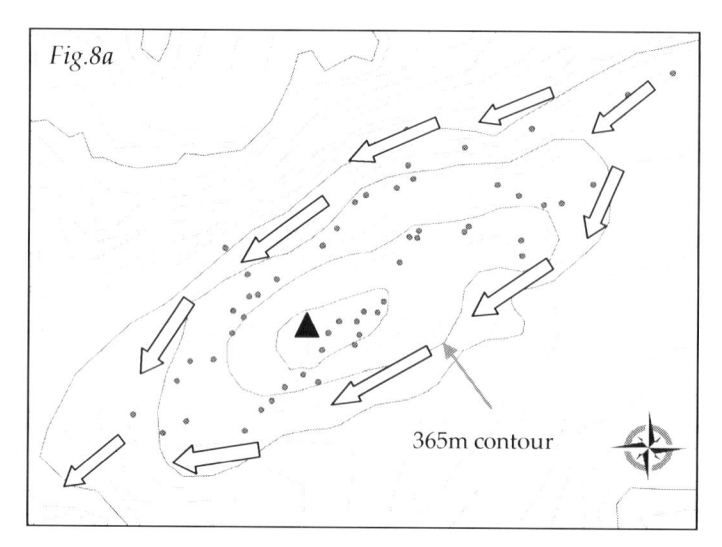

365m contour

Figures: P8 and 8a show the distribution, or geological scatter, of gritstone outcrops and glacial erratic boulder groups on the higher slopes of Boulsworth Hill.

These would be extant before the last glacial period and survived in situ because they were located above the glacial surface.

The grouping patterns indicate the edge of the glacial flow line (arrowed). The outcrops are evident above the 356m level and are aligned along the direction of flow. Intermixed erratic boulders would have been deposited during an earlier phase of glaciation when the ice surface reached a higher level.

At Windy Hill (two miles south of Blackstone Edge and to the south-east of the Boulsworth district) a number of Palaeolithic tools were discovered. This group, consisting of eighty flint flakes and twenty chert tools of the Aurignacian Series, was found on the hill in the lowest layer of a site occupied before the deep layer of peat had been laid down. Among the tools were two large carinated planes, a large parrot-beak graver and two hammer stones.

The scarcity of very early evidence for the presence of people in Lancashire reflects the difficulty experienced by countless generations who lived through the alternating glacial and temperate periods of the Palaeolithic. The south of England escaped much of the Devensian ice, and probably the glacial cover of earlier, ice periods, and so we see a richer archaeological record for the Palaeolithic here. It would appear that people from the south migrated in and out of our northern district as the ice sheets grew and receded.

Recently, the *Ancient Human Occupation of Britain Project* has discovered evidence on the Norfolk and Suffolk coasts to show the presence of human activity in Britain dating back to around 900,000 BC. At this time the area would have had a climate similar to that of southern Scandinavia today which contradicts the traditional thinking that early humans could not tolerate such cold conditions.

MESOLITHIC
8,500 BC TO 4,000 BC

FOUR

The Palaeolithic and Mesolithic periods are concerned with the fundamental developments in physical and cultural evolution which brought humanity from its very earliest hominin ancestry to a stage (the Neolithic) at which agricultural food production became the economic norm. These developments took place over an enormous extent of time - several million years - and against a backdrop of major climatic, geophysical, and ecological changes during the Pleistocene and early Holocene (Bell, M. and Walker, M. *Late Quaternary Environmental Change: Physical and Human Perspectives* 2005).

A distinguishing feature of Mesolithic archaeology, in contrast to that of all later periods, is its low visibility within the archaeological record – there are very few sites known by anything other than surface scatters of lithic (flint/chert/stone/quartzite) artefacts. Mesolithic habitation evidence, apart from being relatively ephemeral in the first place, is far more vulnerable than that of any subsequent period to the ravages of time. Permafrost, changing sea levels, coastal erosion, alluviation, peat growth and colluviation have all contributed to its destruction or concealment.

The distinction between Early and Later Mesolithic in England was defined on the basis of artefact typology in the 1970s. The separation date between Early and Late was adopted as c. 6,750 cal BC, and the defining characteristics were, essentially, that early lithic tools and weapons were of relatively large microlith types (especially obliquely blunted points and isosceles triangles) made on *broad blades*, while later tools were elaborately retouched *narrow blade* microliths, including small 'geometric' and other edge-blunted forms.

By and large it can be said that the Palaeolithic travellers brought their own supply of raw flint, and finished tools, with them when venturing into the north western districts of England. It is perhaps fortunate that Lancashire does not have a native geological flint source as this means that when flint is found hereabouts it can readily be identified as having been introduced from outside of the district.

Besides flint the other main source of tool and weapon manufacturing material was chert. Like flint, chert is a silicate, the essential components of which are silicon and oxygen. Flint and chert are aggregates of microscopic crystals of quartz found in calcareous sedimentary rocks. The quantity of silica varies within different limestones at a local level, and fine-grained black cherts, as well as coarse white cherts, can be found in all the Carboniferous limestone areas of Northern England. The gritstone geology of the Boulsworth district does not contain native limestone although glacial limestone deposition occurred in a number of localities here. This means that outcrops of chert can be found, especially in the area around Pendle Hill, and these find their way into hillside colluvium and stream beds. However, although a local source of chert was available to the Early Mesolithic people of Boulsworth this does not mean that they used the material in any meaningful quantity.

Chert seems to have had correspondingly fewer applications than flint. It is rarely used for cutting tools, though flake knives do occur occasionally. However, large blanks are frequently retouched to form scrapers and piercing tools, such as awls. It is often chosen alongside, or in preference to flint, for scrapers with steep retouch, awls, and fabricators, and it is often an alternative to flint for microliths within the Later Mesolithic. A rough survey of Mesolithic sites within the Southern Pennines indicates that chert made up some 6% of lithic assemblages in the early period while this figure rose to 61% in the Late Mesolithic. It could be argued, therefore, that there was a change in the way chert was worked from the Early to the Later Mesolithic sub-periods, and that chert was increasingly used for retouched artefact types (Hind, D. *Chert Use in the Mesolithic* Paper).

Fig:P9

4.5CM	8CM
Chert Core	*Chert bar end-scraper*

Fig:P9 shows the high quality chert core discovered by the author beneath a stone within a stone circle on the Pendle Ridgeway *(see Ringworks section)*. This material appears to be of Derbyshire or Norfolk origin and not local Pendleside chert. While yet to be confirmed the circle appears to have contained burials and the chert core was almost certainly a deposition (ritual?). The end-scraper came from a site at the Watermeetings in Barrowford and this material appears to have been sourced locally.

Dating evidence for the material culture of the Mesolithic is dominated by tools and weapons; these occur in a wider range of lithic materials than those of the Palaeolithic. Mesolithic tool types include: microliths, scrapers, burins, piercers and gravers with micro burin flakes an important waste element. Insofar as these are indicators of phases within the Mesolithic some diagnostic types point to Early and Later horizons as follows:

7,500–6,800 cal BC:
   This period exhibits predominantly broad blade production: obliquely blunted point microliths, 'large' isosceles and equilateral triangle microliths, micro burin technology.

6,800–3,800 cal BC:
   A period of predominantly narrow blade production, though also broad blade forms: small geometric microliths, especially scalene triangles and crescents, platform-struck cores and bipolar anvil-struck cores, obliquely blunted point microliths, micro burin technology, blade technology, conical and cylindrical blade cores, scalar (bipolar) cores, scrapers of various forms, hammerstones of various types including bevel ended pieces and very small pyramidal bladelet cores of the later Mesolithic tradition (Hind)

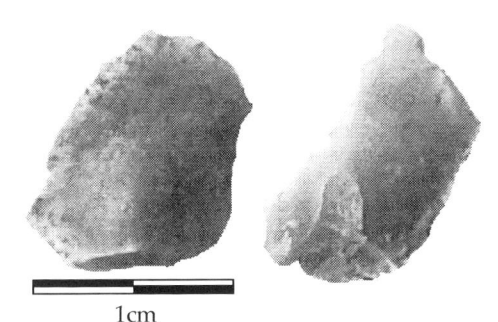

Fig: P10 - Microlith blades (formerly known as pygmy flints) from Boulsworth Hill

These tiny blades were used in composite weapon manufacture where pitch, or glue from birch tree bark, were used to fix a number of them into the haft of a spear or arrow

1cm

Other tool types, and organic materials, surviving from the Mesolithic include: non-silicate stone tools such as hammers, and maceheads - bone tools including points and needles - antler tools including barbed points and mattocks - animal teeth such as boar tusk chisels – shell utensils including scoops and scrapers - ornaments of coal and jet and natural silicas - colouring pigments including ochre - fish-hooks - baskets - nets - rope - hide or skin - wood including bows and arrows, logboats, fish-traps, bark containers and timber structures.

Flint Scatter Sites

Within the Mesolithic there were essentially three dominant cultures; the Maglemosian *broad blade* operated across a large swathe of land stretching from North Germany to East Prussia and as far south as Boulogne in France. This culture can be traced into the Derbyshire uplands and northward along the Pennine fringe into Yorkshire and Lancashire. Within the later *narrow blade* culture were two related, but separate, types of microlith, both of which originated in France - the *Tardenoisian* came from the north of the country and the *Azilian* from the south. It appears that the Azilian had little impact in the north of England while the Tardenoisian culture made its way into the Yorkshire Moors and Pennine hills via the north-east coast.

Maglemosian (Early Mesolithic) blades have been found in the Edinburgh district of Scotland and are thought to date to before 7,500 BC – however, it is difficult to assign a firm Scottish cultural occupation to this date. The Maglemosian people who inhabited Doggerland (now beneath the North Sea) and southern England were moving in and out of the north of England and Scotland according to the warmer and colder spells of the *Loch Lomond Stadial* period.

Around 7,500 BC the climate settled into a long period where temperatures were higher than today; woodland spread across the herb and shrub dominated landscape and the Mesolithic migration into the north became permanent.

The tool making technology of the Mesolithic people changed as the period progressed and it is argued that this can be considered to have been a consequence of population replacement. It is possible that a new wave of migrants, displaced by rising sea levels, introduced the new technology although it is equally possible that a slow absorption of technology from other cultures took place among the settled population. The adoption of new tools was perhaps a reaction to a shift in territorial exploitation patterns due to environmental change.

A particular feature of the Mesolithic period is that intensive flint working sites abide even in adverse conditions. When a site was used for manufacturing lithic tools a great deal of waste was generated – the making of a single tool can create around two hundred waste chippings. Many flint 'workshops' have been discovered throughout Britain; some appear to have been working areas separated from the settlement activity while others were part of the settlement foci.

The extended areas of Boulsworth, and the uplands of Calderdale, are the finest in Britain when it comes to surviving evidence relating to the Mesolithic period. The earlier Mesolithic migrants carried a French/Belgic tradition of tool making into the north of England and Scotland and it appears that these travellers preferred sandy or rocky landscape in which to live and hunt. This is probably the reason why axes do not appear in any significant numbers in earlier Mesolithic tool assemblages.

Within the One Metre BNC Survey we find an apparent concentration of Mesolithic activity; in the northern parts of the Survey area scatters of flint tools and weapons have been found along the fringes of Boulsworth Hill while the southern area around the Worsthorne moors is particularly rich in Early Mesolithic finds.

Fig: P11 - Mesolithic flint 'workshop' or 'scatter site' on Boulsworth Hill

The most prolific source of Mesolithic flint implements within the Boulsworth area is a site found by historian Peter Whalley at the end of the nineteenth century *(Figure: P11)*. Described as a flint 'workshop' the site is located on a spur of land overlooking Hey Slack Clough on the lower SW slopes of Boulsworth Hill. Sitting a few metres on the Burnley side of the Trawden Forest boundary the site was described as being a hundred metres in length and seven metres wide. At the time of discovery the upper peat layer had shifted due to heavy rain and it was in the exposed sub-layer that Whalley found a wealth of flint and chert tools and weapons – these are largely of the Early Mesolithic *broad blade* type with a smaller number of later *narrow blade* examples.

The site was taken to have been a place where flint manufacturing took place, away from the settlement foci. Due to the depth of peat the surrounding area does not seem to have been subject to any particular archaeological survey. LiDAR and aerial imaging indicate a circular patch of ground-cover discoloration within which is the suggestion of a rectilinear feature *(Fig: P11)*. It is possible, therefore, that the 'workshop' was actually a Mesolithic occupation site covering a long period of use.

Fig: P12   Flint manufacturing 'wasters' from the Boulsworth scatter site

The Boulsworth site was re-investigated during the 1950s and 1970s when more flint was discovered; these later collections are not readily available for assessment but are likely to reflect the Whalley assemblage. The find area has now assumed a natural cover through erosion and slippage of the upper peat layer.

Scatter sites, then, are a vital resource in the archaeology of the Mesolithic period. Small sites indicate the temporary presence of hunter gatherer groups as they made their way through the landscape. Larger sites can offer evidence of structural remains and possibly a wider chronological range of artefacts through which the period can be better understood. To this end it is possible that the Boulsworth site would reward any field survey that might be undertaken there.

Fig: P13 – Waste grey and black chert material from the Boulsworth site.

Gratitude is extended to the Heritage Trust Northwest (Barrowford) for access to the Whalley collection

The difficulty in field assessments of peat districts is that the peat cover can extend to some three or four metres in places and only where land slippage has taken place can evidence for the Mesolithic period be observed.

Roughly speaking the peat cover began to be laid down after the Mesolithic and this suggests that a great deal of evidence for the period lies on the post glacial bedding layer, unseen and unknowable. Millions of hectares of our British upland landscapes are covered in a blanket of peat and this, of course, means that the upland sites available to archaeology are extremely limited. This makes the earlier lithic discoveries all the more important but, unfortunately, many of the antiquary collections are now scattered far and wide.

Fig: P14   *Reworked flint cores from the Boulsworth site.*
A) Cortex flake: B) Transverse arrowhead: C) gravers: D) Micro burin: E) Backed blade/graver: F) Discoidal scraper

With regard to modern site visibility within the Pennine uplands it can be said that, to a certain extent, there is good news and bad news. Pollution from large industrial areas, erosion caused where sheep gather and ramblers tread, peat extraction for compost and lower water tables all contribute to erosion of the peat layer. In some areas, then, where the original ground surface is exposed, more archaeological evidence for the Mesolithic (and rarely, the Palaeolithic) is coming to light.

Fig: 15 - Illustration from W. Bennett's 'History of Burnley' Vol 1 1946

The scraper (Fig: 15a) is from Boulsworth and is of a similar design type to number 5 in the illustration.

This is a retouched cortex strike from a Yorkshire chalk flint nodule. This material is inferior to southern chalk flint and this is why the tool was made from a single strike flake

Fig: P15

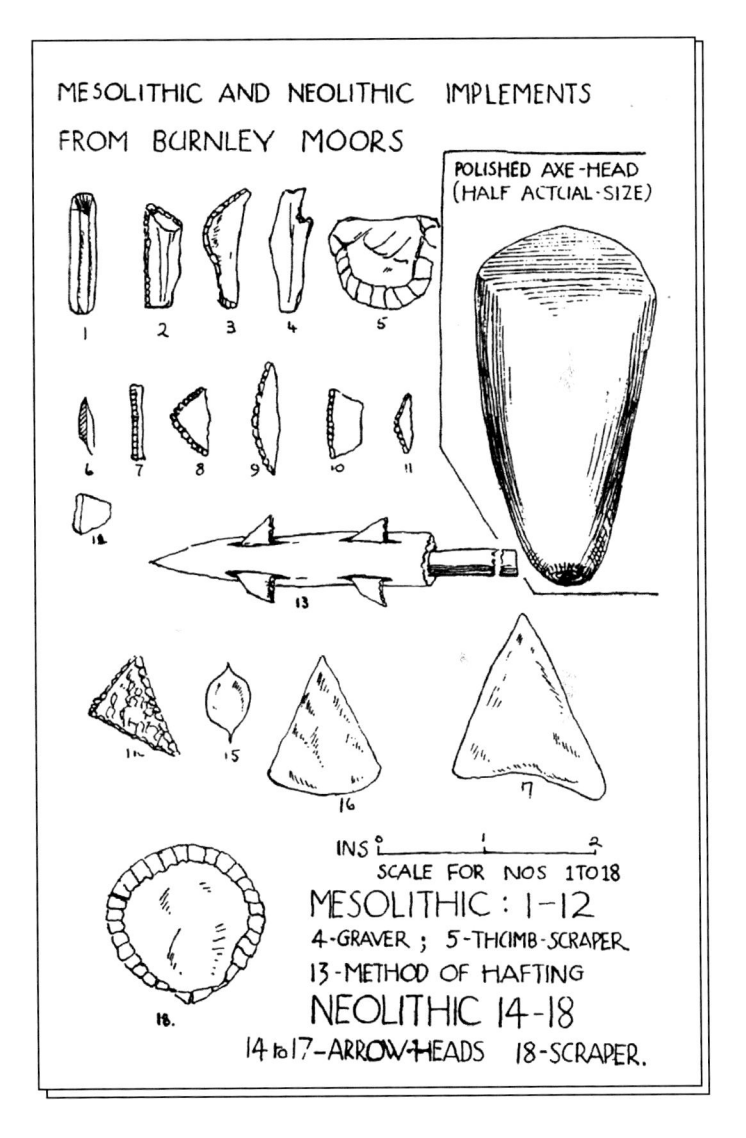

FIG: P16 — P. WHALLEY COLLECTION

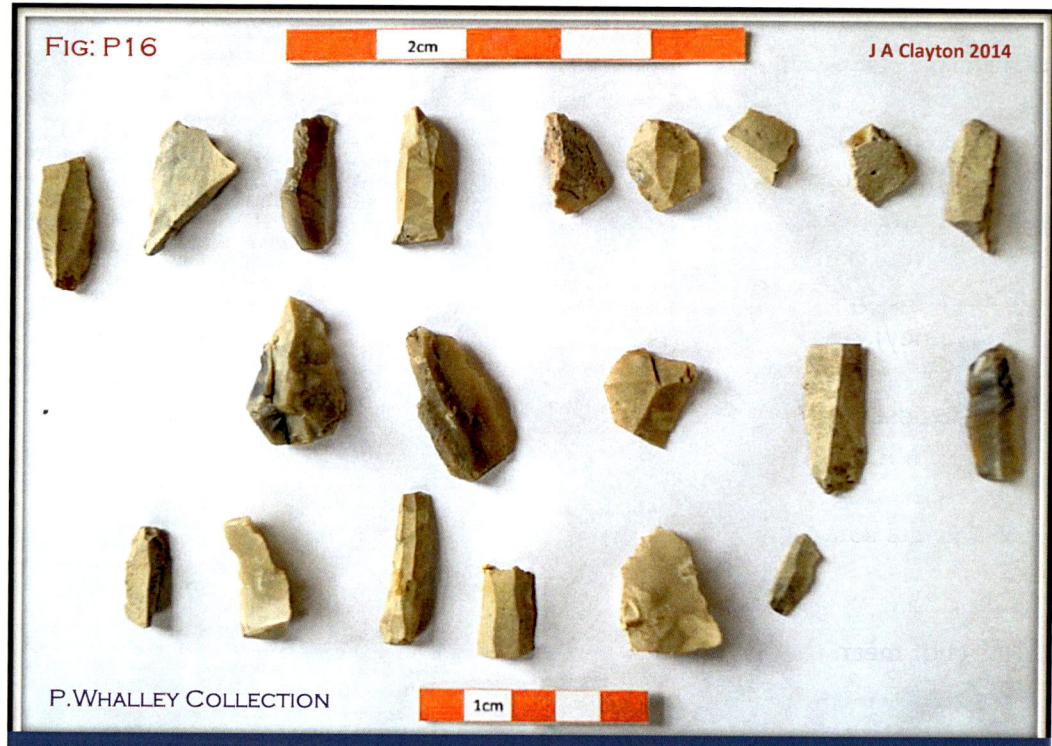

MESOLITHIC FLINTS FROM THE CASTERCLIFFE HILLFORT SITE

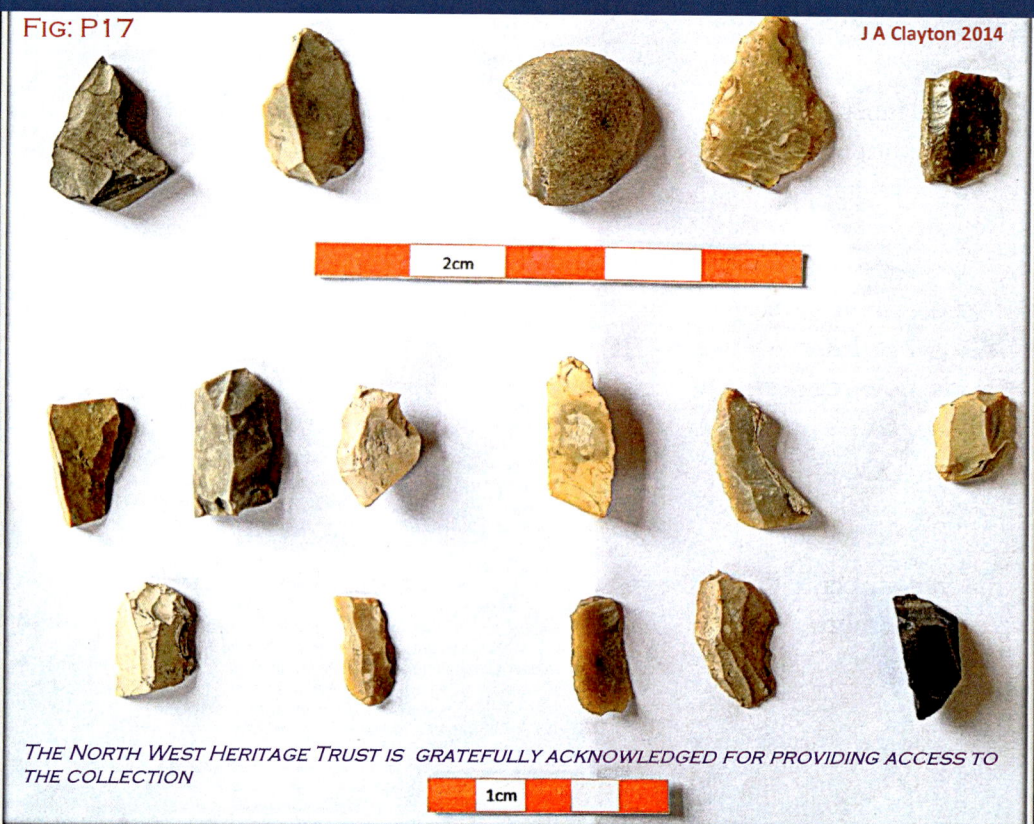

FIG: P17

THE NORTH WEST HERITAGE TRUST IS GRATEFULLY ACKNOWLEDGED FOR PROVIDING ACCESS TO THE COLLECTION

MESOLITHIC — REGIONALITY

As the Late Upper Palaeolithic era faded into the mists of time increased rainfall and glacial meltwater caused sea levels to rise and the nature of the British coastline changed. By the beginning of the Early Mesolithic the low lying coastal regions of Lancashire were submerged; a twenty kilometre wide stretch of forested land disappeared along much of the Lancashire coastline leaving a few scattered islands (such as Walney).

The land exposed by the retreating glaciers was initially devoid of tree cover and would present a slightly alien aspect of vast open grasslands. This began to change as the Mesolithic period dawned when low scrub species took hold; gradually the climate and the soil became more suited to the species of birch, elm, oak, hazel and lime trees.

This does not mean that the Mesolithic period saw a steady improvement in climatic conditions – we have seen that changes in sea level occurred leading to the flooding of the former rich hunting grounds of Doggerland (the land bridge connecting Britain to the continent). Not only did this reduce the land area to the east but it also impacted upon British communities by isolating them from the continent.

Perhaps the most severe environmental impact, however, came from the Storegga tsunami of about 6,300 BC - this may have caused the final flooding of the land bridge and might have caused the deaths of around 700-3,000 people.

As the ice-blasted terrain settled down a covering of grass and then low shrubland began to invade the open plains – this was superseded by deciduous woodland. A new method of hunting evolved to take advantage of the game to be found in the woodlands. Low regions of the hinterland, and the coastal areas, were largely swampy areas of bog, mossland and fen which were difficult for the traveller to cross but rich in game for the hunter. Occupation sites within the lowlands tend to be located on sporadic areas of relatively raised ground.

The massive auroch was to be found on the coastal lowlands and the higher ground while red deer migrated between the two according to season. Hunting in the uplands would have been at its most prolific during the summer and this probably explains the camp sites such as that on the lower Boulsworth Hill slopes (*Fig: P11*).

It almost certain that many other transitory camp sites lie beneath the Boulsworth peat; also, the boulder groups scattered across the higher hill slopes would have made ideal shelters (*Figs: P8 and 8a*). A number of these groups display a similar trait to other groups around the Widdop area where shattered glacial boulder erratics have been formed in circles and sub-circles. These foundations could easily be transformed into permanent shelter enclosures to be reoccupied each season.

It is, perhaps, significant that the boulder groups on Boulsworth Hill fall almost entirely above the 360m contour (*Fig: P17*). It was suggested earlier that this was a result of pre-Devensian glacial deposits being undisturbed by the last glacial period and it is interesting that the groups fall within the area that would have been subject to woodland clearance by the Late Mesolithic hunters.

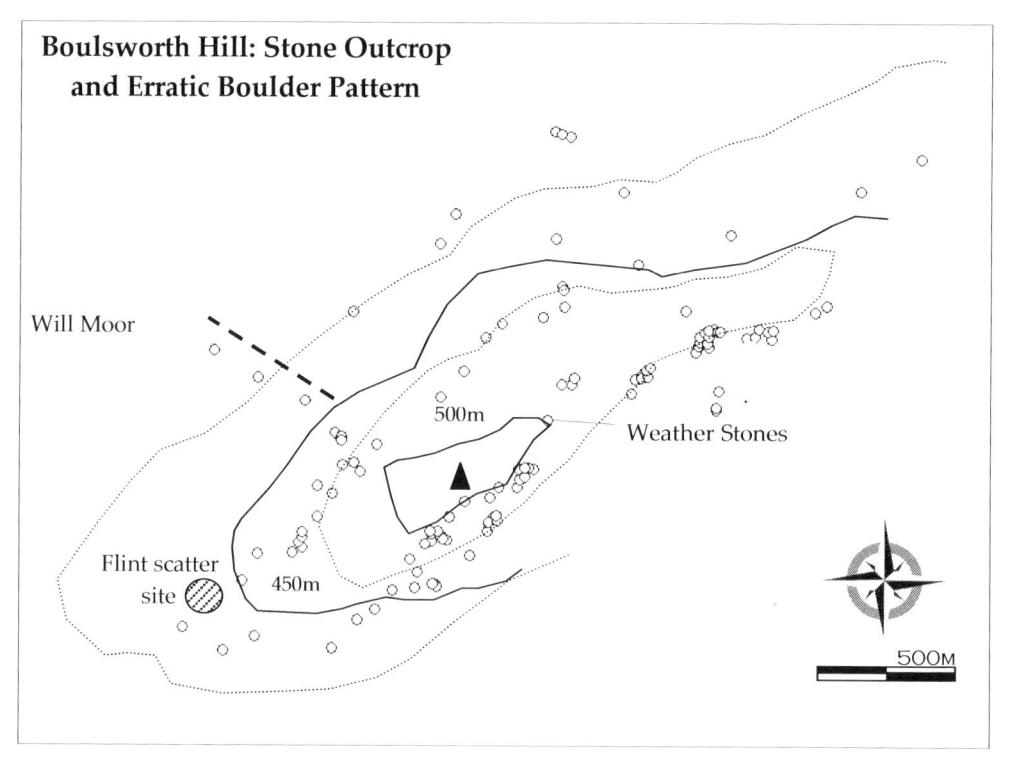

Fig: 18
The circles represent stone group sites within the woodland clearance level. At least one of these stone groups was utilised by hunting groups for shelter and possibly for more permanent dwellings. The dotted line indicates a line of orthostats (some apparent on the 1847 OS map and others extant) arrayed along the line of an early trackway from Will Moor onto the upper hill – Mesolithic and Neolithic tools have been found in this location which was possibly a very early route used by hunter gatherers

Fig: P19

A 20m diameter circular pattern of stones on Boulsworth Hill (far right) and a 26m diameter example near Widdop reservoir

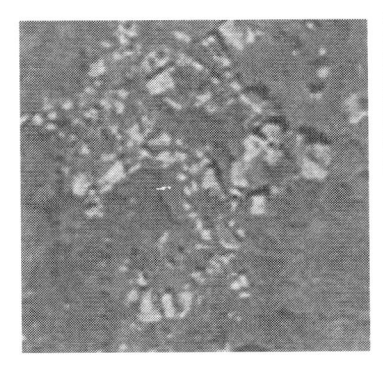

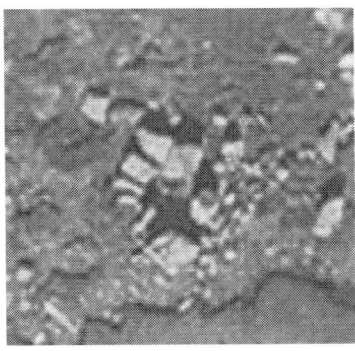

The Later Mesolithic saw a marked increase in the number of hand axes within the lithic material and this coincides with the evidence of charcoal layers across swathes of higher ground. It appears that Late Mesolithic hunters burned off the tree cover above the 360m contour line in order to create an environment suitable for grazing animals (Barrowclough 2008). These open areas of upland would have been eco-managed on a regular basis and would provide a regular source of protein during specific periods of the hunting year.

Although there is not enough evidence at present there is potential to recognise earlier and later Mesolithic occupation from their specific siting patterns in relation to upland forest cover. It appears that a favoured location in later sites was on the edge of land plateaux on south facing slopes at a height of around 360 metres to 430 metres, particularly where a camp could be set near to a stream or a particular landscape feature.

The later period also saw a general pattern of smaller, more widely distributed sites with a marked increase in the presence of microliths. Early sites tended to be set around fifty metres below their predecessors. (Spikins, P. *Palaeolithic and Mesolithic West Yorkshire* Paper 2010). •

A structured system of migration and trade routes is evidenced by the Early Mesolithic importation of the raw materials employed in tool and weapon manufacture. This can be seen in the flint, chert and stone assemblages recovered from the western districts of Lincolnshire and East Yorkshire (Barrowclough 2008) - this is also true of the area around the mouth of the Mersey and into the Central Pennines.

However, as the Late Mesolithic period progressed the material evidence suggests that movement of materials became more stilted. It is possible that the population expansion across a wider landscape at this time indicates a growing need for land to manage as a more pastoral way of life developed.

This is furthered by the suggestion that Late Mesolithic materials were sourced from a more localised area (Barrowclough 2008). People from north of the River Ribble appear to have sourced their materials from Yorkshire and Northumbria while the Pendle and Boulsworth people commonly used local Pendleside chert. This, perhaps, suggests a reduction in population movement resulting from a lifestyle shift where the migratory tendencies of the Mesolithic changed in favour of a more local and settled existence.

Subsistence resources would have influenced population numbers across the Mesolithic period but the provision of accurate head-count figures is not possible. Ethnographic specialists have postulated that a reasonable population figure for the Mesolithic may be around 0.01 people per square kilometre although this figure can be easily skewed when various environmental factors are taken into account (Smith, C. *Late Stone Age Hunters of the British Isles* Routledge 1992). It is probable that the end of the Late Mesolithic saw a widespread increase in birth rates and population coinciding with the change to a pastoral existence.

Fig: P20   *A favoured Mesolithic landscape*
Looking north-east from Worsthorne Moor across Extwistle Moor to Boulsworth Hill

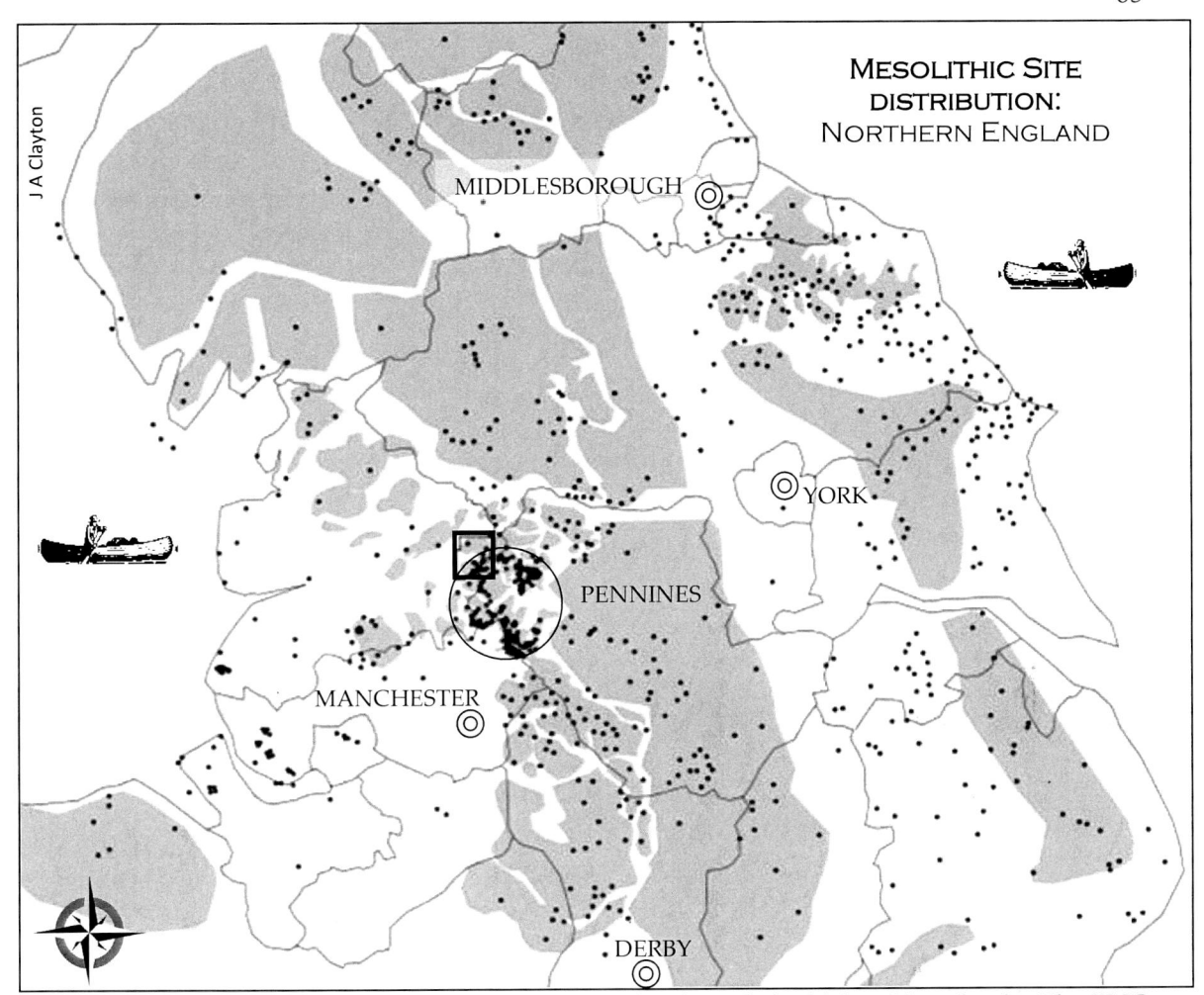

Fig: 21 The shaded areas represent Pennine uplands and the higher hinterlands. The BNC Survey area (boxed) cuts into the north-west quadrant of a sharply defined cluster of Mesolithic sites within Calderdale (circled). Yorkshire data after Spikins, 2010

Fig: 21 illustrates the distribution patterns of Mesolithic sites across the North of England. The data here is somewhat generalised in that there is no distinction made between Early and Late Mesolithic; nor is there account taken of the type and size of site (camp, findspot, lithic scatter site etc.). Some sites indicate the recovery of 'loss' where artefacts were dropped by the traveller while other sites were transitory settlements occupied on a seasonal basis and enduring within the landscape for a long period of occupation. Although the data cannot be employed for an accurate ethnographic study it does, nevertheless, provide a valuable insight into the *presence*, (spatial occupation/movement/regionality) of people within the Mesolithic period.

Fig:22

SURVEY AREA
SITE CLUSTERS

PENDLE
BURNLEY
LANCASHIRE
CALDERDALE

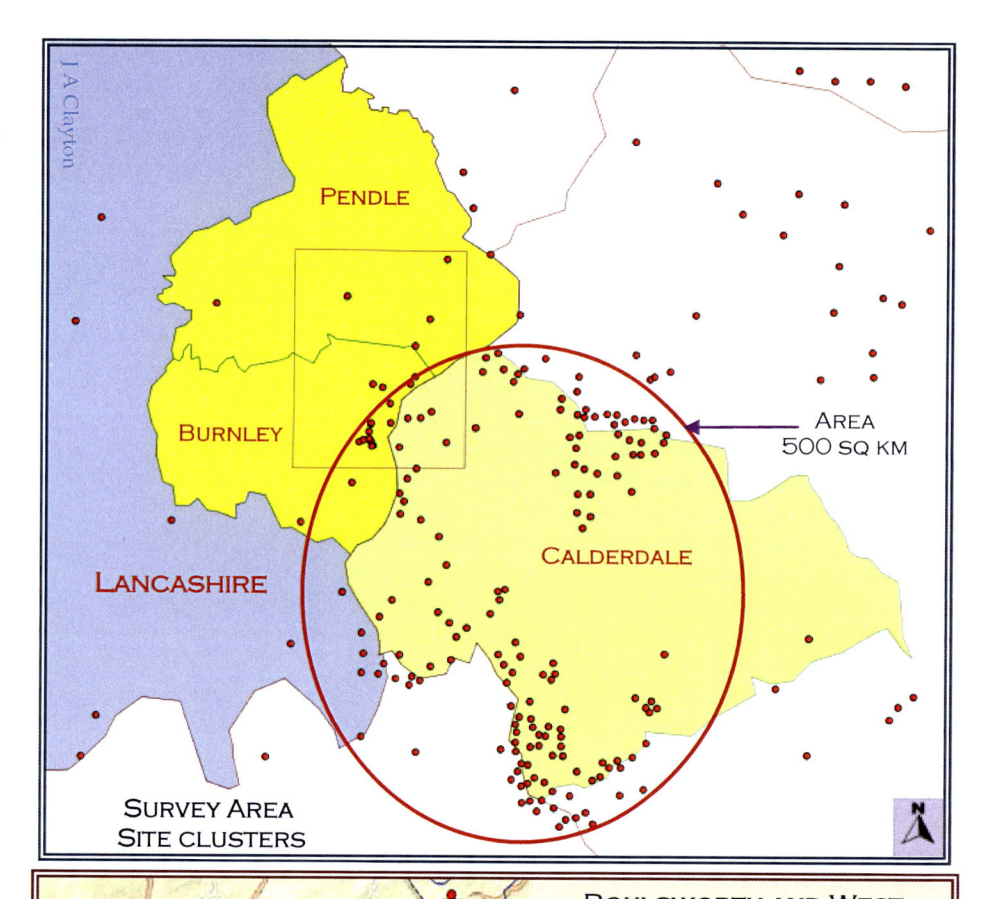

AREA 500 SQ KM

Fig: 23

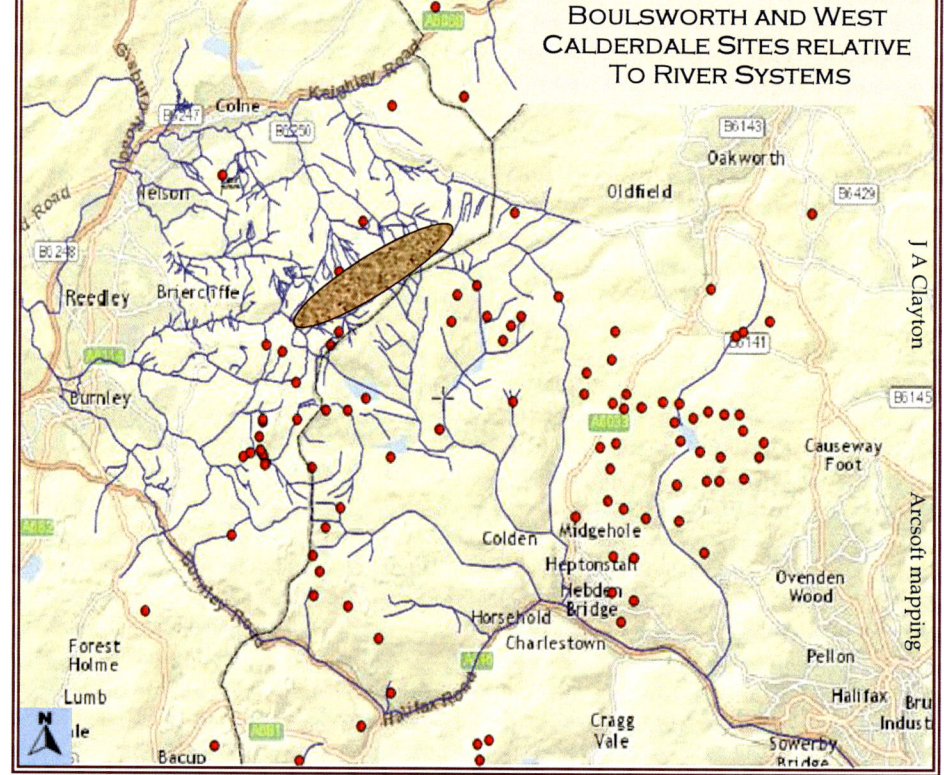

BOULSWORTH AND WEST CALDERDALE SITES RELATIVE TO RIVER SYSTEMS

It is apparent in *Fig: 21* that Mesolithic site incidence across the North of England displays defined grouping patterns and linear 'corridors.' The majority of sites can be seen to cluster around the North York Moors and coast, along the western edge of the Central and South Pennines and, particularly, on the north/south/west boundaries of Yorkshire Calderdale.

The linear site scatters possibly relate to the main groupings and it is suggested in *Fig: 21* that the sites within these 'corridors' would possibly have been semi-transient camps occupied by members of the communities involved in migratory hunting expeditions.

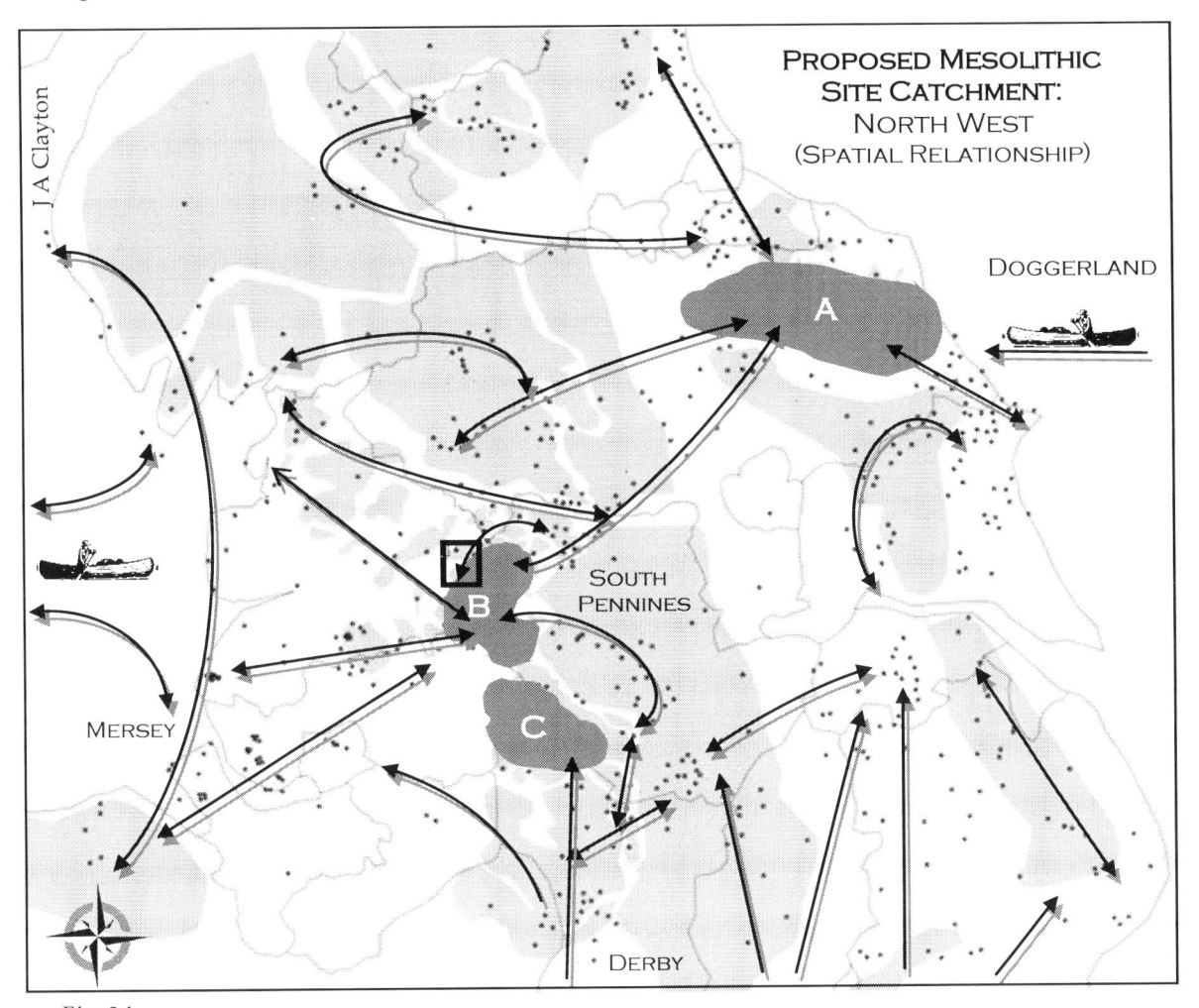

Fig: 24
Primary regional groups: **A)** *North York Moors* **B)** *West Calderdale* **C)** *Sheffield/Glossop*

Two lithic assemblages from Filpoke Beacon, to the north-west of Hartlepool, have been found in association with broken and charred hazelnut shells (clearly collected for food) and dated to 8,810 BC ± 140. All the tools are microliths of either narrow rods trimmed down one side or both sides, or scalene triangles of the narrow blade type. This group represents the earliest part of the Mesolithic industry identified in England and is earlier than any from mainland Europe. Occupation of the famous Star Carr site, five miles south of Scarborough, North Yorks, has been dated to the period from 8,770 BC to 8,460 BC. In North Wales Early Mesolithic sites have been dated at Rhuddlan (6,789 BC ± 86) and Aberffraw (6,690 BC ± 150).

In the Pennines, on the low ground of east Yorkshire, Lincolnshire, Durham, and the crests of the Cleveland Hills, it has been possible to identify a strong commonality of tool and weapon manufacture. An Early Mesolithic flint assemblage from Money Howe, on Bilsdale East Moor, North Yorkshire, has been dated by associated charcoal as 7,480 BC ± 390 while Pennine sites at Warcock Hill and Lominot date to roughly the same period. Generally the lithic assemblages from upland and lowland sites conform to a common general transition between the Early and Late Mesolithic – the main differences between the two can be seen as ones of proportion and not of types (Berger, R. *Radio Carbon Dating* Paper California Press 1979).

West Yorkshire can boast of having the highest density of Mesolithic sites in England and Wales – the district also contains the earliest and latest known upland sites in England along with the smallest dimensional flint assemblage and highest resolution sites yet recorded for the Palaeolithic/Mesolithic (Spikins 2010). As we have seen, particularly high concentration of Mesolithic sites occurs within the Two Metre BNC Survey of west Calderdale and this washes over into the One Metre BNC Survey.

Because the Mesolithic period is devoid of recognised monumental dating evidence the polities and religion of the period are particularly unfamiliar to the modern mindset. Mesolithic peoples were constantly mobile, living in small groups, with day to day lives which seem to be different in fundamental ways from our own. Apart from the lack of architectural evidence there is also a distinct lack of principle artefact dating evidence. Where these have survived in later periods we can relate to objects such as jewellery, grooming implements and pottery and, therefore, we are able to form an archaeological theory of culture. However, the post-glacial Mesolithic occupants of Britain were living some 6,000 to 10,000 years ago and this means that little material evidence has survived (with the notable exception of lithics - sometimes bone and, rarely, wood).

In *Fig: 26* an attempt is made to isolate particular Mesolithic social groupings but spatial location alone cannot provide a universally acceptable view of the societal structure that might be expected in an area of such extreme physiographic and economic variability as northern England. Lithic evidence must be taken in tandem with biological material and other associated datable material.

The Early Mesolithic period appears to have been one of substantially mobile populations evidenced by the movement of raw materials from the North East to the Southern Pennines. It has been suggested that almost all of the north of England was a single territory within the Mesolithic (Barton, R. & Roberts, A. *The Mesolithic Period in England* 2004). This is also suggested by the cluster and corridor patterns apparent within *Fig: 21* and it seems logical, therefore, to suggest a model based upon the available spatial and material evidence.

Fig: 25 - Site clusters running north-south from the BNC Survey include a group around the uplands of the Huddersfield area (circled). The Mesolithic sites within this district have been subject to systematic investigation over a long period – the most important sites being: Windy Hill, White Hill, Lominot, March Hill, Cupwith Hill and Dean Clough.

South of Huddersfield large numbers of narrow blade microliths have been found on the moors west of Penistone and Sheffield at heights ranging from 300 metres to 400 metres *(Fig: 25)*. A number of these implements are made from chert and lydian stone originating in Derbyshire. Although these Later Mesolithic implements resemble the *Huddersfield Series* of the earlier period in general character, they suggest a northward movement of their makers, rather than a southward one from the Huddersfield area (Kendrick, 1932).

Given the available site pattern there seems to be little doubt that a defined concentration occurs at the northern tip of the proposed northward migration *(Fig: 25)*; there is a suggestion in this that regionality had developed here. Further to this, Kendrick suggested in his *Archaeology of Yorkshire* (1932) that a narrow blade industry existed that was *'more or less peculiar'* to the Pennines, probably developed from the Aurignacian culture of the Upper Palaeolithic.

It is possible, then, that a region-specific Mesolithic culture existed along the Central and Southern Pennine ridge between the Rivers Trent and Ribble. These sites were contained within a northward-trending upland corridor that narrowed markedly towards the northerly extent and peaked towards the Lancashire/Yorkshire boundary in west Calderdale.

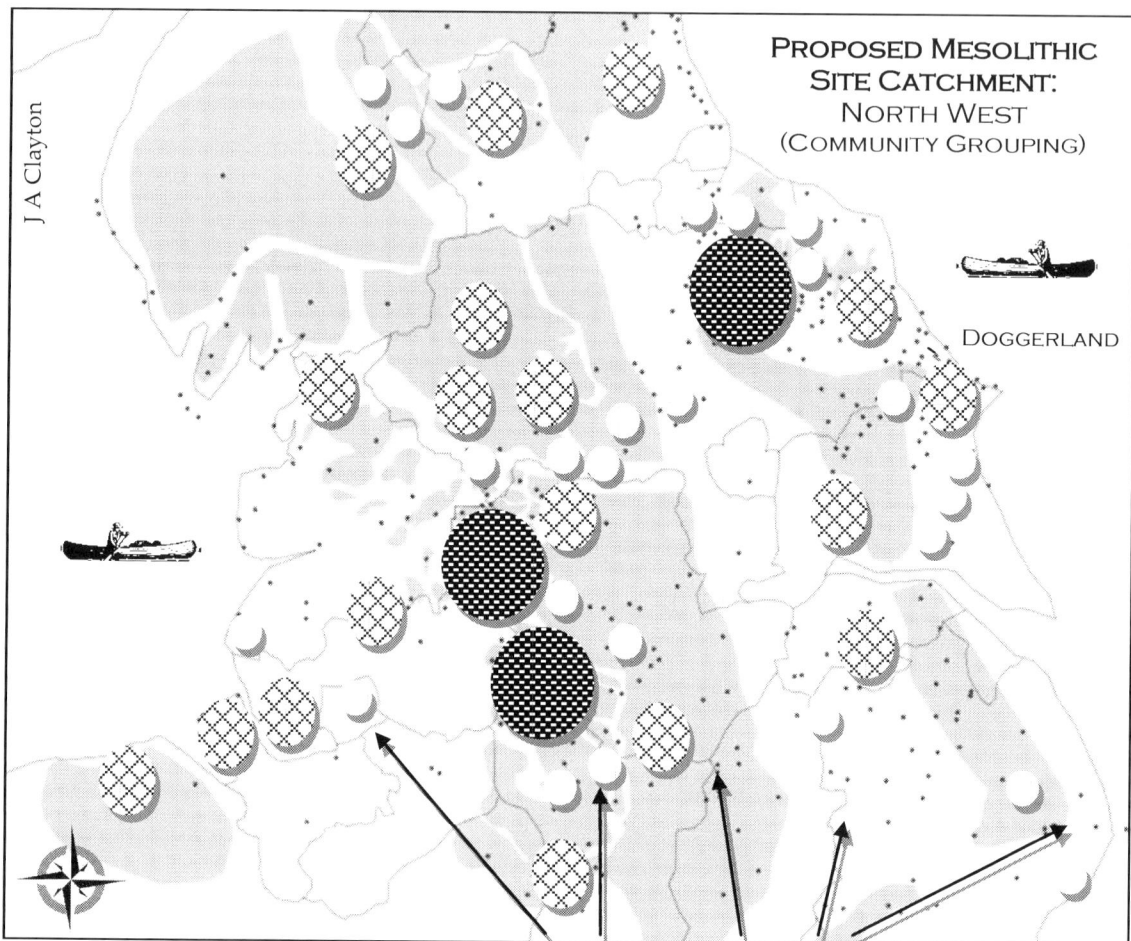

Fig: 26 A tentative model for possible Mesolithic regionality. Three primary groups are seen on the North East coast and in the Southern/Central Pennines. The former was probably occupied by displaced occupants of Doggerland and the latter by early movement from Derbyshire/Nottinghamshire/Lincolnshire

● *Primary grouping – 27 kilometres diameter   54.700^2 hectares - 135,166^2 acres (after Schulting)*

▦ *Satellite communities – 13 kilometres diameter*   ☽ *7 kilometres diameter*

Many models have been advanced for the Mesolithic occupation of Northern England and no claim is made for the models suggested here being more accurate than any other – in fact, the very nature of the beast defies any single theory. The most valuable source of evidence for early settlement and society is found in skeletal material – biologists can study recovered human bones to show the background of a particular individual. Unfortunately bones do not survive in any quantity from the Mesolithic; those found by antiquarians have usually been lost or are completely out of archaeological context and, therefore, of little use.

Where a few bones have survived recent study has been able to form a lifestyle picture. Samples from a cemetery site at Avelines Hole cave in the Mendips have been dated to $8,400 \pm 200$ BC. The people were smaller in stature and shorter lived than the modern population and did not appear to have led easy lives. An elbow joint displayed signs of severe wear-and-tear, possibly from repetitive action such as rowing and spear throwing. Dental samples showed that periods of stress occurred in childhood – this is usually caused by periodic food shortages related to the pre-harvest period for farmers and the late spring for foragers. Eight tooth samples showed that the people had all grown up near to their burial site thus suggesting a limited annual range of movement. Carbon and nitrogen isotope analysis showed a land-based diet (as opposed to shellfish) and faunal remains suggest that the main prey animals were red deer and pig (Schulting, R *What The Bones Say*: Oxford Lecture 2007).

Similar tests have been carried out on coastal islands and inland sites in South Wales and Ireland both of which show that the coastal groups had either marine diets or mixed diets but people of the inland groups were eating a land-based diet only – despite being near to plentiful supplies of river fish and only thirty kilometres from the coast. The inference within these results is that groups were utilising small territories over long periods of time. This is of interest to spatial occupation models in northern England as groups within Scottish coastal areas appear to have moved between the coast and the uplands on a seasonal basis.

It may be that people living along the west coast of northern England followed the pattern of neighbouring Wales and Ireland where inland and coastal groups adapted in different ways, with specialised knowledge of their particular environment – this would mean a degree of exclusivity for each regional group which may have culminated in territorial and social stress. This might also explain the difference in adaptation to the new Neolithic culture seen between different areas in the Late

Mesolithic. Schulting suggests from dietary evidence that each territory would be approximately 25 kilometres in diameter (*Fig: 26*).

Perhaps the best evidence we have at present for the Mesolithic lifestyle is that coming from Denmark and southern Sweden. Here it has been found that there was a long continuation of the same flint technology and skeletal shape indicates stable populations. Human bones display little disease and, coupled with site density, this is suggestive of well nourished people. Seeds and nuts were a staple as were small mammals caught in traps. Coastal groups were trapping fish and the remains of shark and whales may be an indication of offshore fishing (or shoreline scavenging). Large numbers of seals were killed and it is very possible that there was a substantial trade in seal oil. Selective hunting of deer, pig and auroch was commonplace and it appears that herd management took place on a small scale.

The Danish data can be run against other models of hunting behaviour and the results indicate that British hunters were being highly selective in the animals they stalked and killed – they were under little pressure to bring back meat from every trip. The Danish evidence shows that the population was living a lifestyle akin to much later periods (e.g. the Bronze Age); their subsistence strategy was so efficient that they were relatively sedentary which enabled the development of a rich culture.

It is possible that the early period scatter of early hunter-gatherer, and later foraging groups, began to coalesce within the landscape in reaction to climate change (*Oasis Theory*). A more recent ecological model indicates that an increase in population through the Mesolithic meant that prime areas utilised for floral and faunal resource began to show signs of distress. Groups were forced to live off decreasing areas of quality land and this gave rise to the growing of limited crops and storing the proceeds in order to supplement wild foods in lean periods (*Hearth Theory*).

The *Positive Feedback Model* sees broad-spectrum foragers spreading out into more isolated regions of marginal land where they begin small scale farming. As population increased so farming practice spread and eventually the foraging lifestyle became untenable.

It seems probable that the change from the hunting and foraging lifestyle resulted from factors seen in all of the above models, to one degree or other. It is clear that the trend was toward a proliferation of more settled communities and this led to the unavoidable growth of a social hierarchy - the sense of regionality became fixed.

The site catchment model proposed in *Figure: 26* may reflect the later Mesolithic period where territorial settlement was stabilising. Although the model features circular territories around group sites, in reality each area controlled by the primary community would reflect the local topography. In the primary grouping territories we can see that an area was largely chosen for its particular qualities i.e. height, level plateau, well drained, water supply, proximity of herd migration routes, proximity of primary trackways, micro-climate etc. By choosing an area where it was possible to maximise efficiency in gathering resources the expenditure of energy would be minimised thus allowing manpower to be employed in other directions.

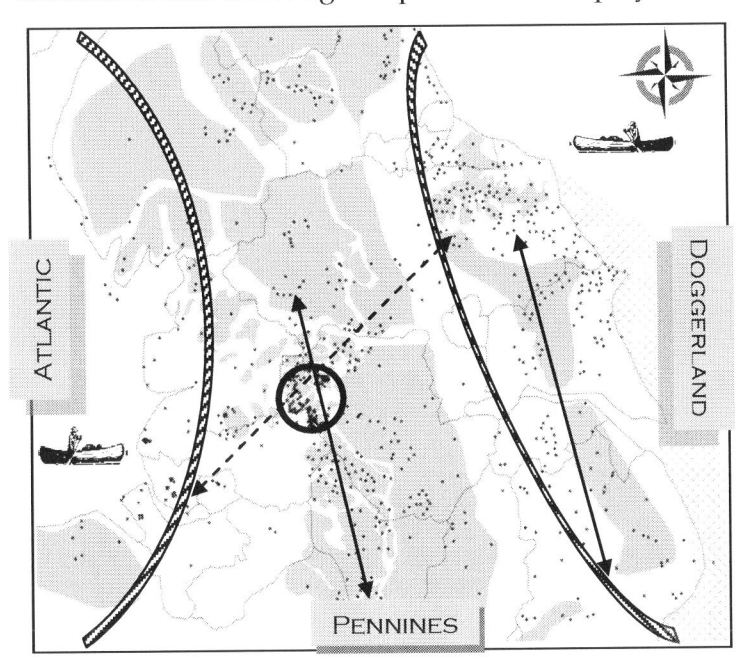

Fig: 27

Given the location of proposed Mesolithic communities within northern England (Fig: 26) it is possible to suggest movement patterns within site groupings.

This can be taken further to divide the subject area into the three distinct territories illustrated - these will still be apparent in the tribal territories of the Iron Age

A defined corridor is apparent between the important coastal locations of the North East and the Mersey. It is unclear as to whether displaced settlers from Doggerland moved south-west through the landscape, thus linking to the Isle of Man and Ireland, or whether a specific Atlantic culture moved north-east in order to access the rich landscape of Doggerland. The answer, perhaps, lies somewhere between the two.

The apparent NE-SW corridor crosses the N-S Pennine corridor at the maximum site density of west Calderdale (circled in *Fig: 27*). It is perhaps significant that the site clusters within the Calderdale region fall along this NE-SW axis – this strongly suggests that the Calderdale catchment was important because of its geographical location at the 'crossroads' of the two primary transit routes within the northern half of England.

Assessment of the linear corridor routes is particularly interesting in that some of them follow later pre-historic and even modern routes. An example of this is the Pennine route northward from Derbyshire into Calderdale and the Burnley district of the One Metre BNC Survey area. Having passed through the Marsden district in the Yorkshire Pennines this route follows north over Blackstone Edge to Todmorden where it passed through the Calder Gap and northward onto Blackshaw Head. It then crossed into Lancashire and over the Kebs Road (west of the Hawkstones) then carried on its northward line for another three kilometres into the One Metre BNC Survey area at Cant Clough (Worsthorne).

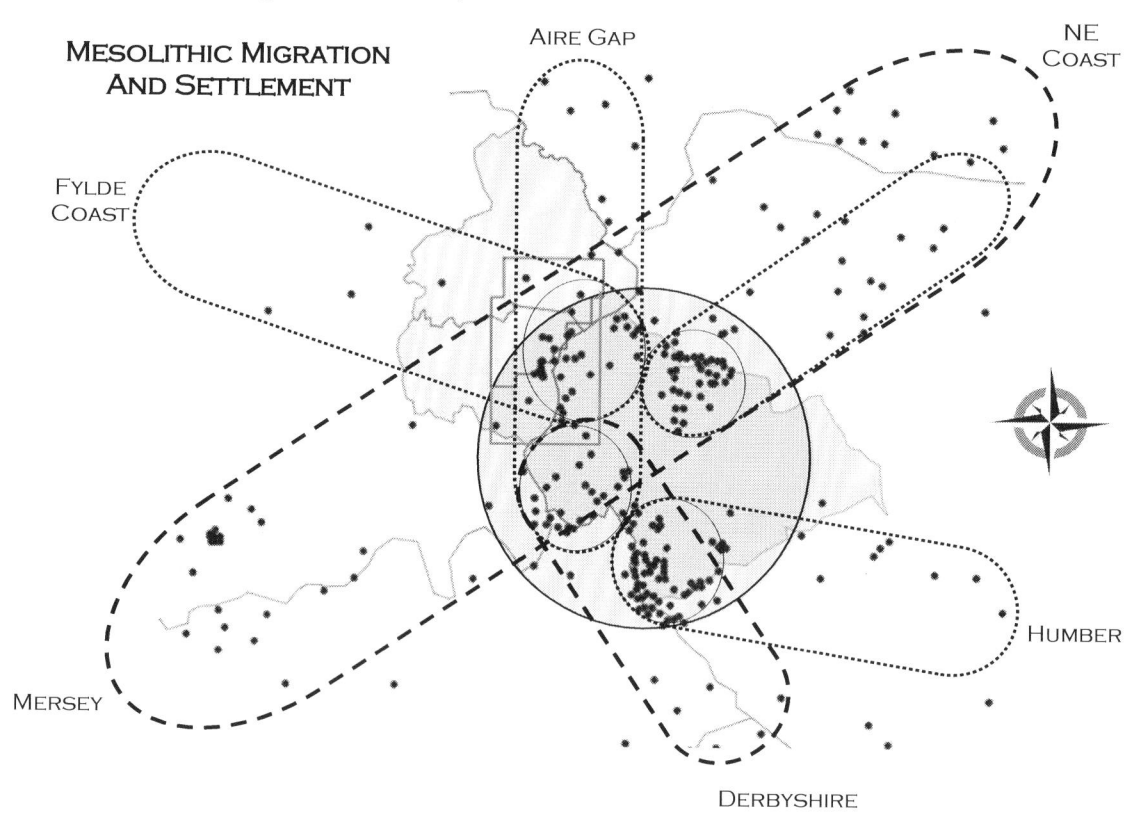

Fig: 28

– – –   *Direction of proposed primary routes*

....   *Direction of proposed secondary routes*

◯   *Area of main site clusters in Calderdale and Burnley (27k diameter)*

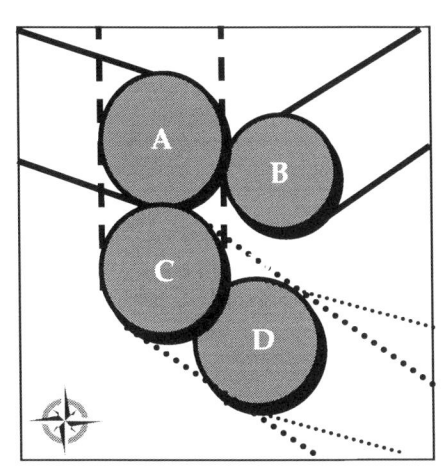

Fig:29

Within the central site cluster in Fig: 28 the terminal of each secondary route can be seen to create four sub-districts within the intersections. A particular group of sites falls within each intersection.

Group A: East of Worsthorne: Group centred on the high ground around the Widdop, Gorple Upper and Gorple Lower reservoirs. Coordinates: X 392397 Y 433298 Lat 53.795936 Long -2.1168952 (WGS84) SD 92397 33298

Fig: 30

200-300m elevation   350-400m   400m +

*At the centre of group **A** is a defined ridge of high ground to the north and west of the Widdop reservoir forming a narrow valley head.*

Surrounding this site are steep ridges descending to the valley floor and each of these ridges is scattered with large glacial erratic boulder groups of the type commonly utilised to provide shelter during the Mesolithic period.

Widdop Reservoir

Fig: P31

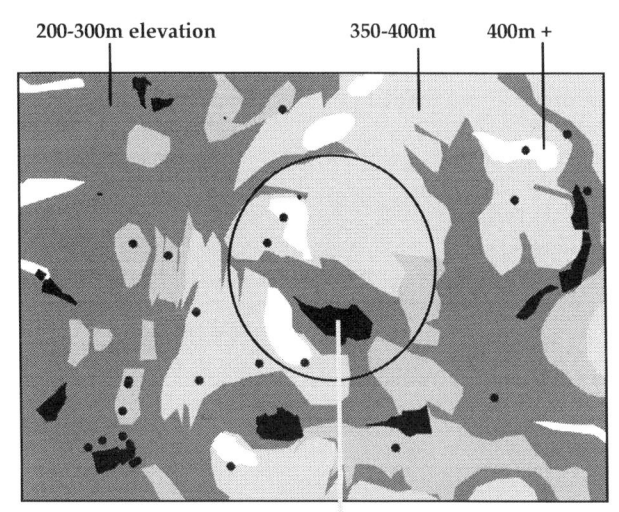

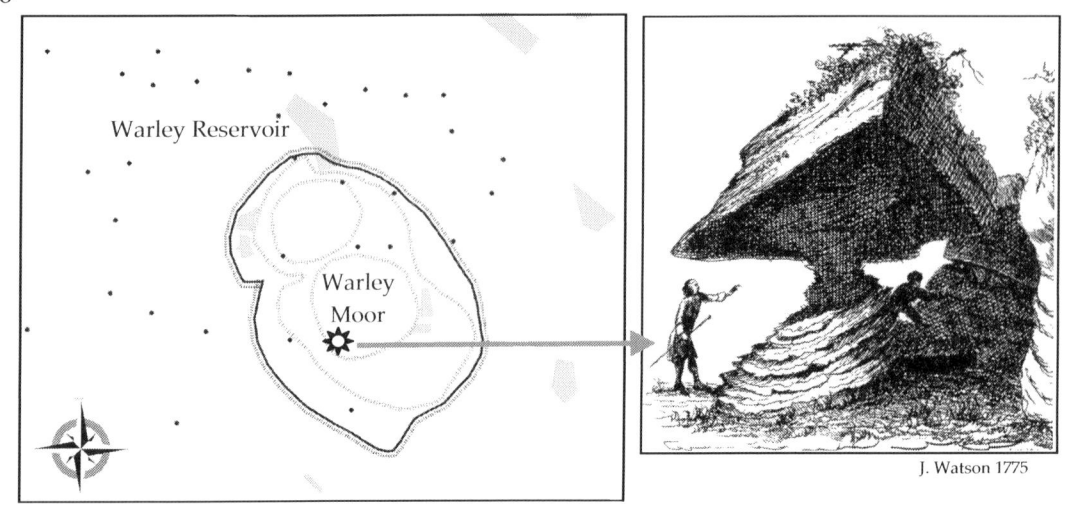

*Fig: 32   Centre of group **B**   Fig: 33   The Rocking Stone*

At the centre of group **B** is Warley Moor: the topography of the moor takes the form of a defined hill with two distinct areas of high ground. It can be seen that a number of Mesolithic sites occupied the hill. Near the summit of the southern apex is the glacial erratic known as The Rocking Stone – this special landscape feature would have been of particular ritual importance to prehistoric communities.

Group B: Midway between Oxenhope and Hebden Bridge - adjacent to Warley Reservoir. Coordinates: X 403423 Y 430218 Lat 53.768297 Long -1.9495494 SE 03423 30218

*Fig: 34   Centre of group **C**   Fig: P35   Looking towards Noon Hill*

The centre of group **C** falls on the Calderdale border south of Todmorden. Here we find a group of defensive hill sites, the principal ones being Rough Hill and Noon Hill (not to be confused with the Noon Hill near Chorley).

Group C: South of Todmorden between Whitworth and Walsden.
Coordinates: **X** 391139 **Y** 420247 **Lat** 53.678612 **Long** -2.1356227
SD 91139 20247.

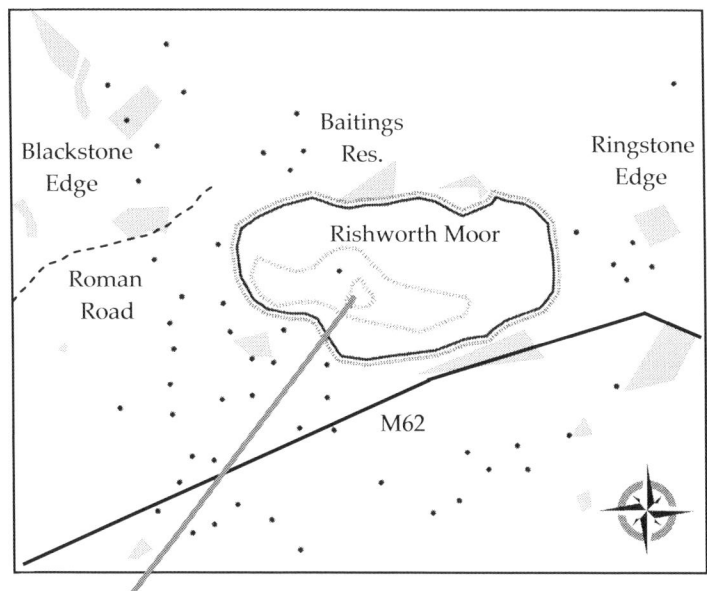

Fig: 36

*Centre of group **D**. As we have seen in A, B and C, group D is centred on a defensive hill site.*

Besides the cluster of Mesolithic sites in the area there are also a number of Neolithic and Bronze Age burials - notably around Ringstone Edge

Fig: P37

Looking over Baitings Reservoir to the Rishworth Moor upland

Group D: West of Rishworth and between the Baitings and Booth Wood reservoirs.
Coordinates: **X** 400692 **Y** 416722
Lat 53.647 **Long** -1.991
SE 00692 16722.

MESOLITHIC DISTRIBUTION MODELS

From an ethnographic point of view it is possible to suggest that the site groupings illustrated in groups **A, B, C** and **D** might offer an insight into the development of Mesolithic culture in the East Lancashire and Calderdale districts of the South Pennines. It is clear that the central area of each group is occupied by a defensible hilltop location within a water catchment area. This can be seen in the number of Mesolithic sites falling within areas of high reservoir density (*Fig: group 38*).

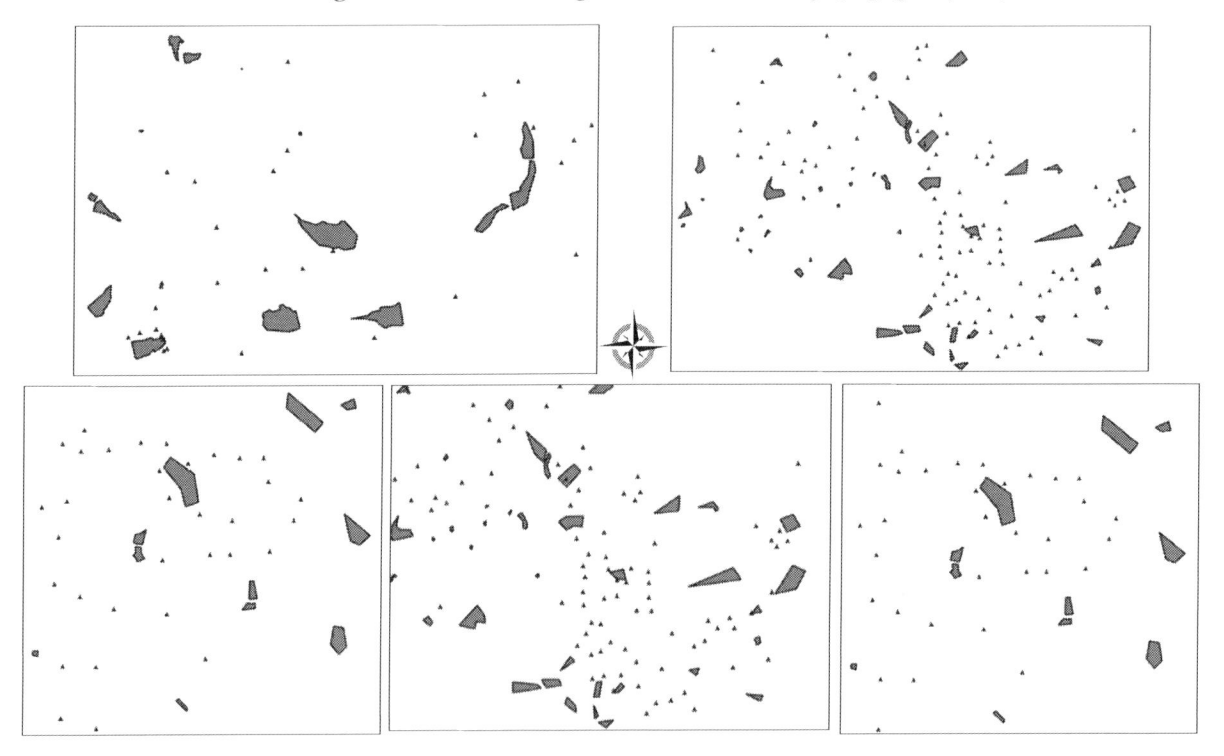

Fig: group 38 - Selection of Mesolithic sites in relation to reservoir density in East Lancashire and Calderdale ▲ *Mesolithic site* ▬ *Reservoir*

The central sites were carefully chosen to conform to the standard upland criteria of contour height and plateaux with the additional requirements that the site should be of a possible defensive nature with good water source. As always there is a caveat in assuming a defensive nature within Mesolithic sites - in most cases these sites were continually occupied through to the Iron Age and any defensive structure (banks, ditches and stone revetments etc.) could have been created during the Neolithic, Bronze and Iron Ages.

Fig: 39

Groups **A** to **D** - *areas of high reservoir density*

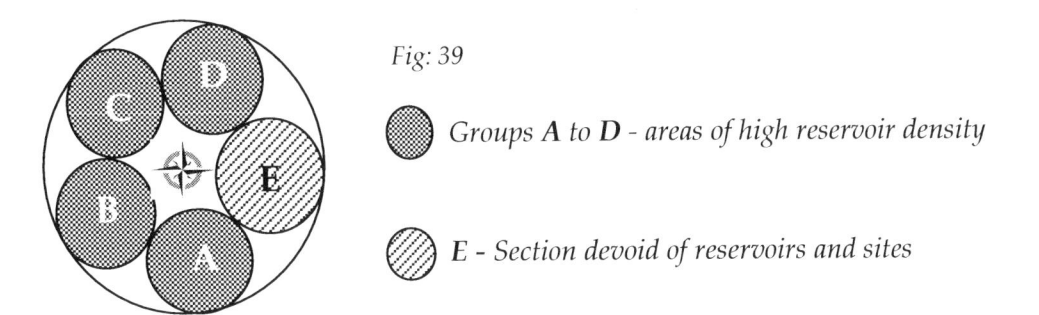

E - *Section devoid of reservoirs and sites*

The group cluster in *Fig: 39* suggests that there should be another sub-group in the eastern sector. However, this is not the case - another group here would tidy up the diagram but in reality **E** covers the lowland area running from the edge of the Pennines to Halifax. There are no prominent hills or water catchment areas here and hence no Mesolithic sites to speak of.

It is very possible that the central sites within groups **A** to **D** were not actually chosen for defensive reasons by the Mesolithic occupiers. In some cases the hillsides were utilised by farmers during the Iron Age thus leaving a lynchet pattern of terracing on the slopes; this could also have occurred during almost any period to the eighteenth century. However, an *element* of defence might have been a priority during the late Mesolithic as there is evidence from some sites nationally to suggest that a degree of inter-communal violence was present during this period (Spikins 2010).

It is possible to suggest, then, that the central sites within groups **A** to **D** may have been chosen by the initial occupiers of this landscape - possibly as early as in the Upper Palaeolithic. We have seen that the site group location falls upon the crossing of at least two important primary routes and within a compact area of hills around the 400 metre contour level within a district containing numerous water catchment areas.

Having been chosen for their particular landscape advantages early sites would have developed over millennia. They would have been reoccupied on a seasonal basis by erecting wood and brush shelters and creating particular areas for specific purposes - such as hearths to supply warmth for the living areas, fires for cooking and heating and small furnaces to heat flint prior to working it. Other areas were used for butchery, tool and weapon manufacturing, growing herbs and plants, latrines, small stock enclosures and, in a small number of known cases, pit burial 'cemeteries.'

In other words, these sites would abide in the landscape as *persistent places* even though they were probably not occupied through the year (certain sites were the exception to this as at Star Carr). Palaeolithic hunters would have fixed their transient camps in the landscape and their descendants would have followed the same lifestyle in following traditional routes and camping in the same places. This is seen in the large number of Mesolithic flint scatter sites and camp sites where evidence in the form of artefacts and burials from the Neolithic, Bronze Age, Iron Age and even the Anglo Saxon periods are gathered within a small area.

As far as the evidence can show the Mesolithic saw a steady population increase over the four millennia covered by the period. It would not be surprising if the central sites within the local groups had been fixed within the landscape by the start of the Mesolithic and we are seeing in the scatter sites of each group a radiating spread within an extended social group. The central site may have acted as a foci for particular families and, as the family expanded over generations so new sites were created within the accepted region occupied by that family. Perhaps we are seeing in the site scatter patterns the rough extent of a culmination of hunter-gatherer and forager lifestyles - the pattern of settled and transient occupation sites of a people slowly developing a different lifestyle to that of the past 250,000 years.

It has been suggested above that within the general linear scatter of Mesolithic sites a number of circular groupings can be discerned and, while some may fall within the realms of chance, a case can be made for these groups having been part of a related community. Taking the area of land covered by the sites, and the postulated Mesolithic population count of 0.01 people per square kilometre, the population in the north of Mesolithic England would amount to approximately 520 people. This amounts to .071 people per *known* site and far less than this when we consider that we are aware of only a fraction of the Mesolithic sites that must exist. Taking an arbitrary (but conservative) figure of one site in ten having been discovered we arrive at a figure of .0071 people per site which equates to a grand population total for the whole of Calderdale of one very lonely (albeit busy) person.

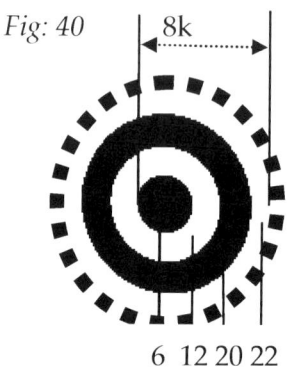

Fig: 40

6 12 20 22
Group site count

Obviously there is something very askew with the numbers here. Taking another approach, the largest group cluster (group **D**) was divided into four equal concentric circles and the number of sites within each sector counted.

It can be seen in *Fig:40* that the number of sites within each two kilometre band increases towards the periphery of the group. If it is indeed the case that the group centres were the original settlement foci then it would appear that the more central the site and the higher its status in terms of space and desirable location.

The central area of group **D** extends to 3.1 square kilometres within which are six known sites. It is difficult to assign an accurate number of people to each of the central area sites as the number will differ according to which spatial distribution model is employed. We could say that the central area was the longest established in the extended group and would be of highest status; this may result in an established family hierarchy where higher numbers occupied each central site with dwindling numbers per site towards the periphery of the extended group (**Model 1**).

Alternatively, the older the site the more possibility there is of an ageing population and subsequently less people per site. It could be that succeeding generations would move to the group periphery when starting a family and the further out from the centre each site is located the younger and higher the individual site population may be **(Model 2)**. Given these scenarios there would be an inverse population for each area:

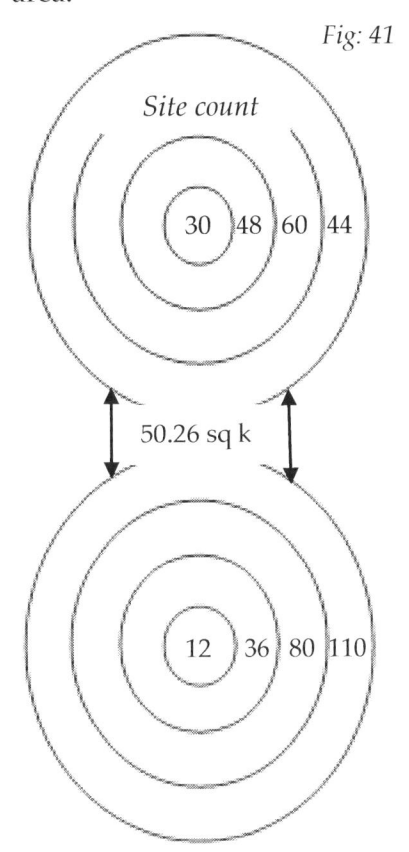

Fig: 41

Site count

30 | 48 | 60 | 44

50.26 sq k

12 | 36 | 80 | 110

Model 1

Postulating a number of five people per site within the central group decreasing to two per site on the periphery we would have: 30 people in the central area: 48 in the 2-4k section: sixty in the 4-6k section and forty four in the 6-8k section.
*Group population total = **182***
*Equating to population per square kilometre of **3.6***

Model 2

Here we would see two people per site in the central section increasing to five per site in the 6-8k section hence: twelve in the centre: thirty six in the 2-4k section: eighty in the 4-6k section and 110 in the 6-8k section.
*Population total = **238***
*Equating to population per square kilometre of **4.7***

If we take the mean of **Models 1** and **2** as 210 people per square kilometre then rolling this across the Calderdale and east Burnley site cluster **A** we would have a projection of approximately 840 people within the middle period of the Mesolithic.

It has to be said there is not enough archaeological evidence for an accurate diachronic assessment of the Mesolithic population (change X time); the connection between sites, the environment and economic strategies is also clouded by our lack of evidence. Also, a third model of spatial settlement was proposed (*CPT*/Christaller) where *Central Place Theory* assumes that as the landscape fills up, settlements will be spaced evenly throughout it. Settlements of roughly equal size reflect a fairly equal society and this theory can be applied to **Model 1.**

Obversely, considerable variation in settlement/site size reflects a hierarchical society where the larger places perform a central function and provide a range of goods on behalf of a cluster of satellite sites. In **Model 2** we see that there are a smaller *number* of sites in relation to outlying satellite districts but we have no indication of site size. Nevertheless, there is a spatial complexity working here and a version of *Central Place Theory* might be at play.

All spatial models suffer from the fact that they are, by default, idealised in their conception of the social, cultural and topographical influences of their subject - they are further limited by the conception of their creator. And here is the rub within **Models 1** and **2**; by fitting all the known sites into a weak diachronic hierarchy the analysis of the Calderdale settlement/site patterns can be said to be one of archaeological discovery rather than a true assessment of the social elements at work in the past.

Some sites may have had a ritual or religious use and, although small in size, would have been of disproportionate importance within society. Other sites would have been relatively large but used only sporadically (on social occasions) while sites of a political nature ('moot' sites) would have played a significant role without actually ever having been occupied.

A model, then, is a synthesis of reality and must fail when certainty is required of it. The principal value in the primary function of the model is to help generate questions and hypotheses that can be tested against archaeological data rather than attempting to fit the data to the model. While no claims of scientific accuracy are claimed for the foregoing Calderdale models it is hoped that they provide at least an ethnographic flavour of the region. The emerging story suggests that Boulsworth and Calderdale could have supported a very similar number of Mesolithic families per square kilometre as did the Forest of Pendle within the sixteenth century.

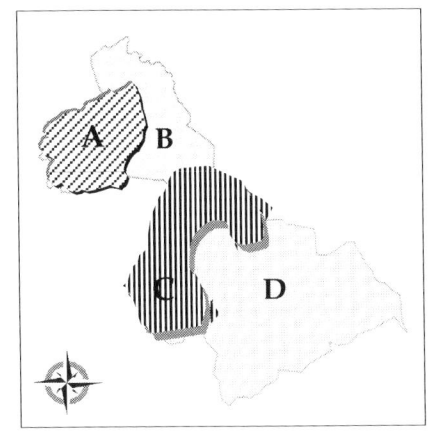

Fig: 42 - Comparison of proposed Mesolithic population density between the One Metre and Two Metre BNC Survey and Early Modern Pendle Forest. This suggests that the Boulsworth area was not the 'empty' landscape that is often suggested

A: Pendle Forest **B**: Pendle Borough
C: Area of site cluster **D**: Calderdale

Before leaving the thorny question of spatial settlement and population numbers during the Mesolithic it may prove interesting to look at a panel of rock 'art' discovered in 1973 on the western slopes of Creag Mhor (NM 8222 0270), Ormaig (Scotland) - *HMS site number NM80SW 8*. The eastern rock displays distinct rosette motifs along with a number of cup-and-ring designs (Beckensall, S. *The Prehistoric Rock Art in Kilmartin* Kilmartin House Trust 2005).

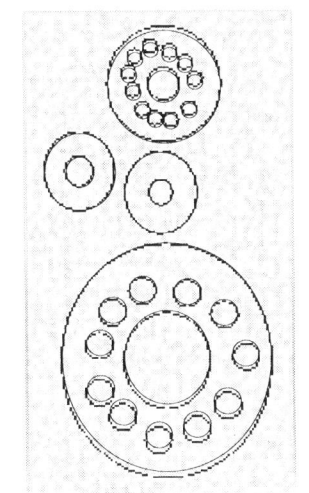

Fig:43 - The Ormaig rosette panel - art or pragmatism?

The dial motif is located on high ground overlooking an entry point into the Kilmartin Valley. The carving arrangement is similar to that found on Ilkley Moor and around the Milfield Basin. The carving is considered to date from the Neolithic or Early Bronze Age and opinions as to its purpose vary widely. C. Waddington (Cup and Rings in Context Cambridge Archaeological Journal 8 [1] 1998) argues that they 'inscribed grazing areas' by demarking secure upland summer pastures for particular groups.

It is clear that there is a remarkable similarity between the satellite rings encircling a large central ring and the spatial site patterns suggested in ***Models 1*** and **2**. Were these inscriptions actually denoting settlement within a defined territory? This raises the possibility that the rock 'art' actually fulfilled a pragmatic need for 'mapping' the landscape.

Territorial Patterns

The hills skirting the north/west/south borders of Calderdale appear to have been highly favourable to Mesolithic people. There appears to have been a greater density of settlement and occupation here than in any other region of the North West of England. The overwhelming majority of sites within Calderdale occupied the periphery of upland plateaux at around the 350 metres to 450 metres.

We saw earlier that there is a noticeable dichotomy of early landscape settlement patterns between the Lancashire district to the north of Pendle Water (Pendle Forest) and the Boulsworth Hill area. This does not mean that Pendle is devoid of Mesolithic human activity; a number of lithic tools and weapons have been discovered throughout the district but, generally, these take the form of 'loss' as opposed to evidence of settlement or protracted landscape use. The handful of recovered artefacts cannot be representative of the real picture but, nevertheless, we do not currently see the density of prehistoric evidence that many other districts exhibit.

There are marked differences in early landscape patterns between Pendle Forest and Boulsworth and it appears that the answer may lie in the story of the Mesolithic. The distinct impression gained from the site patterns of the One Metre and Two Metre BNC study areas is that the landscape stretching from the top of Boulsworth Hill (Lad Law) to Hebden Bridge in Yorkshire was a single landscape entity. The Lancashire boundary now cuts along the eastern slopes of Boulsworth Hill, thus separating the hill itself from Calderdale. The uplands to the south of Nelson and Colne fall within the Blackburnshire curtilage of the Lancashire side of Boulsworth and for centuries have been taken to be a part of the district to the north of Pendle Water.

This raises the question as to why two neighbouring areas of the same district can display such different patterns of early occupation? The answer appears to lay within the Mesolithic site pattern which dictates that Boulsworth Hill was firmly situated in the settlement district we now know as Calderdale. Taking the major rivers encircling the Boulsworth catchment area a strong case can be made for an enclosed district or territory having existed *(Fig: 44)*. This territory extends to approximately fifteen kilometres NW-SE and fourteen kilometres NE-SW (210 square kilometres); the site cluster group **A** is contained within this territory. It is interesting to note that the proposed territory is bounded by a series of defensive hill features along its western, northern and eastern perimeter while the deep Calder Valley/Cliviger Gorge delineates the southern boundary.

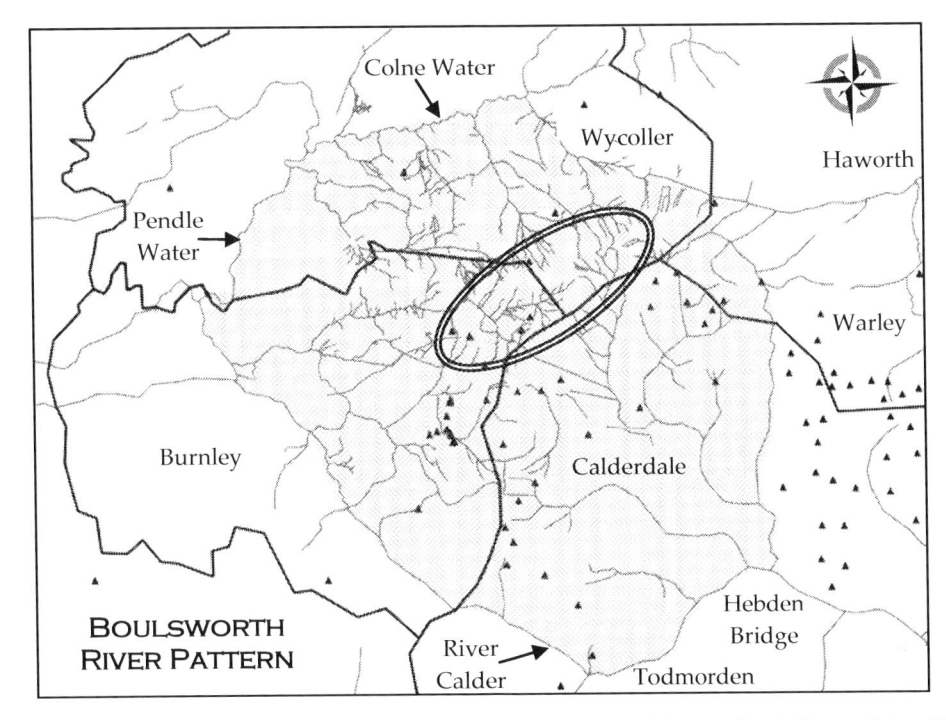

Fig: 44 - It is apparent that the outer drainage rivers of the Calder, Colne Water, Wycoller Beck and Pendle Water form a natural territorial enclosure (shaded area). ◯ *Boulsworth Hill*

The proposed territory in *Fig: 44* stretches from Colne in the north to Todmorden in the south and from Burnley in the west to Warley Moor in the east. Boulsworth Hill falls roughly within the centre of this area with the district boundaries of Burnley, Pendle, West Yorkshire and Calderdale radiating outward from it.

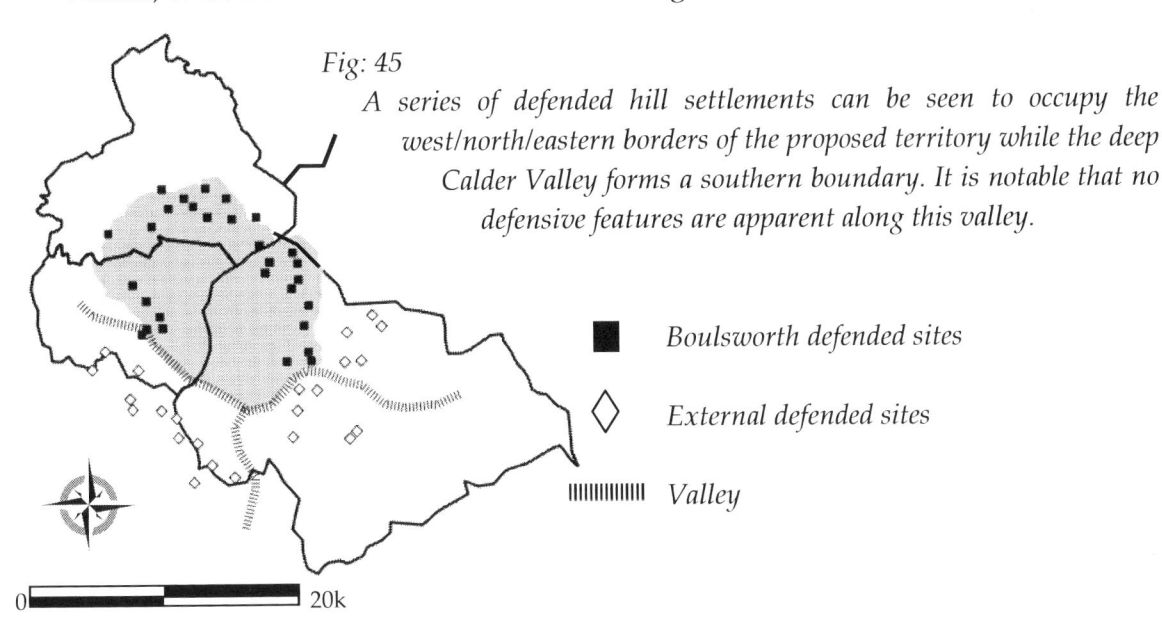

Fig: 45
A series of defended hill settlements can be seen to occupy the west/north/eastern borders of the proposed territory while the deep Calder Valley forms a southern boundary. It is notable that no defensive features are apparent along this valley.

■ *Boulsworth defended sites*

◇ *External defended sites*

|||||||||| *Valley*

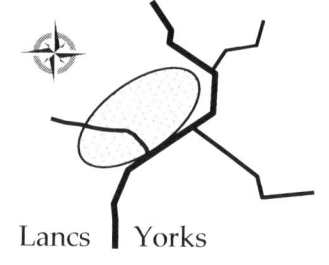

Fig: 46
Two counties and five sub-districts radiate out from Boulsworth Hill. This suggests that the hill formed a centrality within the landscape

It is very possible, then, that a territory was defined within the water catchment area around Boulsworth Hill. A separate territory here is strongly indicated by the Mesolithic site pattern, the location of defensive sites around the proposed territory borders and a strip of 'no-man's-land' running around the outer periphery. This strip is defined by a minimum space of two kilometres between defensive sites on the borders of the Boulsworth territory and neighbouring regions.

We have seen that a specific group of Mesolithic sites can be assumed within the Boulsworth territory but does this mean that the Mesolithic people actually practised the enclosure of territory? Is it possible that the defined area existed in the Late Upper Palaeolithic and that later occupants of the landscape respected it?

It has to be said that current thinking would negate the need for a such an enclosed or 'owned' parcel of landscape in this period. Although population numbers were probably higher than most ethnographic models suggest the lack of archaeological evidence for significant population numbers within the Palaeolithic suggests a later date for any enclosure.

Along with the defensive hill sites illustrated in *Fig: 45* a number of other such features are scattered across the Calderdale and Boulsworth districts *(Fig: 48)*. When a correlation is run between all of the apparent defensive sites, and all of the Mesolithic sites in the district it is found that fewer than 5% of the Mesolithic sites fall within 500 metres of the core of the defensive enclosure. A further 10% fall within a kilometre, many of these being within the extended defenses; however, it cannot be taken that Mesolithic sites were deliberately located in defended areas. Because Mesolithic and later sites shared a commonality of site requirement (level high ground etc.) we are probably seeing the result of long continuity within a shared landscape. Close inspection of the defended hilltop sites shows that Mesolithic people were generally occupying the slopes on the levels below the highest ground - these were flat areas of plateau near to streams and the water catchment areas now occupied by reservoirs while the highest ground was utilised in later periods.

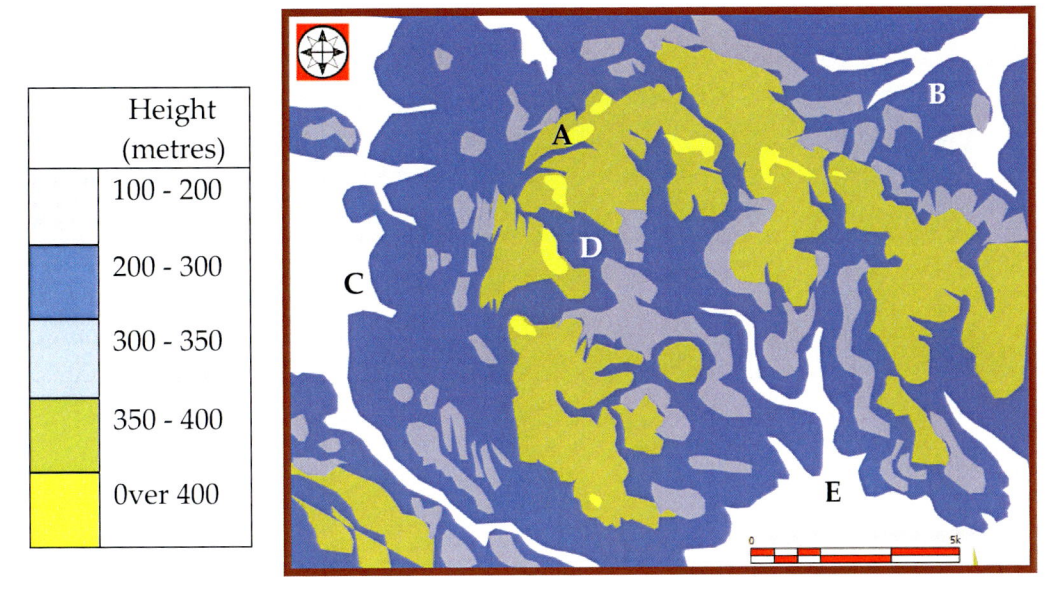

Fig:47 **A**: Boulsworth Hill **B**: Haworth: **C**: Worsthorne **D**: Widdop **E**: Hebden Bridge

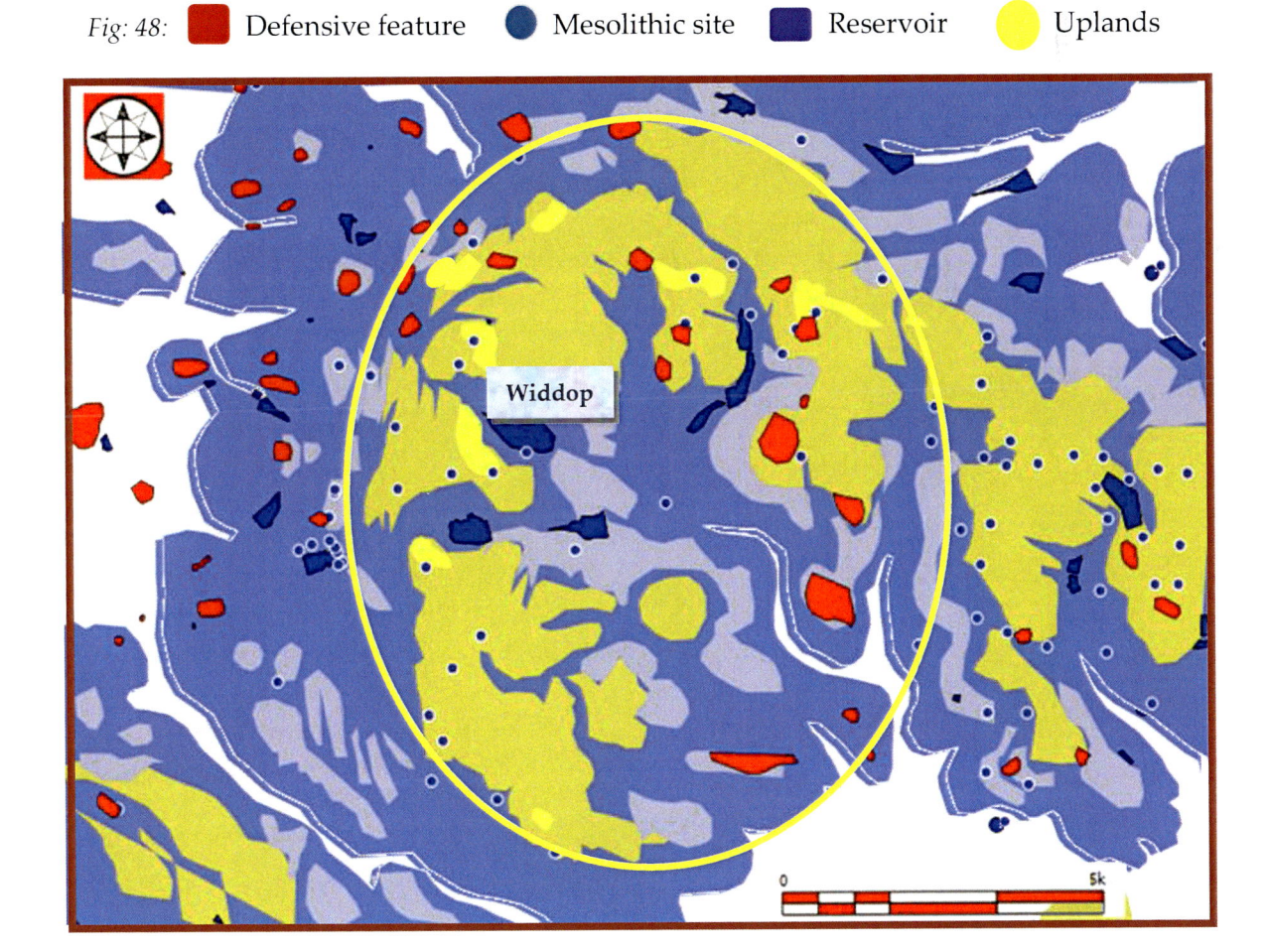

Fig: 48: ■ Defensive feature ● Mesolithic site ■ Reservoir ● Uplands

The correlation between Mesolithic sites and defensive sites is, then, likely to be a superficial one. We are seeing in the Mesolithic pattern the results of a long period of occupation within a specific landscape chosen to suit a specific lifestyle of hunter-gatherer and forager. Succeeding cultures occupied the same landscape albeit with different requirements. The later Bronze Age viewed the former Mesolithic settlements on the highest ground in a different light as new political stresses were present - to a large extent the highest ground became the reserve of the defender.

Until there is firm evidence for a system of defensive landscape features within the Mesolithic it is probably wise to assume that this was a time of relative political stability.

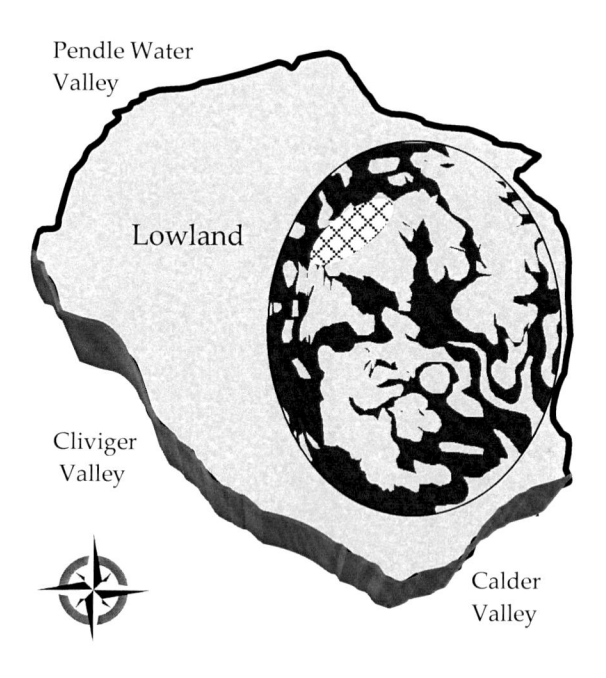

Fig: 49

The concentration of upland areas within west Calderdale (encircled in Fig: 48) forms a defined area in the proposed 'Boulsworth territory'

This has the effect of dividing the territory into two roughly equal districts of lowland to the west of Boulsworth Hill and upland to the east

⋈⋈⋈⋈ Boulsworth Hill

The One Metre BNC Survey covers the strip of upland running roughly north-south between Wycoller and Worsthorne - this is demarked by the urban fringes of the towns of Colne, Nelson and Burnley in the valley and the upper slopes of Boulsworth Hill. Along this strip we see a handful of known Mesolithic sites and this contrasts sharply with the defined clusters on the Yorkshire boundary and into Calderdale. This suggests that the lowland sites were transitory camps used by local Mesolithic hunters or travellers following routes between Calderdale and the north and east.

A good example of this can be seen in the results from a small excavation carried out at Beaver, on the outskirts of Wycoller by Lancashire archaeologist, John Hallam (Barrowclough 2008) and the late Colne historian, Bert Hindle. The site contained a flint assemblage thought to have originated in Yorkshire along with patinated flint, grey and black chert and some burnt flint. Evidence of burning was also found on gritstone and the conclusion was that the site was a transient Mesolithic hunting camp, possibly used only in a single season.

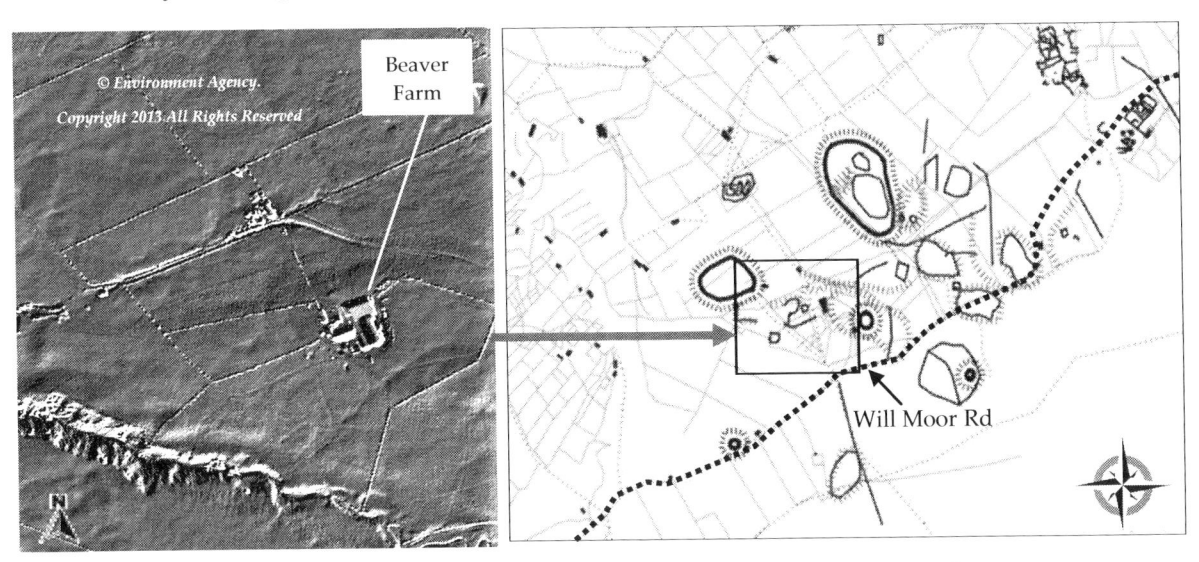

Fig: 50 Beaver Farm LiDAR   *Fig: 50a*   *Beaver Farm LiDAR features*

Fig: 50 is a one metre LiDAR extract. *Fig: 50a* illustrates that the Beaver Farm site occupies a landscape of concentrated archaeological features. The Will Moor road runs through the site and the fact that this area was occupied during the Mesolithic indicates the probable age of this routeway

The Mesolithic was a fascinating period where modern humans had no other choice but to adapt to a rapidly changing environment. Following the withdrawal of the ice sheets hunter-gatherers were faced with a largely open tundra-like landscape but this was quickly changing to a landscape of deciduous woodland and coniferous forest. During the very early Mesolithic period sea levels were low and the hunter enjoyed a larger and richer landscape in which to operate. This was not to last as the North Sea gradually inundated the low-lying area of Doggerland; the displaced population occupied the newly formed island of Britain and a long series of technical advancement and cultural development began that would stretch to the present day.

At the time when the area now covered by the North Sea was utilised by nomadic peoples from the Continent the Pennine hills were much higher and more formidable in relation to the lowland than is now the case. As the displaced peoples began to occupy their new landscape they adapted to a lifestyle on higher ground and the Pennines were no longer the dominant barrier they had once appeared to have been. Because of the diversity between an upland lifestyle, and that of the hinterlands and the new coastal plain, a new economy grew through mutual necessity. An example here being where the coastal and lowland dwellers of East Yorkshire traded the brown and chalk flint materials found in their district with their Pennine cousins.

A gradual change took place through the period which saw the pure hunter-gatherer lifestyle adapt to the increasing forested landscape by manipulating their environment. Occupiers of the Pennine uplands began to burn off swathes of tree and brush cover in order to create controlled open areas for hunting, corralling animals and cultivating certain plants.

In his Oxford University thesis on the Mesolithic Central Pennines (2012) author Paul Preston shows that the Central Pennine Mesolithic sites were persistent places that were repeatedly visited to exploit local plant and animal resources, had significant levels of site investment, were situated on Trans-Pennine pathways that linked rivers (which are argued to have been the main navigable transit routes), and were close to culturally significant 'handrail' landmarks.

The tools and weapons found on the persistent place sites were exclusively imported from a hinterland covering Northern England. This hinterland can be compared with population density models and displays a commonality of lithic styles across the Mesolithic period. Preston argues that this hinterland reflects a socio-ethnic and linguistic territory that implies a mobility throughout Northern England, with the Pennines being the core of increasing resource and mobility networks. This challenges formerly accepted models showing a defined east-west mobility and smaller separate interior and coastal social territories.

Raw materials were imported into our Pennine area and this resulted in a distinctly different way of making and using tools to that of the lowland areas. Occupants of our Pennine uplands did not display the same level of on-site flint knapping as their lowland neighbours while the amount of blade tool importation, and reworking of tools, was much higher. Further, as the displaced peoples of the former land bridges spread out and fixed their territories so the old transit routes changed in favour of the new demographic - this is reflected in changes in the raw materials imported into the uplands.

Preston also shows that a specific technology, and a localised cultural tradition developed in the Pennines. Living in the Pennines presented particular problems in that imported raw material for tools was often not suited to the uplands; however, the upland dwellers were extremely resourceful people and adapted their hunting, foraging and tool making techniques to their particular needs.

As the Mesolithic period advanced it can be seen that regional differences became more obvious. There are many complex reasons for this but on a basic level the availability of lithic material, and a more stable climate, probably became increasingly divisive as settlement patterns became fixed during the Later Mesolithic. A diversity of subsistence patterns meant that different tools and equipment were necessary to operate within riverine and lowland areas to the uplands and this served to accelerate regional diversity. Late Mesolithic society became increasingly complex which led to defined social identity, ethnic grouping and territorial affinity (Bailey, G. & Spikins, P. *Mesolithic Europe* Cambridge University Press 2008).

It is interesting to note that the Mesolithic site locations across the north of England form different patterns according to location. We see linear clusters westward from the North Yorkshire Moors, similar linear corridors from Derbyshire into Lancashire and closely defined clusters in Calderdale. Wider distribution scatters coincide with relatively low-lying areas of hinterland between the coasts and the Pennines.

Hunter-gatherer groups would have operated within a limited distance from their base camp as a balance was necessary between the expenditure of energy against the energy value of food acquired in the hunt. As the Mesolithic period advanced it appears that an increasingly pastoral lifestyle reduced the distance travelled on hunting expeditions markedly. Studies of modern nomadic and pastoral lifestyles have shown that a 25-30 kilometre radius from base might have been the norm within the earlier part of the Mesolithic - also, those following a stock herding lifestyle rarely travelled beyond a 5 kilometre radius.

It is possible, then, that the more widely distributed Mesolithic sites within the north of England were predominantly transient hunting camps that fell within the spatial extent of primary/base settlements on the higher ground.

While there may indeed be value in questioning the dichotomy of patterns between the densely clustered sites of Calderdale, and the scattered sites of East Yorkshire and East Lancashire, there may equally be nothing more telling here than the fact that the terrain had a marked influence on site location. The hinterlands of Lancashire and Yorkshire were covered in sporadic woodland, were often boggy, difficult to navigate and home to several unfriendly scurrying and flying creatures – pursuit of game was different in this environment to the uplands.

A great deal of Mesolithic evidence in the lowland areas comes from the banks of major rivers. Sites along the Alt, Lune, Ribble and Mersey show that activity along the rivers included fishing alongside hunting the larger animals as they congregated at the river.

Animal migration patterns into the uplands could be predicted and Mesolithic hunters who occupied the high ground were able to observe their prey from a distance. A favoured hunting technique for catching small animals was to trap them while larger animals were ambushed in 'chokes.' When herds of elk and deer moved through the landscape they would habitually choose traditional routes through the undulating hills and moors; the cloughs and gulleys formed by river activity were favoured routes across the hills. Certain places, where a promontory of land overlooked a narrow valley, were ideal positions from which the hunter could control and kill their target prey.

Fig: 51 – Illustration of a game choke - based on a GPS survey of the Watermeetings, Barrowford/Blacko. This route alongside Pendle Water is used by deer to this day

The Mesolithic sites indicated within the BNC Survey mark only the locations where lithic material of the period has been found and recorded. It is certain that a great deal of evidence has been discovered and discarded over the past centuries – it is equally certain that a mass of evidence lies buried beneath the upland peat cover.

As the deep valley of the River Calder cuts through the Pennine hills it bisects the cluster of Mesolithic sites within Calderdale. The route formed by the river joins the Lancashire lowlands with the lowlands of East Yorkshire and this would have been a distinct advantage to the early nomadic populations of northern England. We have seen that other important early routes converge on the Calderdale area and this would have been a contributing factor to the high population density here.

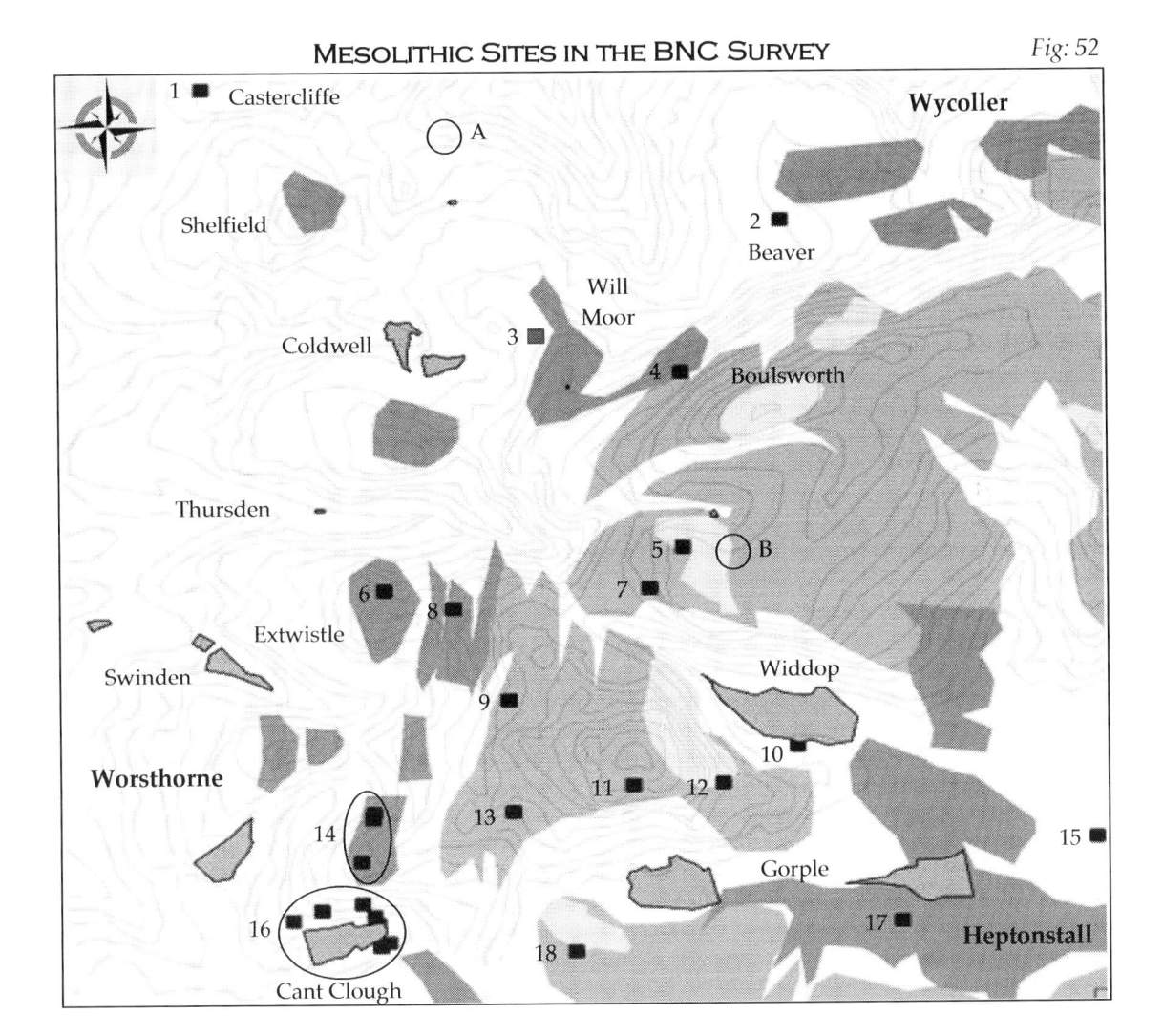

Fig: 52 MESOLITHIC SITES IN THE BNC SURVEY

SITE DETAILS IN FIG: 52

1) Castercliffe

Location: **SD** 88500 38456   **X** 388500 **Y** 438456
Lat 53.842222 **Long** -2.1762636

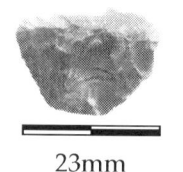

Fig: P53

23mm

Castercliffe is a Class A hillfort dating to the early Iron Age. The site extends over a large area on the Nelson and Colne boundary but flint artefacts have been discovered largely within the confines of the fort enclosure.

The extended Castercliffe area can be divided into two equal geological sections – the southern half produces quality sandstone in well-bedded sections while the northern half has long been mined for coal. The hillfort enclosure is to this day pock-marked by the circular bell-pits created by surface mining: local historian, Peter Whalley, took advantage of this in the early twentieth century by searching the spoil left by miners on the edge of the fort enclosure.

This policy paid dividends as Whalley found flint and chert material dating from the Mesolithic through to the Early Bronze Age. A small number of stray lithic finds from Castercliffe have come to light over the centuries; the black chert thumb scraper (centre in *Fig: P53*) was discovered at Hill End Farm in 2012 but most finds have now been lost. This makes the Whalley assemblage all the more important.

Fig: P54

The Castercliffe hillfort enclosure (looking north-west towards Pendle Hill)

2) Beaver (Farm)

SD 92872 37337   **X** 392872 **Y** 37337
Lat 53.832245 **Long** -2.1097877

Beaver Farm sits on the boundary between a swathe of grazing land stretching south from Trawden and the moorland sweeping down from Boulsworth Hill. The site is located on an ancient routeway connecting East Lancashire, via the Burnley area, with the Yorkshire areas of Keighley and Skipton.

Evidence for pre-Metal Age occupation of the Beaver area can be found in a series of probable cairn burials at nearby Brink Ends, the remnants of a stone hut circle at Beaver Scar, a local Mesolithic flint assemblage and Neolithic implements along with a number of circular mound features. A Bronze Age spearhead has also been found in the area.

The Mesolithic material consisted of unpatinated grey-brown-black flint and grey flint with inclusions (possibly of Yorkshire origin), patinated flint, grey and black chert and a small amount of burnt flint (Barrowclough 2008).

3) Will Moor
SD 91107 36103
X 391107 **Y** 436103
Lat 53.821125 **Long** -2.1365669

Fig: P55

45mm

Will Moor is a raised plateau of moorland on the plain directly below Boulsworth Hill. There is evidence of settlement on the highest part of Will Moor and other plateau areas in the vicinity. The patinated green flint waster *(Fig: P55)* was found by the author next to the Will Moor road in a stream that feeds the Lower Coldwell reservoir. A number of small chert chippings were also present in the exposed peat layer of the stream bank. It is likely that the flint and chert have been deposited at this position through water action.

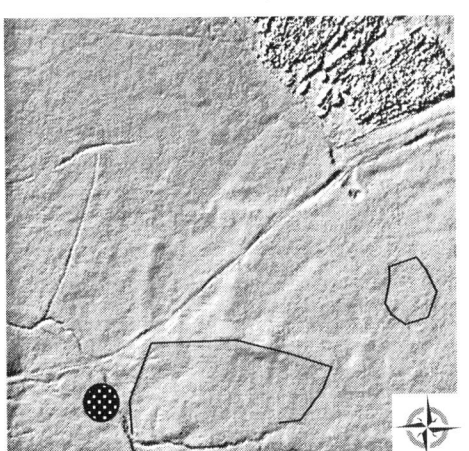

Fig: P56- One metre LiDAR extract from tile D5

● *Flint findspot*

4) Boulsworth Hill (western slopes)

Fig: P57

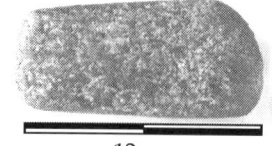

SD 91645 36060 **X** 391645 **Y** 436060
Lat 53.820745 **Long** -2.1283931

Mesolithic flint tools and a Neolithic polished stone axe *(Fig: P53)* probably of Langdale origin) were found by Peter Whalley in the early twentieth century. The exact location is not recorded but the area was around the 475 metre contour on a small plateau on the Boulsworth Hill slope between Will Moor and Lad Law. This site is adjacent to the ancient route running from Will Moor onto the hill summit.

Fig: 58

The Mesolithic flint implements found on this site could have been related to a number of apparent enclosures on the upper reaches of Lad Law

▲ *Lad Law summit*   ■ *Flint find area*

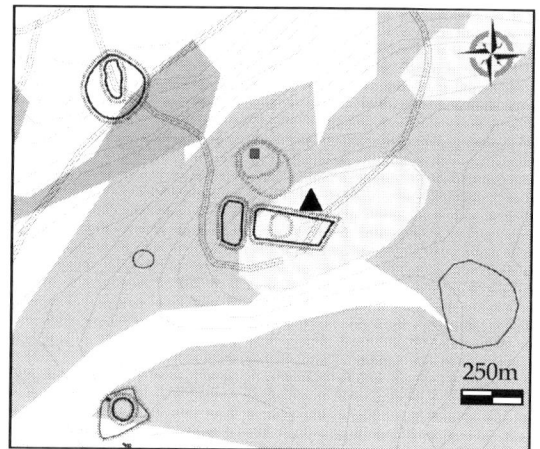

5) Boulsworth Hill 'Flint Workshop' - Scatter Site

SD 92108 34881 **X** 392108 **Y** 434881
Lat 53.810154 **Long** -2.1213319

See earlier section on flint scatter sites

Fig: 59

■ *Mesolithic flint scatter site to the north of Hey Slacks Clough (430 metre contour). A possible enclosure is located nearby to the south of the Clough*

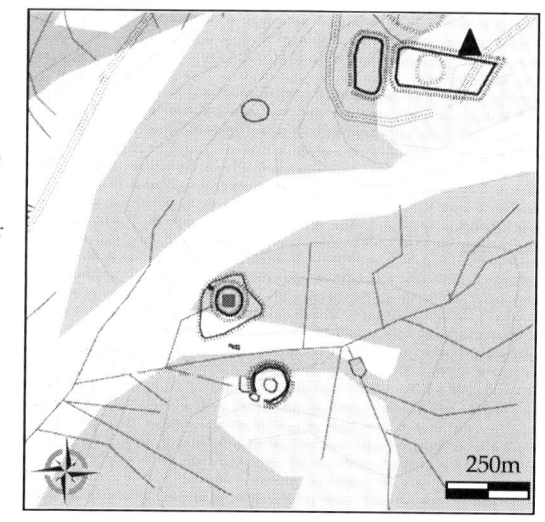

George Bernard Leach 1951: Draft site records currently in the possession of the Pendle District Landscape Archaeology Society and intended for the Transactions of the Lancashire and Cheshire History Society:

'Between 1935 and 1945 the writer investigated a number of flint sites belonging to the Mesolithic, Neolithic and Bronze Age, on Worsthorne Moors, near Burnley. The Mesolithic material belonged in general to the Tardenoisian culture. Site Number 20 is situated at the head of the Thursden Valley and near a ruined building known as Robin Hoods House. The overlying peat bed is eighteen inches deep and the top two inches of underlying soil have been washed away. This bared area is 100 yards long by 7 yards in width. White and grey flints, chert flakes, small quantities of clear brown, dark brown and reddish flints were scattered over the surface when first visited.'

'There does not appear to be the mixture of cultures which is so evident on many of the other sites in the district. What was found can be assigned to the Mesolithic period and shows Tardenoisian influence: 3 dark brown flint flakes, lightly trimmed at one edge of point - 2 grey chert flakes with blunted edges - 1 broken flint flake trimmed to an oblique point - 3 micro burins of white and grey flint - 1 triangular microlith of clear brown flint - 11 narrow blade microliths, most of them broken brown, grey and white flint with grey chert - 1 white flint graver - 3 light grey flint flakes - 2 flake end scrapers of mottled yellow flint - 2 brown flint cores - 3 chert thumb scrapers - 1 mottled grey flint scraper - numerous flint and chert flakes and chippings were also found.'

6 + 8) Extwistle Moor *Fig: 60*

6) SD 90203 33838
X 390203   Y 433838
Lat 53.800752 Long -2.1502222

6) Mesolithic flint find area recorded by G.B.Leach in 1952: 1 calcined microlith curved longitudinally - 1 black chert microlith - 1 mottled grey flint flake also curved longitudinally

8) 1 grey chert triangular microlith - 3 grey flint flakes - 1 flint core - 3 small flakes - 1 black chert microlith

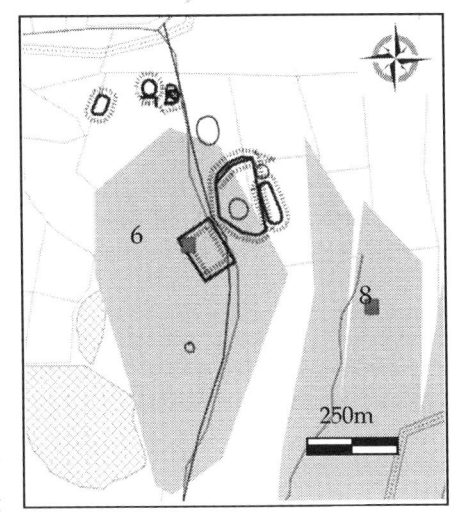

7) Thursden Valley

SD 91474 34338
X 391474 Y 434228
Lat 53.805263 Long -2.1309450

Mesolithic implement find area marked on third party map on edge of Thursden Valley. The findspot sits on the western perimeter of a possible 11 hectare enclosure at 450 metres.

▪ *Uncorroborated flint find area 700 metres south of* **Site 5**

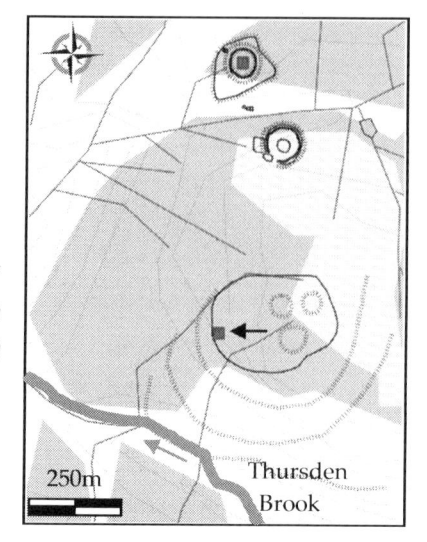

Fig: 61

9) Near Head of River Brun

SD 90163 33040   X 390163   Y 433040
Lat 53.793579 Long -2.1508015

'Mesolithic flint' find area near trackway on edge of valley. Third party information - uncorroborated.

10) Southern edge of Widdop reservoir

SD 92849 32722
X 392849 Y 432722
Lat 53.790765 Long -2.1100287

One of many Mesolithic findspots in the Widdop area.

Fig: P62

Image: Chris Heaton - Creative Commons

11) Gorple Stones

Fig: P63

SD 91663 32144
X 391663   Y 432144
Lat 53.78548   Long -2.1280069

Mesolithic flint find area recorded by G. B. Leach in 1952: Site on the Gorple Stones outcrop on the Lancashire/Yorkshire boundary at 1400 feet ASL: 2 black chert microliths - 1 small chert scraper - 1 thin flat white flint flake.

Image: Chris Heaton - Creative Commons

12) Gorple Gate

Fig: P64

SD 92605 32404
X 392605   Y 432404
Lat 53.787900   Long -2.1137227

G. B. Leach 1952: 1 narrow mottled-grey flint - 1 light-brown flake - 1 dark smoky-brown leaf-shaped flake - 1 chert graver - 2 flint microlith cores.

Image: Malcolm Streeton - Creative Commons

13) Rams Clough

SD 91062 32017   X 391062   Y 432017
Lat 53.784401   Long -2.1371248

Mesolithic flint find area recorded by G. B. Leach in 1952: Evidence of non-geometric industry shown in white, light-grey and mottled brown flints: 1 light-grey chert flake trimmed hollow at end and notched near base - 2 small trimmed flakes - 1 black chert micro core - 1 small bead of weathered grey silt stone - 1 small tranchet arrow tip of rock crystal - 20 good flint flakes - 1 flint core - 1 black chert core.

14) Site group near quarry north of Cant Clough reservoir

SD 89317 32207   **X** 389817   **Y** 432207
Lat 53.786087 **Long** -2.1660306

Mesolithic flint find area recorded by G. B. Leach in 1952: 1 grey flint microlith - 2 broken white flakes each with a notch on one edge, probably from preliminary work in manufacture - a number of microlith cores which all point to the Early Mesolithic - 9 triangular and leaf-shaped arrowheads and a beautifully worked grey flint willow leaf pattern arrowhead, all of the Windmill Hill cultural tradition - 1 fragment of a polished stone celt of finely grained grey stone.

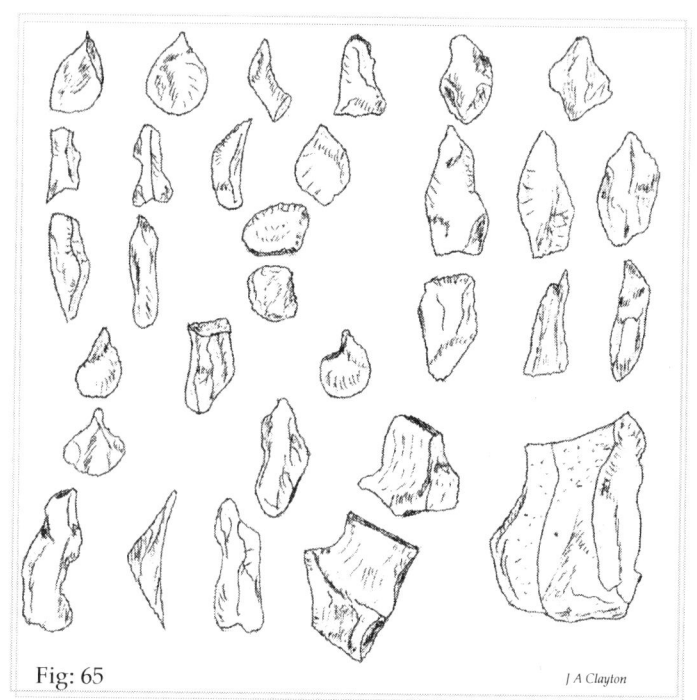

Fig: 65   J A Clayton

In the top three inches over three square yards of peat stained soil were found 4 micro-burins - 2 microliths of clear light-brown and clear smoky-brown flint - 2 lightly trimmed flakes of grey and clear light-brown flint - 2 reddish flint flakes (one trimmed) - 1 broad brown flake - a few broken flakes and chippings.

15) Ridge on southern edge of Lower Gorple reservoir

SD 91528 30762   **X** 391528   **Y** 430762
Lat 53.773129 **Long** -2.1300305

G. B. Leach 1952: Level area of ridge top sitting on Lancashire/Yorkshire boundary. Possible early occupation site: 1 micro burin - 3 small lightly trimmed flakes - 1 small light-brown flint chisel flake - 1 black chert microlith - 1 flat flake - 1 brown flint microlith core - numerous flint flakes and chippings.

16) Group of seven sites around Cant Clough reservoir
(group centre): **SD** 89741 430996   **X** 389741 **Y** 430996
Lat 53.775196 **Long** -2.1571498

Group sites all recorded by G. B. Leach in 1951:

Site 16a) East of Cant Clough keeper's house to reservoir wall and up steep slope to top of hill. The quarry road bisects the site. The site was occupied in the Mesolithic, Neolithic and Bronze Age. 15 non-geometric and geometric flint microliths of light-brown, slightly patinated, clear-brown, white and mottled-grey - 1 bead of cannel coal with picked hole (not drilled) - 35 thumb scrapers - 4 other scrapers - 2 hollow scrapers - 1 brown chert side and end scraper - 3 borers - 10 flint flakes - 2 leaf arrowheads - 2 tranchet arrowheads - 2 beautifully worked tanged-and-barbed arrowheads, one of which is unusual being of black chert and the other of light-brown flint (both of these worked to a convex finish) - 1 large leaf-shaped implement of horn coloured flint is possibly a spear head - 1 chopper of grey and black banded chert, the chopping edge is trimmed and the back steeply faceted. There were numerous flakes and chips from this site but only 2 cores found.

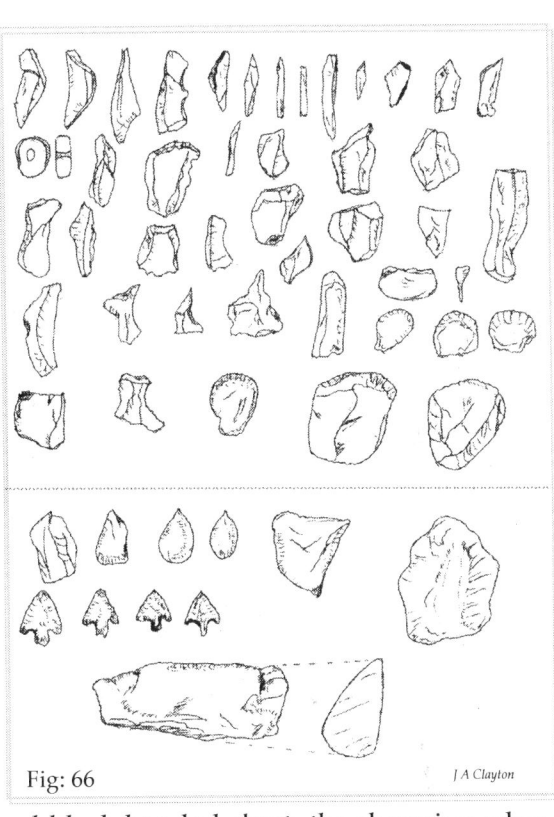

Fig: 66   J A Clayton

Site 16B) Site near near quarry road. Half of an oval mace head with hourglass perforations found. This was sent to Dr. J. R. Earp of the Geological Survey. He considered it to be of fine grain white silica stone which had been quarried from a alleged 'roadway' (Lancs 55 SE1) which he believed most certainly was not in fact a road but a quarry specially excavated for this type of stone. In a recent Paper W. F. Ranking has shown that mace heads of this kind in South East England have Mesolithic associations.

Fig: P67 - Many mace heads do not display signs of wear - this may indicate that they had a ceremonial purpose

Site 16C) Site on knoll to the north of, and close to, the cant Clough quarry road: 3 clear flint microliths - 1 white flint microlith - 5 micro cores (2 of good quality chert) - 5 arrowheads, 3 leaf-shaped, 1 triangular, 1 barbed-and-tanged light-grey flint - 12 small scrapers - 22 ridges and polygonal flakes - 3 pointed implements worked along one edge and tip - 1 thin symmetrical flake of pink flint roughly round at edges (it is difficult to see what purpose this had).

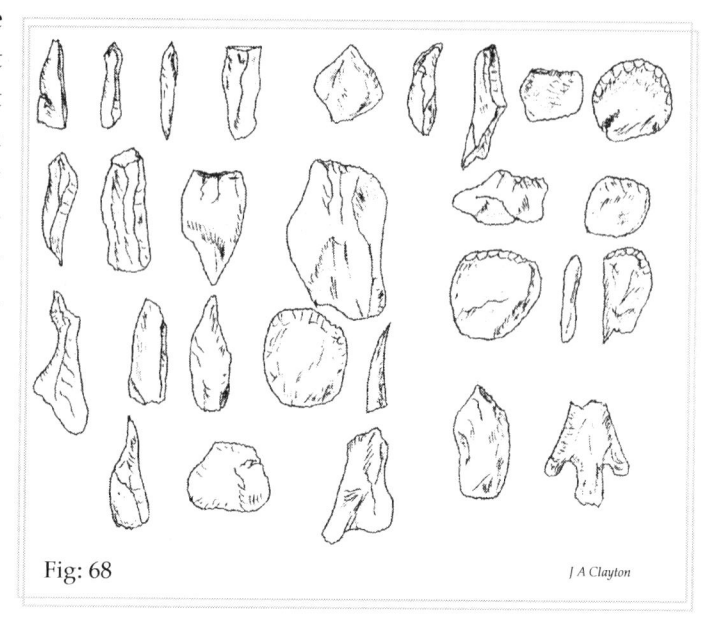

Fig: 68

16D) Site near north end of ridge above Cant Clough reservoir: 3 microliths, 1 white flint, 2 clear light-brown - 2 lightly trimmed flint flakes - 1 mottled-grey obliquely pointed flint implement - 3 flint flakes - several flint flakes and chippings.

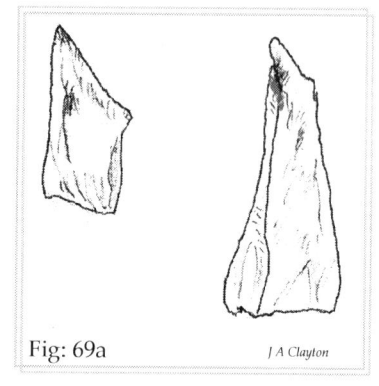

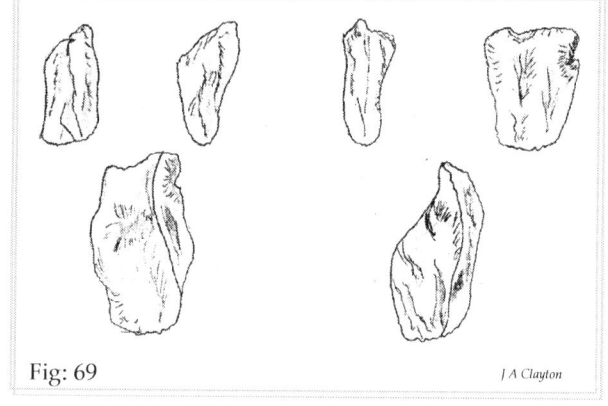

Fig: 69

Fig: 69a

16E) Site on ridge to south of end of Cant Clough reservoir: 2 implements were found: 1 white flint microlith - 1 grey flint graver.

16F) Area find of 4 microliths of white and grey flint.

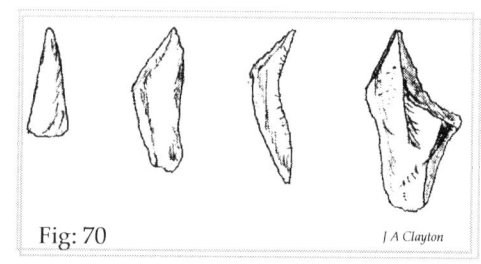

Fig: 70

16G) The site area begins at the quarry north-east of Cant Clough reservoir and continues northward. At the centre of the site is a cairn over a prehistoric burial. Finds were: 3 white flint microliths - 1 white flint graver - 1 black chert flake lightly trimmed along upper part of right edge - 3 smoky-brown flint flakes worked at the edges - 1 smoky-brown triangular flint arrowhead - 2 fine side scrapers of grey flint - 2 discoidal thumb scrapers of clear-brown flint - 14 good flint flakes - 14 small flint flakes - 4 small flint scrapers.

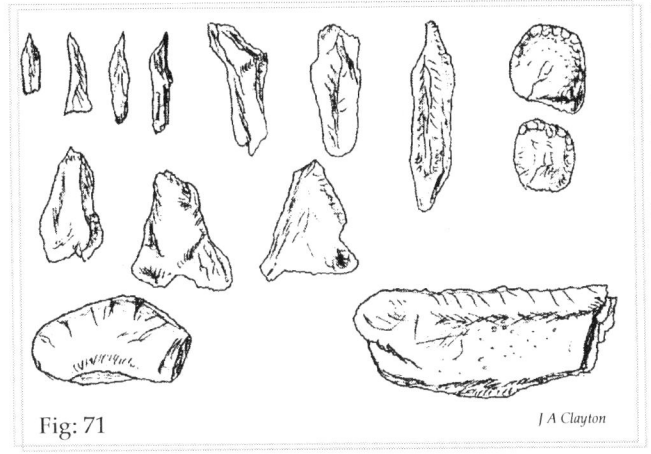

Fig: 71   J A Clayton

17 + 18) Small numbers of Mesolithic implements including white flint flakes and a scraper - find areas.

A) Stone axe found in Fox Clough on the Colne/Trawden boundary in 1957 - 150mm x 62mm x 6mm. Type of stone not known - report appears to suggest Mesolithic date. Reported in *The History of Colne* Pendle Heritage Centre 1998.

B) Rock shelter found on 'upper reaches of Hey Slacks Clough' with more than 100 flint implements discovered on the hill slope in front of the site - report appears to suggest Mesolithic date >A/B Reported in *The History of Colne* Pendle Heritage Centre 1998<

MESOLITHIC: DISCUSSION

The foregoing lithic assemblages contain a similarity in implement type and materials but this is to be expected given the close proximity of the sites from which they originated. That said, when lithic groups from across the north of England are studied it can be seen that Mesolithic society within the Boulsworth area appears to have echoed the traditions apparent within the wider area - to a certain extent at least.

White patinated and brown flint tools and weapons appear along with chert implements on almost all sites across the Pennine district. However, as the Mesolithic period progressed so a subtle difference appeared within tool types and materials employed within the Pennines in relation to the lowlands and coastal regions. If a Mesolithic Boulsworth 'territory' did indeed exist within a Pennine penumbra of settlement then material imports suggest that the area exercised closer ties with the Lincolnshire and Nottinghamshire districts than it did with its neighbours in the eastern and western lowlands. Further to this, ethnographic studies, backed by stable isotope analysis, has revealed that the coastal and inland occupiers of the north of Mesolithic England were, in fact, two distinct cultures *(YAS - Europa Day Lecture)*.

The Early Mesolithic people who inhabited our Pennine district were little different to their Palaeolithic ancestors who had lived off the land here for countless generations. The nomadic lifestyle of this latter period had continued over a mind-boggling length of time; southern Britain could possibly have been inhabited by early humans as early as 850,000 years ago. A recent project carried out by Oxford Archaeology at Ebbsfleet (Thames estuary), Kent, saw the excavation of an elephant that died somewhere around 400,000 years ago. Remarkably, the elephant can be shown to have been killed and butchered and was almost certainly the victim of a hunting party whose flint tools and weapons litter the site.

It is not know exactly which species of human ancestors were responsible for the death of the elephant but the probability is that they were *Homo heidelbergensis*, close cousins of *Homo erectus*. Although their brain volume was only around 75% of that of modern humans they walked upright, used fire and manufactured lithic weapons. Gradually the early hominine occupants of Britain gave way to modern humans but the ancient nomadic hunter-gatherer lifestyle actually changed very little.

Fig: 72
After Grant, Goring & Fleming

Winter fashion - Ötzi was discovered as an ice mummy who had lived in the Alpine region around 3,300 BC - although he lived in the Copper Age he would have sported the same winter clothes as Mesolithic people across Northern Europe. He wore a grass cape over skins lined with grass to trap air for insulation. His hat was of bearskin as were his boot soles with deerskin being used for his boot uppers - his boots were stuffed with straw. Other garments were of leather. He carried a flint blade with an ash handle, a longbow and a leather quiver filled with arrows along with special fungi used for lighting fires and for medicinal purposes

To the modern mindset, where recorded history covers a mere two millennia, the Palaeolithic is almost unfathomable. If an individual were to have lived throughout the period they would have witnessed at least ten major Ice Ages where glaciers advanced across the land before gradually retreating. These were interspersed with climatic episodes that are not classed as Ice Ages but were, nevertheless, harsh periods that would have placed undue demands on flaura and fauna - often for thousands of years in a single episode.

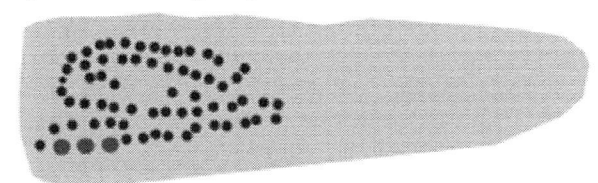

Fig:73 A representation of the Abri Blanchard Bone Plate. Dating to around 30,000 BC the artefact was found in the Dordogne. It has been suggested that the carved pattern of circles represents the waxing and waning moon and could have served as a form of crude Upper Palaeolithic calendar. It is generally agreed, however, that the pattern was created to record lunar events as they occurred rather than as a predictor of future events

Modern archaeology is increasingly providing evidence for a defined social structure within the Mesolithic period and this gives the lie to the traditional views of the post-glacial peoples who populated our islands. Evidence from sites at Vespasian's Camp, Wiltshire, and Star Carr in East Yorkshire shows that Mesolithic communities gathered together in large numbers at certain times of the year - probably in relation to a specific, or a series of events. This suggests an acknowledgment of a common time-frame and, therefore, a means of timing the organisation of gatherings.

Recent work by Prof. Vince Gaffney of the University of Birmingham has raised the fascinating possibility that Early Mesolithic astronomers were able to utilise the phases of the moon, in conjunction with sophisticated adjustments relating to the solar year, to reckon time. Excavations in Warren Field, Aberdeenshire, have uncovered a series of twelve large pits of varying size and alignment arranged around an arc. Two of the pits had contained timber uprights and it was found that the pit and post complex corresponded with the landscape horizon of Warren Field where a defined notch formed a pass through the surrounding hills.

Viewing the sunrise on the midwinter solstice from a specific pit within the complex shows the sun to appear in the base of the notch V - as the seasons progress the sun rises higher within the notch and appears to roll up the side of the hill. Other sight-line permutations allow for an accurate subdivision of the lunar cycle. It is thought that this time reckoner was begun around 8,500 BC - 8,000 BC and reached full operational mode around 7,800 BC - thus predating the earliest known formal calendars of Babylonia by around four millennia. (The Warren Field 'calendar' is reported in *Current Archaeology* No. 283 October 2013).

It is clear that our view of the 'simple' lifestyle of the Mesolithic is changing rapidly. It was previously thought that a lack of evidence for monumental structures within the period pointed to a fully nomadic culture where time restraints dictated a short period spent at each seasonal site. In other words, because the lifestyle only allowed a fleeting visit to each camp on the seasonal cycle the people had no will to erect permanent monuments within the landscape.

This view has now been shown to be inaccurate; during the Mesolithic an initial phase of Stone Henge was marked by massive timber 'totem poles' on the site. Also, evidence for permanence of landscape occupation is increasingly coming to light with wooden structures and markers being discovered, especially within the northern half of Britain. A recent find in the Rhondda Valley appears to be the oldest known decorative wood carving in Europe. A wooden timber post measuring 1.7 metres in length, and dating to the Late Mesolithic, was discovered in a waterlogged peat deposit. It is thought that the post, carved with wavy and herring-bone pattern lines, was erected as a territory or 'significant place' marker or possibly used as a votive offering. It is certain, then, that a great deal more evidence, in the form of Mesolithic timber artefacts, has yet to see the light of day.

The end of the last Ice-Age (Devensian) ushered in a new interglacial period known as the Holocene and this is really where we begin to pick up the story of the early inhabitants of the British Isles. In the six thousand years or so from the retreat of the glaciers, to the final throes of the Stone Age, the Mesolithic people can be seen to have developed a lifestyle that is sometimes referred to as a 'revolution.' The very gradual evolution of humanity and technology to the Late Upper Palaeolithic gathered pace, firstly across the Middle East and then across Europe. The inhabitants of the new British Isles adapted the routes and landscapes of their ancestors to suit a rising population and this further developed into a more settled semi-pastoral lifestyle. The Late Mesolithic peoples had developed their own tool technology and now they were manipulating the land itself.

Controlled burning of the tree and bush cover created attractive grazing areas and attracted prey. Having been gathered within a predefined area the animals could then be trapped, ambushed or corralled into enclosures and here we see the initial stages of true pastoralism. The herding of wild animals required a degree of skilled stock management, including growing and gathering specific feedstuff; this meant that the stock-keeper would need control of a defined area of land, at least during the growing and harvest season. Fences (ditches, banks, boulder, hurdles) became necessary, not only to contain the domestic herd but also to keep wild animals from the growing crops. The field limits would rapidly become fixed land boundaries and former transient camps became more settled in order to at least endure through the planting, growing and harvest season.

Stock-keepers quickly realised that selective breeding of the finest stock animals would allow for improvement in particular genetic traits, such as increased meat yield and greater strength in draught animals. And so the energy input into stock keeping became such that it was no longer feasible to move on to distant winter hunting and foraging grounds. Summer crops were grown close to the base camp for winter feed and this meant that highest ground was no longer such an attractive place to set up camp. More permanent sites were created on the periphery of the established group territory where a greater range of crops could be cultivated. The new farming groups improved their livestock, grass and corn and remained on the lower hill slopes, heading into the higher grounds in summer to graze their animals. And so the Late Mesolithic community groups developed into non-nucleated socio-economic territories where certain members of the extended groups farmed while others built and maintained the necessary infrastructure required by a settled agricultural way of life.

This is not to say that there was a headlong rush into farming during the Late Mesolithic. It was probably more a case of a very gradual realisation that the increasing population was tending to settle for longer periods which, in turn, meant expansion and 'ownership' across attractive parcels of the landscape. This reduced the capacity of the land to provide shared resources between the 'owner' population and incoming foragers and so it became necessary to squeeze the maximum production out of the land available to each group. This was a slow reaction to a changing world that would only be obvious to someone looking back from the beginning of the Neolithic period (c. 4,000 BC) over the previous 1,000 years or so.

Landscape evidence for the Mesolithic period is not readily apparent in the aerial data of the BNC Survey, although it is fair to say that it does exist. We may yet find that certain extant moorland landscape features (enclosures and stone monuments) are actually of a formerly unrecognised Late Upper Palaeolithic or Mesolithic origin.

| FIVE | # NEOLITHIC AND EARLY BRONZE AGE
4,000 BC TO 1,500 BC |

Settled agriculture was being practiced in the Near East when Late Upper Palaeolithic people were establishing their hunting patterns within the British landscape. During the Mesolithic the Atlantic coast of Britain was frequented by marine traders from the Eastern Mediterranean and with them came the ideas that would shape an embryonic farming system that would take around two millennia to take a firm hold. Towards the end of the Mesolithic the landscape was supporting a wide scatter of *small* farmsteads but a system of wider communal cooperation was yet to come.

Organised farming on a larger scale would eventually lead to a firming of society within defined territories, along with the associated political difficulties of disputes over land ownership. Towards the end of the Mesolithic, however, the focus appears to have been on agricultural experiment within a subsistence tradition.

Mesolithic people are not generally recognised as having had a particular burial practice but, before the onset of the Neolithic, communities within certain districts at least were practising formalised burial. Stone tombs have been dated to around 4,3000 BC through to 4,1000 BC in the British Isles and this serves to illustrate the difficulties in assigning a particular period to a certain cut-off date.

The Neolithic period is different to the Mesolithic in a number of ways; population expanded as widespread settled farming became established, ritualistic behaviour began to leave monumental evidence within the landscape, attitudes towards the dead changed and the use of pottery became commonplace. The speed of subsistence and cultural change is, however, open to much debate. Shulting and Richards (2000) provide isotopic evidence to suggest that the change-over period was marked by a rapid change in coastal populations where domesticated resources replaced marine resources. Unfortunately this does not fit with the archaeological evidence for a gradual change over the Late Mesolithic and the Early Neolithic.

It appears from the archaeological record that the Early Neolithic societies can be viewed as having been much the same as their Mesolithic predecessors. The main initial change can be seen where the Mesolithic tools and weapons evolved from broad blade to narrow blade over the first half of the period so we see in the Early Neolithic that leaf-shaped arrowheads replaced narrow blade microliths as the favoured hunting weapons.

Fig: P74

Neolithic implements found on Shelfield Hill, Nelson (P. Whalley collection)

Material: green flint

Left to right: Leaf-shaped arrowhead: Multi-purpose tool: Spearhead: Scraper

During the British Mesolithic there was a defined 'cultural stirring' within the Near East; from the evidence of impressed pottery farmers from the region were moving into Greece. They had colonised Crete from the sea around 7,000 BC and advanced into Southern Italy around 6,000 BC. The migration continued along the Mediterranean coasts into Spain and France. Around 5,500 BC a second wave of farmers, who had settled in Hungary, migrated into Central Europe via France and by 4,000 BC the new farming methods had replaced the indigenous hunter-gatherer culture of the south of England. It took longer for the full impact of the 'revolution' to arrive in northern England and Scotland but by 3,500 BC the Neolithic can be said to have been in full swing.

Perhaps it is fair to say that the idea of herding mobile groups of animals between the best grazing areas, and growing fodder to feed domesticated animals in the winter, did not shock the indigenous people of the Late Mesolithic. After all, they had been exposed to the strange stories of agri-culture in foreign lands for many generations. It is not clear exactly how the new Neolithic culture gained a hold across Europe. Were the native Mesolithic societies overwhelmed by numbers of farming migrants who eventually supplanted them or, more likely, was a there steady trickle of migrants whose ideas were highly attractive to the indigenous populace? If this was indeed the case then it is easy to assume that a small skilled band of Neolithic venturers would carry their methods from one district to another where they would be appreciated for their knowledge and allowed to assimilate rapidly into their new environment.

It has to be remembered that each successive pre-historic period advanced at a faster rate than the preceding era. The vast amount of time over which early humans evolved into modern humans stretched back over hundreds of millennia; within the final 200,000 years of this this era modern human development became complete and people looked increasingly to the skies; they manipulated their environment and eventually began to migrate over large distances in search of a better quality of life.

Following the end of the Devensian Ice Age a 6,000 year period saw the hunter-gatherers of Europe develop methods of controlling the flora and fauna within their environment and this engendered a sense of permanence.

The following 2,000 years covered the final stone age and was a time when new ideas were introduced, not only of farming but also of 'religion.' Entirely new methods of dealing with the dead, and the erection of permanent monuments in earth and stone, firmly fixed the idea of settlement and the concept of land ownership that we see today. The first true metal age endured for 1,250 years and can be seen as an ongoing development of the cultural practices, and material technology, of the preceding era.

The final metal age lasted for 700 years and gave way to the Roman period of occupation which covered 367 years. Whereas ideas of culture and religion has formerly taken numerous millennia to become accepted within extended districts it took only three centuries for Christianity to become a serious contender for the hearts and minds of the British people.

The Neolithic, then, was a period when this 'stepped acceleration' became unstoppable - a period when 'modern' concepts were rapidly superseding the ways of the 'noble hunter.' As one antiquarian observer was moved to write on the subject; *'No longer would man enjoy the bounty of the Garden of Eden, he was forthwith sentenced to a life of drudgery, earning his existence by the sweat of his brow.'*

As a caveat on the subject of integration between the middle and new stone ages it is worth noting that the transition from hunting to farming allowed the population to quickly rise by up to a factor of twenty in certain areas. Early farmsteads often had defensive features in the form of ditches, banks and fences; it is possible that these were necessary to prevent the petty theft of live-stock by naughty neighbours but, equally, these fortifications may indicate that the intentions of the newcomers were not entirely peaceful.

However it was accomplished, by around 3,500 BC the Neolithic was firmly established and a new system of ideology and social relationships flourished. The upland sites favoured during the Neolithic were much the same as those occupied during the Mesolithic; this is evidenced by the many sites where Neolithic implements and burials overlay Mesolithic sites.

Neolithic England enjoyed a climate similar to that of the South of France today. Seed corn was now widely grown, including wheat, and the stock-breeding capabilities of the farmers had resulted in highly domesticated animals. Concepts of ownership meant stable and expanding settlements and many of the upland boundaries, paths and trackways used today were fixed at this time. Hunting was still carried out but this became a specialised skill probably practised by small groups of young men. Farmers and growers, warriors, craftsmen and miners all became an integral part of society while the role of the shaman, story-tellers and ritual-keepers grew in stature.

The old and the sick could be cared for in a settled society. It is highly unlikely that the Mesolithic people did not follow cults of one type or another but the Neolithic way of life lent itself to an appeasement of the entities considered to have been responsible for the return of the sun each spring, the bringing of rain, good growing seasons and fertility of the fields.

At the dawn of the Neolithic a new building phase swept along behind the agricultural 'revolution.' From around 4,000 BC, but only over a period spanning two generations, a number of massive halls were constructed across the British mainland. The archaeological evidence suggests that some of these halls were of cruck frame construction and could extend up to 70 metres by 30 metres, thus rivalling the latter day Anglo Saxon halls in size and construction. It has been suggested that the erection of these halls was a statement on behalf of a new social order. Larger communities (or kin groups) were being created and the new buildings would have been designed to bring people together in the build and to act as a community meeting hall on completion. The erection of such buildings on a hitherto unknown scale would have impressed the indigenous people - the buildings would be seen as a form of monument within the landscape.

It is apparent, then, that the new farmers from Europe were either arriving in Britain in sufficient numbers to form their own communities or small bands of pioneers wielded enough influence over the natives to cause them to rapidly adopt a new culture.

It is interesting to note that the mindset of the hall builders was extremely short-lived and that, in some cases, the halls were purposely destroyed. At Dorstone Hill, Herefordshire, two neighbouring halls was partly dismantled by removing the large timbers and then the remainder was burned. Two long barrow funerary monuments were created on the site of the halls and the ashes from them were incorporated into the mounds.

The indication here can be interpreted as the replacement of one type of monument with another. Where the halls could have been a foci for rituals relating to the dead so the newly created long barrows allowed for the congregation of people at burial ceremonies. The long barrow can be seen as the first structure type that still abides within our landscape.

The earliest 'earthen' barrows were actually constructed of numerous materials - some were of turf and soil, some of chalk while others were built with large quantities of small stones. The barrows were marked by flanking ditches from which the material was dug to raise them. The majority range in length from 12 to 121 metres, from 9 to 43 metres in width and of varying height. Another type of long barrow was the menhiric or chambered tomb where the mound contained a chamber, or chambers, formed by upright stones or timbers (*Fig: P75*). Long barrows were communal tombs, holding from one to fifty adults and children. Not only were they tombs, but they also served as centres of religious activity within a cult of the dead and fertility. Often, the bones of the dead were used in ceremonies performed at the recessed entrance to the barrow. The dead were usually interred after a certain period of excarnation or, sometimes, after the bones had been burned in a form of cremation ceremony.

Fig: P75
The Trevethy Quoit, Bodmin Moor.

These monuments were originally thought to have been covered by earthen mounds but are now considered to have been 'stand alone' monuments. The capstone (3.7m long) is supported by six massive uprights and reaches a height of 4.6m. A hole cut into the capstone was possibly of astronomical significance

The long barrows were roughly pear-shaped in that they were built with a bulbous end, commonly orientated roughly to the east, and a narrower tapering end towards the west. This is possibly related to ritual observations of the rising and setting sun - the burials were placed within the eastern end of the barrow. The burials contained very few grave goods other than pottery shards and arrowheads.

It is not clear how the Early Neolithic societies disposed of the vast majority of their dead, as only the bones of a very select few were interred in the barrows. Of the other 99.9% of the population, there is no archaeological record. Given that the early halls at Dorstone Hill were 'converted' into long barrows it might be suggested that the barrows were intended to represent a hall or house of the dead where the ancestors dwelt in the otherworld.

From the Late Neolithic the accepted method for disposal of the dead was by either cremation or inhumation in a single grave. In Early Neolithic period, however, a completely different practice took place - the body was disposed of in one place and then was subjected to a secondary burial of either the whole body, or part of it, elsewhere.

The settled aspect of the Neolithic peoples saw a predisposition toward the use of stone to create permanent dwellings and monumental structures and this was reflected in the tombs they built. Long barrows/passage graves/chambered tombs of the period typically contain an apparently jumbled mass of bones from numerous bodies. The skeletons are often disarticulated and frequently bones are missing. In other words, the evidence shows that Neolithic communities did not dispose of their dead in a one-off burial; they handled the remains repeatedly and moved them around.

It was traditionally considered that the scattering of human bones showed a distinct lack of respect for the dead and, worse, some antiquarians suggested that this was evidence for cannibalistic practice. However, modern archaeology has proven that the reordering of skeletal remains was the result of careful arrangement.

Neolithic bodies were given a secondary burial in three ways. The whole body could be entombed and re-arranged at a later date or certain parts (particularly skulls) could be removed to be used elsewhere. Bodies could also be placed on mortuary platforms outside the tomb until the clean bones could be placed within the communal chamber. To the modern mindset the handling of dry white bones, picked clean by the actions of nature, animals and birds, seems to be at least understandable. People have suggested that the decomposing flesh of the dead was recognised as a biological hazard and this meant that the body needed to be moved outside of society. Others are of the opinion that the soft wet flesh corresponds with ideas of femininity while the hard dry bones relate to the masculine. It might have been considered that the male was more closely allied with the earth and that all decomposed bodies assumed a masculine identity – this being useful for physical adventures in the otherworld.

Mary Baxter, a postgraduate student at Cambridge University, is a human-bones specialist and her study of Neolithic burial practice has convinced her that bodies were not fully decomposed when moved between initial mortuary and secondary burial. Rather, they were handled in a semi-decomposed state when flesh and muscle still adhered to the bones. In many cases the limbs were cut from the body or even torn away and this suggests the action of defleshing before secondary burial.

In an article for British Archaeology, entitled *Dancing with the Dead in a Mass Grave*, Mary Baxter addressed the question of why secondary burials took place in the Neolithic:

> *There may be, in some cases, a link between the place of burial and association with land - just as today many people abhor the idea of being buried in a 'foreign field' away from home. The removal of Neolithic body parts from the tomb for reburial elsewhere may relate to claims of ownership of several places. Partial or complete Neolithic skeletons, perhaps removed from tombs, have been found at other monuments such as causewayed enclosures - as if Neolithic communities wished to invest the monument with the spiritual power of the dead person.*

Excarnation, or the natural de-fleshing of bones, is a form of temporary burial that is still widely practised. The exposure of a corpse in the branches of a tree by tribes in Central Australia, or inside the house of the living by certain Papuan and Bantu tribes, or on a specially raised platform by Polynesians, all have the same object: to offer the deceased a temporary residence until the natural disintegration of the body is completed and only the bones remain. The transformation process changes the character of the corpse, turns it into a new body, and is, consequently, seen as a necessary condition for the salvation of the soul (Milliken, S. Paper Oxford 2011).

It is possible that excarnation was widely practised at various times in British prehistory. In the Early Neolithic period (4000–3000 BC), bodies appear to have been left to decompose before the bones were scattered inside settlements or carefully deposited inside tombs; in the Middle Bronze Age (1500–1250 BC) excarnation often preceded cremation on the funeral pyre; and in the Early to Middle Iron Age (800–120 BC) bodies were exposed to the elements and then selected parts of the skeleton, such as pelvises, skulls or, in the case of children, the upper half of the body, were buried in pits, as at Danebury hillfort (Milliken 2012).

The foregoing discussion relating to the transition from the Mesolithic to the Neolithic is a general overview of the changes wrought by an incoming culture. The edges of the new Neolithic blur into the preceding period and this is well illustrated in the Lancashire district. That is to say, as the Neolithic period took hold nothing much seems to have happened! It appears from the archaeological record that it was a case of 'business as usual' for the Early Neolithic occupants of the Lancashire coastal plains and uplands.

Sea level rise decelerated throughout the Neolithic from the peak levels seen in the Early Mesolithic, the levels being, perhaps, five metres below those of today. Inland lake levels slowly declined from 7,900 BC in response to infilling and the prevailing dry climatic conditions. Low levels then persisted until the beginning of the Neolithic when a rise in the water-table led to a major rise in lake levels. Taking Haweswater (Lancashire) as an example it is clear that human activity around the lake rose significantly - possibly reflecting the migration of coastal Mesolithic communities inland in response to lost coastal areas. (R.T. Jones, Paper 2009 Department of Geography, University of Exeter).

A shift of focus from the higher plateaux to the lower slopes during the Late Mesolithic appears to be marked by the density of sites around the moorland periphery. Mesolithic find concentrations at Worsthorne and Extwistle are overlaid by Neolithic implements but this probably reflects an uptake of the latest tool technology by a primarily Mesolithic society. It could well have been the case that the early Mesolithic occupants of the Lancashire Pennines were operating small scattered farming units on the dryer ribbons of the lowland/upland edges while maintaining their traditional hunter-gatherer lifestyle across the whole district.

At the end of the official Mesolithic period a marked reduction in elm tree numbers occurred across north-west Europe and there has been much speculation as the cause of this *elm decline*. The start of the elm decline event lies between 4,341 BC and 4,305

BC indicating that the onset was rapid. The end of the event lies between 3,288 BC and 3,418 BC, a period of 130 years. The probability distribution indicates that the elm decline was a uniform phased event across the British Isles. It appears that the decline can be explained to a large extent by the outbreak of disease. However, recent research on palaeoclimatic change and the nature of the transition from the Mesolithic to Neolithic in the British Isles suggests that both climatic change and human activities were implicated. It was probably the interplay between these factors, rather than any in isolation, that catalyzed the widespread, catastrophic decline of elm populations during the mid-Holocene. (*A review of the Mid-Holocene Elm Decline in the British Isles* Progress in Physical Geography March 2002 vol. 26 no. 1 1-45).

Pollen sampling over a wide area of western England indicates that post-elm decline woodland grew back in many areas from which it had been cleared, although elm did not always recover to its former levels. Thereafter the woodland was only occasionally impacted by people – and only then on a small scale – until the very Late Neolithic and Early to Middle Bronze Age. It would appear, therefore, that a pattern of shifting agriculture and small scale pastoralism was maintained throughout the Neolithic.

In north Lancashire there appears to have been a short burst of cereal growing activity during the elm decline but the Pennine fringes, and much of the lowland areas do not appear to display any concerted arable activity (Barrowclough 2008). This aids the argument for Early Neolithic people having practised small scale husbandry of animals along with utilising wild resources.

STONE AXES

In the year 1753 the idea was advanced by the Finnish agricultural chemist, P. A. Gadd, that pre-historic agriculture started by man's cutting down the primeval forest and burning most of the trees and branches in order to sow his corn-seeds in the ashes. Since that time the science has advanced and now indicates a different level of woodland clearance across varying periods within Europe.

Woodland clearance, accomplished by the cutting down and burning of woodland and scrub was practised long before agriculture started, it is known to have taken place during interglacial times. Primitive hunters and plant-gathering peoples made use of the crackling flames in order to improve their berry-grounds, to produce better grass for wild animals, or to kill gnats and other insects. It is possible that the cultivation of grain started in Western Iran, on the border line between the highland steppes and the sloping and wooded mountains, when seeds of the wild ancestors of barley and wheat were accidentally blown into the burned-off areas of the hunters, and were found to grow abundantly.

We know that this form of ecological control was being exercised in the Late Mesolithic but was a lack of tool technology responsible for the apparent low level of woodland clearance apparent within the Lancashire Pennines? In other words, where Late Mesolithic people might have wished to clear large areas of thick primeval forest, would their somewhat crude flint axes have allowed them to do so? To answer this question, in the 1950s an experiment was run in the deciduous forests of South Jutland, Denmark (Axel Steensberg *Some recent Danish Experiments in Neolithic Agriculture* 1956). A number of original Late Mesolithic, and Early Neolithic, flint axe blades from the National Museum, were obtained and these were fixed to a wooden haft in the form of the well-known Sigerslev axe, excavated from a Seeland bog.

The initial tree-felling tests were carried out in February 1952 in a temperature of 3 to 4 degrees centigrade. At the second cut one axe was totally broken, two minutes later the largest blade was cracked transversally and, after three or four minutes, the edge of the third axe was spoilt - a violent stroke split the handle of the last and smallest axe. The lesson was: **A)** that flint axes have to be treated carefully in frosty weather; **B)** that if the haft was not to split it must not be bound to the blade too tightly as allowance must be made for a little sideways play; **C)** that the usual tree-felling technique, in which the weight is transferred through the shoulders into long powerful blows, was useless when using flint tools.

The professional lumber-jacks who tried out the flint tools were unable to change their habits and consequently damaged several axes. The archaeologists soon discovered that the proper way to use the flint axe was to chip at the tree with short, quick strokes, using mainly the elbow and wrist. Having mastered the technique it was possible to use axe blades that remained unsharpened since the Early Neolithic and to finish the tree clearing operation without spoiling the axe edges. Two archaeologists were able to fell oak trees more than a foot in diameter within half an hour. They felled smaller trees by cutting all around the trunk but on heavier ones they had to use the slower method of hewing two notches, one at each side, and one a little more elevated than the other in order to control the direction of the fall. In forest clearance by fire the fallen trees must lay in the same direction; this is determined by local conditions in order for the wood to dry more quickly.

The larger mature trees were not cut down, they were killed slowly by cutting rings through the sapwood. The experiment also proved that the beech tree is by far the most difficult to fell with flint tools but this species was extremely rare in the Mesolithic and Neolithic woodlands and forests. Once the majority of the trees in the clearance area had been felled they were allowed to dry out by raising them from out of the surrounding vegetation and wedging them with branches. The first experiment failed to do this and, because the wood had not dried sufficiently, it proved impossible to set it alight. The ignition of the second phase took place along a ten metre wide belt by means of torches of birch bark attached to stakes. The wood burned well and, once the belt was well cleared, the still burning logs were rolled with long poles in order to set fire to the adjacent area. In this manner the entangled branches of trees were burned off belt by belt. Over four days the fire was controlled and conducted day and night in order to achieve an even and thorough burning of the ground.

The ashes were then evenly spread over the newly exposed ground in preparation for sowing the three kinds of wheat available in the Early Neolithic - small spelt, emmet and nodding six-rowed naked barley. Sowing experiments showed that seed planted in drill holes far outperformed seed broadcast freely on the ground. A good crop was harvested in the first year and a reasonable one in the second but after that the ground became deplete of the minerals provided by the woodland ashes. Interestingly, following the experiment it was pointed out to those involved that there was no need to actually burn the felled trees in order to improve the ground for cereal growth.

The Swedish Professor, L. G. Romel, knew that a method of clearance known as the *assart effect* had been employed by Finnish farmers for centuries. These people knew that it was not so much the wood ash that fed the soil but rather it was something produced by an acidifying or 'souring' of roots of newly-felled trees. Thanks to this assart effect once the mold has been severed from the old spruce even the supposed inactive acid humus (mold) of old and poorly growing northern spruce-woods quickly releases ammonia in great quantity. Samples of such mold stored in a laboratory had up to three per cent of its total nitrogen available after a year and a half in storage. In comparison the best beech mold would have less than one-half of this percentage. According to Romel this assart effect is believed to have a good deal in common with green manuring.

New burnt clearings would be of short-term value for growing seed crops and, once the soil had become exhausted, a lack of nitrates encouraged the growth of certain plants, such as broom and alder. Once abandoned the burnt and un-burnt areas would subsequently develop quite differently. Cleared but unburnt areas would see the regrowth of the same species, although growth would be stronger. Ferns, sedges, and grasses would flourish more than before. However, the burnt ground would display a marked difference. Ferns would regrow but most of the old vegetation, having shallower roots, was killed by the fire. Many new plant species took advantage of the conditions, plantain made an appearance and the wind-blown spores of mosses found their way into the clearing.

The Early Neolithic landscape of the Lancashire Pennines, then, was probably a mosaic of relatively small clearances, abandoned Mesolithic upland clearings in various stages of scrub to woodland succession and relatively undisturbed, perhaps even primary, woodland.

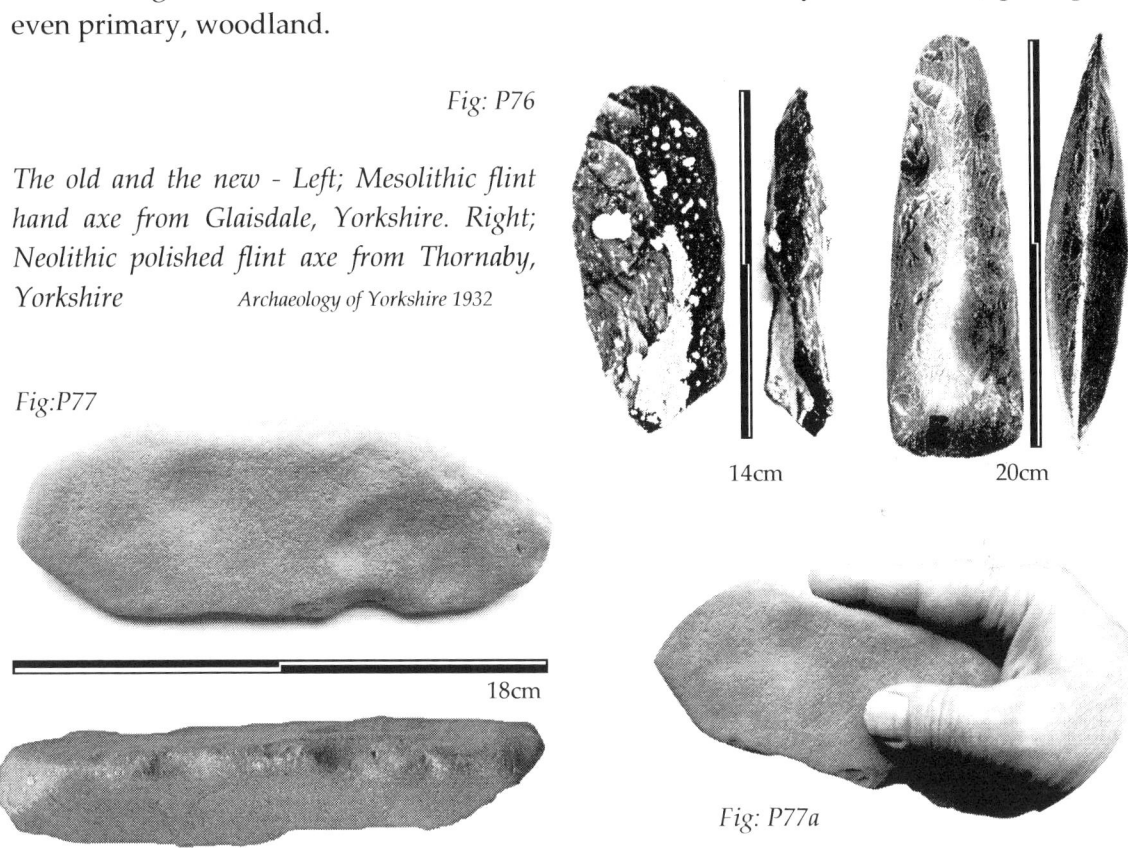

Fig: P76

The old and the new - Left; Mesolithic flint hand axe from Glaisdale, Yorkshire. Right; Neolithic polished flint axe from Thornaby, Yorkshire   Archaeology of Yorkshire 1932

14cm   20cm

Fig:P77

18cm

Fig: P77a

A ground stone implement found by the author at the Water Meetings, Barrowford. The tool displays signs of heavy wear; the blade is badly chipped and a thumb-shaped indentation exists on the side. This was possibly carved into the stone to facilitate grip, or the thumb of the user has worn the stone through continual use. The tool would possibly have been used for dividing or scraping softer material or it may have been a whet stone for sharpening metal blades

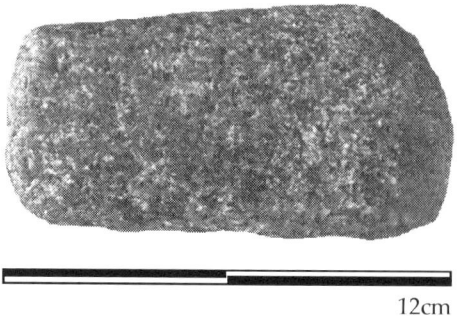

Fig: P78

Polished volcanic tuff stone axe found on Boulsworth (P.Whalley collection)

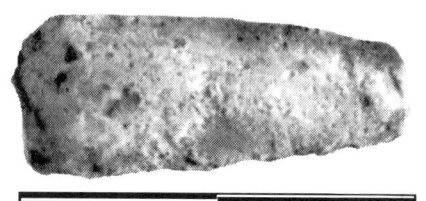

12cm

Fig: P79

Small local stone hand axe found at Stang Top, Roughlee
Photograph: D. Ormerod

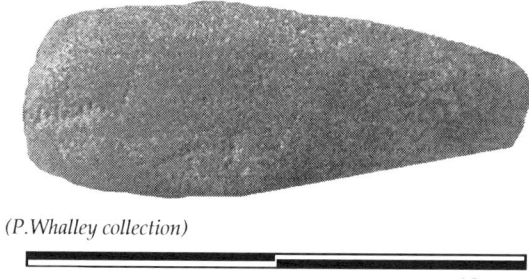

10cm

Fig: P80

Local stone hand axe found on Boulsworth Hill

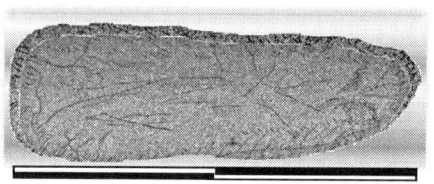

(P.Whalley collection)

18cm

Fig: P81

Sketch of a flint axe discovered in Pendle Water at Roughlee in the early 20th century

(Information: Blakey, J. The Annals and Stories of Barrowford 1929 P.15 - Reprint - Barrowford Press 2013)

13.5cm

In evidence of movement and settlement the stone axe is viewed as the most valuable artefact from the Late Mesolithic and Early Neolithic periods. On a basic level it could be taken that axe find patterns could be used to illustrate the degree to which the land was worked in any particular area. If there were to be more axes within well drained lowland soils than the heavy clay uplands then it would seem that this is where the woodland clearance, farming and settlement foci would be located.

As always, however, there is a caveat in that not all axes were related to a purely pragmatic purpose. Thousands of stone axes have been discovered over the years in Lancashire and Yorkshire, many of these being classed as 'losses.' It could be readily assumed that the axes were dropped by their owners on the site of a clearance operation or on the spot where woodwork was being carried out. In some cases this is no doubt the case but there is also an argument for the axes having been perceived as valuable objects, such as symbols of high status. A well crafted flint axe might never have actually been put to work - considered to have been worthy of passing down the generations the object might have acquired a venerable status (a heirloom).

In this case it is possible that the object was imbued with a sense of ancestral belonging; when the person who owned the axe moved to another settlement, possibly many miles distant, he or she would carry the story of the implement with them. Over time the axe would become firmly associated with the ancestral origin and could have been carried by its new owners to the ancestral settlement as a form of pilgrimage. In many ritualistic cases objects of veneration would be given up as cult offerings by being deposited within a context of monument, dwelling or 'special place.' This could well have been the case with high quality tools and weapons.

Another possible reason for the spread pattern of early axe heads is where they 'fell from the back of a lorry' - it is certain that some implements were lost by traders from their packs while stumbling over the rough terrain. These losses could have occurred at any time between the origin of the implement and its destination - it is clearly impossible to ascertain the percentage of these within the total axe assemblage.

Other ways in which axes may have travelled within the landscape is through exchange of goods between neighbouring settlements or as gifts from farmer to farmer (Barrowclough 2008). In cases other than ritual deposition, then, it can be reasonably assumed that the axe was either mislaid by its owner, left behind on a clearance job, swiped by the local tea-leaf and hidden, dropped in transit from the trader's sack or the woodman's tool pouch or simply discarded as an old fashioned piece of junk. It must be said that the latter is particularly unlikely given that quality flint tools and weapons appear to have been venerated by subsequent cultures.

Many of the 'lost' axes will not have been found in the exact location where they were dropped/hidden/stored as river action and colluviation is responsible for moving many artefacts over surprisingly long distances. However, the find pattern generally illustrates the areas in which axe-wielding settlers were operating.

Later Neolithic

In conclusion, the Early Neolithic models applied to other parts of Britain (southern England in particular) do not fit easily with the Boulsworth district of the Lancashire Pennines. The large scatter and group site patterns evident in the Mesolithic are largely absent; the only real body of lithic evidence being chance finds of Neolithic arrowheads on the moorlands and within historically extant Mesolithic sites.

Early Neolithic material found within the BNC Survey area is largely confined to the flint scatter sites and camps evident on the Worsthorne moors. The signature monument of the period, the long barrow and its variations, is found in relative abundance within East Yorkshire where it is thought to have been influenced by a migration of Neolithic newcomers from the south-east of England. In stark contrast the long barrow is rarely found within Lancashire. As shown below, it is possible that our Survey indicates an example or two of this burial mound type, it is also very possible that there are long barrows yet to be discovered within the landscape. It is clear from the archaeological record, however, that the practice of burying their dead in such specialised monuments was not taken up with any enthusiasm by those Neolithic people who spoke with a Lancashire accent.

The Mesolithic population shift towards the lower ground continued within the Neolithic and it is probable that the sites that lie scattered around the Worsthorne and Extwistle moors represent what were the fringes of marginal grass land at the time. Given that these sites do not show evidence of permanent settlement there are two possibilities as to their purpose. It could be that the semi-pastoralist occupiers of the hinterland travelled here and set up seasonal camps on the moorland edge. In the flint tool and weapon assemblages of Cant Clough, Extwistle and Widdop we could be seeing the implement manufacturing work carried out in preparation for hunting trips into the uplands of Boulsworth and Calderdale.

Just how far these hunters travelled from their base camp is unclear. Had they moved into the area along traditional hunting routes from Manchester, The Fylde, The Wirral, North Wales, Preston or Chorley? As we shall see, from the Later Neolithic onwards the BNC Survey indicates that there was far more activity within the locality of the Boulsworth and Calderdale hills than previously thought; this raises the second possibility that these were not the camps of seasonal incomers, rather they were occupied by people from within a half-day walking distance.

The gradual green slopes leading from Worsthorne down to the River Calder, and from Boulsworth to Pendle Water, would have provided all the necessities for the Late Mesolithic and Early Neolithic settler. This mixture of low plateaux and river valleys offered swathes of well drained land, was close to the ancient upland hunting grounds and was served by important routeways. While a number of ancient lithic and metal implements have been discovered across this valley plain it is certain that the Burnley, Nelson and Colne conurbations have destroyed countless more. The suggestion, then, is that we may see evidence within, and not much further beyond, the BNC Survey boundaries for the small pastoral settlements of the people who began to settle the district in earnest.

The Early Neolithic halls discussed earlier were intended as communal buildings but, by the later Neolithic wattle and daub buildings measuring six metres square, and sited on stone foundations, were more common. By 3,000 BC we see the emergence of an art form in the shape of concentric circles, wavy lines, spirals, swastikas and footprints. Also, the design of a cross within a circle appears to have an origin in the Carpathian Mountains – this design was traditionally taken to be of British 'Celtic' origin but it would appear that it travelled to Britain within a possible exchange of cultural ideas.

Around 3,000 BC the long barrow group of tombs ceased to be utilised for burial and their place was taken by earthen ringworks, sometimes accompanied by flat burial. These rings could be circular or oval enclosures defined by a ditch or bank and sometimes both. These are described as *ring ditches, ring banks* or, if they had both, *henges*. It is significant that 90% of henges have the ditch inside the bank and so were not intended for defensive purposes - Stonehenge is of this type.

There are over 300 known henges in Britain ranging from the Orkneys in the north to Cornwall in the south - most date to the Late Neolithic (2,500 BC - 2,000 BC) and are located within valleys (water association). Some regions, such as the Welsh Marches, the Yorkshire Wolds, East Anglia and much of the south and West Midlands, are largely devoid of henge features. In the later circles and henges there seems to be evidence of alignment ranging from a simple line of three stones in a row to far more complicated 'engine' systems such as Stonehenge. There seems to have been a discontinuity at about this time - tombs were blocked up, camps abandoned and fields allowed to go to waste. Perhaps the rise of chieftainship was causing local quarrels and large scale tribal warfare. Whatever the cause, some stress in society is evident.

By 2,500 BC mines in Sussex, Wiltshire and Norfolk were producing flints for much of England. 'Factories' at Great Langdale in Cumbria, Craig Llwydd in North Wales, Mounts Bay and the Cheviot Hills produced axe heads for use all over the British Isles and almost certainly for export overseas.

The Late Neolithic is marked by the emergence of metal extraction – sources of copper, gold and tin were increasingly being found and this led to the Bronze Age. Tin was being used by 1,500 BC and iron would soon become workable. There is little doubt that the existing export trade in unfinished flints and stone axe heads continued and was augmented by metal and finished metal artefacts. Sea trade routes were firmly established at this time and a sophisticated international maritime exchange of goods existed. (Graham, S. *Notes*)

BARROWS

Where the Early Neolithic was typified by long barrow funerary monuments the monumental architecture of the Late Neolithic and Early Bronze Age (2,500 BC - 1,500 BC) is typically visible in the modern landscape as circular mounds. These tumuli, or burial mounds, are the most common prehistoric monuments in the British landscape. Long barrows were constructed as earthen or drystone mounds with flanking ditches and acted as funerary monuments in the period stretching roughly from 3,800 BC to 3,300 cal. BC. Long barrows often produced the disarticulated remains of more than one individual in a single deposit with few associated artefacts, whereas round barrows often covered primary graves containing single graves, sometimes with associated grave goods.

Round barrows can be divided into the distinctive sub-categories of *bowl, saucer disk* and *bell* by their shape, diameter, height and composition. There are two major classifications relating to monument composition - the term barrow has its root in Old English and means *a mound of earth*, while monuments constructed of stones are usually described as cairns. At first glance round barrows can appear to be similar in shape and construction but they differ widely in size from around three metres in diameter to over thirty metres. Bowl barrows vary according to district and even neighbouring examples can contain burials conforming to different burial practice. This type of barrow usually dates from the Late Neolithic to the Late Bronze Age, most commonly to the period 2,400 BC to 1,500 BC.

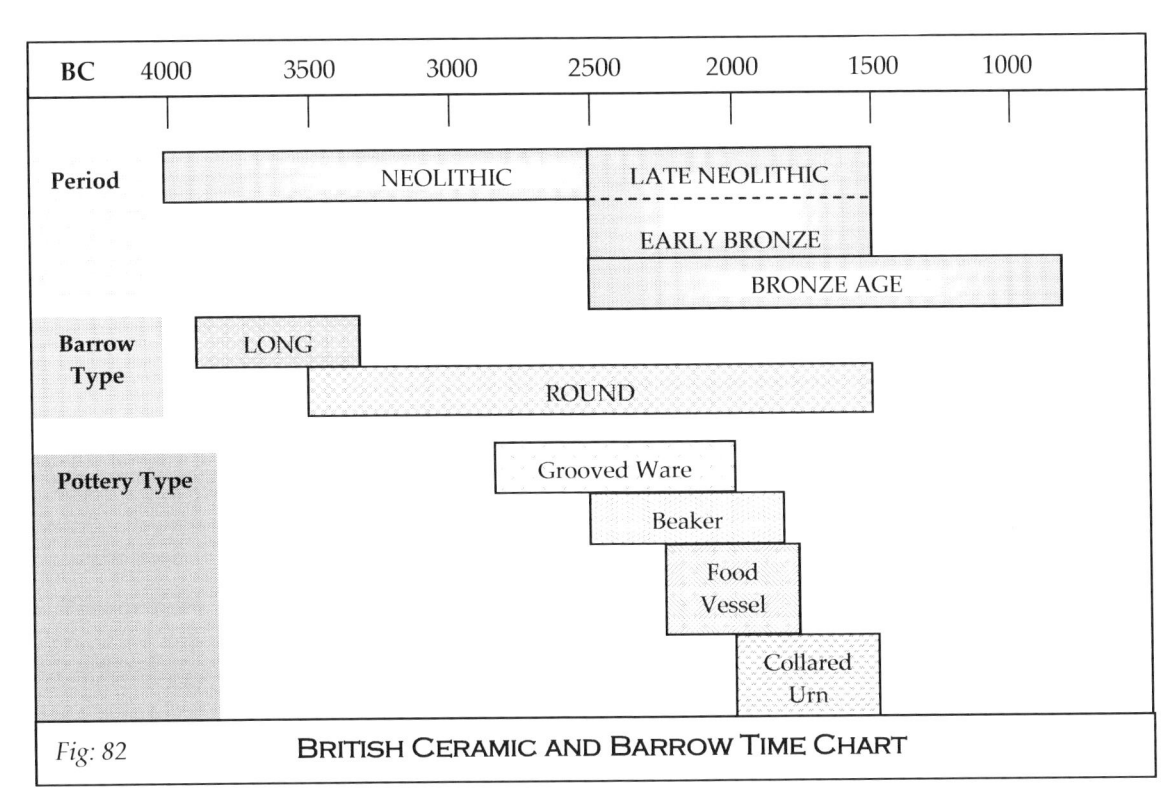

Fig: 82 — **BRITISH CERAMIC AND BARROW TIME CHART**

Round barrows can occur in isolation but where clusters occur they can be viewed as barrow cemeteries. Round barrow cemeteries were created through the gradual addition of mounds within the location of an early single burial - commonly developing from the Late Neolithic, and through the Bronze Age the number of barrows within a cemetery can vary according to national location. The chalkland downs of southern England are particularly rich in cemeteries containing large numbers of bowl barrows.

The appearance of pottery runs roughly in tandem with the development of new burial practice during the Neolithic - the key development being the emergence of Grooved Ware. The diagnostic shape for the style is a flat bottomed pot with straight sides sloping outwards and grooved decoration around the top. The pottery comes in many different varieties, some have complex geometric decorations while others display appliqué bands suggestive of a willow basket pattern. Grooved ware is considered to have developed in Orkney - the exact date of its emergence remains somewhat but it was very probably in use by 3,200 BC. Its emergence seems to be related to the social dynamics of Late Neolithic communities in Orkney, where a system of competitive conspicuous consumption operated. The spread of these ceramics, from Orkney into southern England (around 2,800 BC), and the movement of stone axes from Cumbria into Orkney, may well indicate that marine and inland trade routes had become firmly established during the Late Neolithic. Grooved ware disappears around 2,000 BC.

Fig: P83
Beaker measuring 17cm in height

Before the end of the Late Neolithic the uptake of the Beaker culture became increasingly widespread, probably through absorption of ideas from the Continent by the indigenous population. The Beaker burial culture is named after the type of pottery produced in certain districts from around 2,400 BC to 2,100 BC before falling out of use around 1,700 BC; the beaker ware is thin, and made of clay mixed with sand or powdered stone. They are yellowish, drab or light-brown, more rarely red, and occasionally burnished. Ranging in height from 11cm to 23cm (rarely, as small as 6.5cm) the beakers sometimes have necks encircled by raised ribs or mouldings and a handful of Yorkshire examples have handles attached. Generally, beakers were used to accompany burials as a single deposition in a grave (1m to 1.3m in depth) beneath a round barrow although they have been found in Yorkshire in relation to cist burials.

From the end of the Neolithic the Beaker Folk equipped themselves with bronze knives, flat bronze axes and flint tools including knives, worked flakes and discoid scrapers. Their most characteristic flint implement was the dagger and surviving examples of this 'elaborate' or 'rare' tool form shows them to have been among the best examples of flint craftsmanship ever seen.

Fig: P84 Flint dagger from Lincolnshire

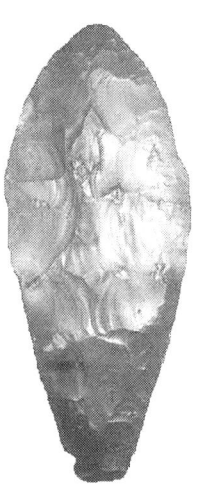

The Yorkshire Wolds was a favoured area for the Beaker culture and there is evidence (such as at Howe Hill, Duggleby) of Neolithic long barrows incorporating both Neolithic and Beaker burials. The Beaker makers spread throughout this part of Yorkshire but appear to have ignored the eastern moorlands. From the Wolds they followed the ridgeways across the Vale of York and pushed into West Yorkshire. The archaeological evidence suggests that the Beaker migration from the Yorkshire Wolds thinned out markedly as it advanced westward. Thin concentrations occur around Shipley in Airedale, Huddersfield and around Grassington (Skipton) but there is no overwhelming record for a widespread Beaker 'invasion' in either West Yorkshire or Lancashire.

It appears that some Beaker ideas were carried into North Lancashire through the trans-Pennine route of the Aire Gap - a beaker found at Portfield, near Whalley could substantiate this although it is possible that this was more of an 'exotic' than an indicator of defined cultural practice. This could also be said of a cremation beaker discovered on Worsthorne Moor and five flint axes of the Beaker tradition found to the east of Worsthorne at Cant Clough, Roggerham, Upper Gorple and Hurstwood. Here we are possibly seeing the result of trade and exchange through the Calder Valley from Huddersfield into Burnley.

MAIN BARROW CATEGORIES

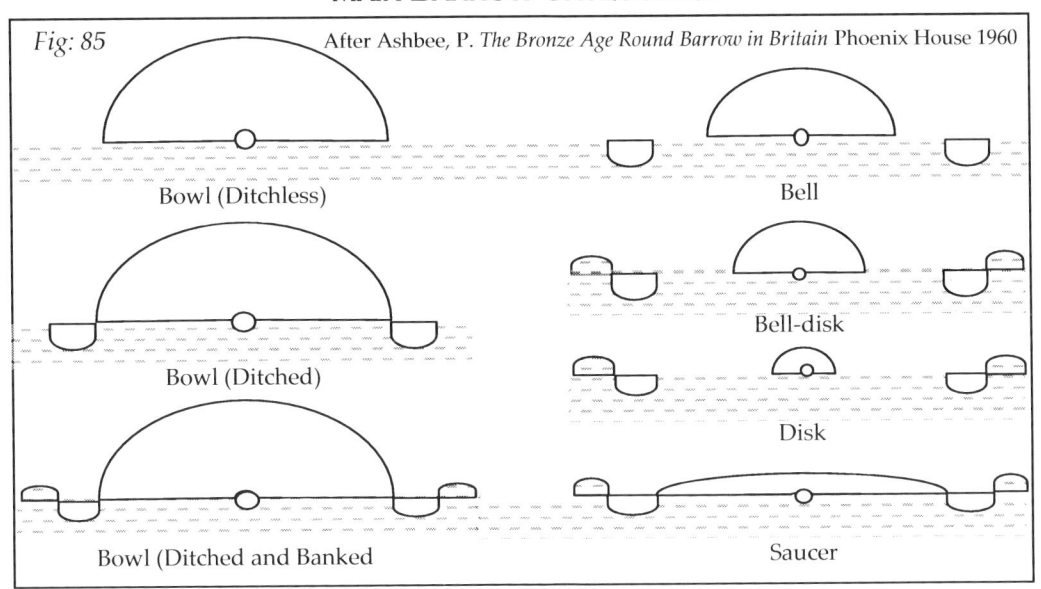

Fig: 85   After Ashbee, P. *The Bronze Age Round Barrow in Britain* Phoenix House 1960

Bowl (Ditchless)

Bell

Bowl (Ditched)

Bell-disk

Disk

Bowl (Ditched and Banked)

Saucer

Nationally, from the very end of the Late Neolithic (2,150 BC to 1,850 BC) round barrows were constructed, elaborated and redesigned on a large scale in relation to existing features in the landscape, often stressing the importance of links with the past through the reopening of graves and the addition of new deposits (Bradley, R. *The Social Foundations of Prehistoric Britain: Themes and Variations in the Archaeology of Power*. Longman Group 1984).

In his study of a large number of Wessex barrow cemeteries and single burials, Simon M. Howarth (*An Investigation Into the Late Neolithic and Early Bronze Age Round Barrow Monuments in the Wylye Valley* - Thesis - Birmingham University 2009/10) showed that there was no correlation between the shape or type of any individual mound and the deposits found beneath it. In a sample of 111 round barrows Howarth found that there were almost three times more primary cremations than inhumation burials. He suggests that the primary burial (the first burial for which the mound was erected) may have been only the first stage in a long ceremonial process stretching from the Late Neolithic into the Early Bronze Age when cremations steadily became more common than inhumations.

It appears that the primary burial was the important event for which a single barrow would be constructed and this might reflect the sense of loss of an individual felt by the community. However, barrows containing a number of burials were continually reopened thus following the Neolithic tradition of ancestral recall. The group-orientated societies of the Neolithic gave way to more 'individualising' societies in the Early Bronze Age where the single burial, accompanied by grave goods, becomes evident (Barrett J.C. and Kinnes I.A. eds. *The Archaeology of Context in the Neolithic and Bronze Age: Recent Trends University of Sheffield* 1988). Beaker burials mark the beginning of the single grave and a shift from a ritual transformation of the dead into the world of the ancestors to a deposition of the deceased as an individual within an 'owned' landscape.

The smaller Beaker mounds were often little more than a low earthen cover encircled by a fence or ditch and this is thought to have ensured a continuity of responsibility for successive generations to tend the burial in order to preserve it. In effect this meant that each successive burial within the mound would be carried out in a manner of rite that either recognised the original primary burial or contrasted with it. In some cases Early Bronze Age burials within Neolithic mounds are distinctly different to the primary burial but others display a marked similarity - they appear to venerate the rites of the earlier period. It has been suggested that this recognition may have been a reaction to social or political change where the social stability of the predecessors needed to be reinforced or introduced (Howarth 2009/10). Late Neolithic and Early Bronze Age barrows often cluster in cemeteries where a number of mounds respect a primary mound (long barrow)) and these are commonly located on scarp edges, where they could be easily seen. Where land units might have existed, they appear on the periphery at the head of slopes.

Fig: 86

Neolithic Sites in the BNC Survey

Fig: 86   ● Neolithic Site   ☐ Mesolithic Site

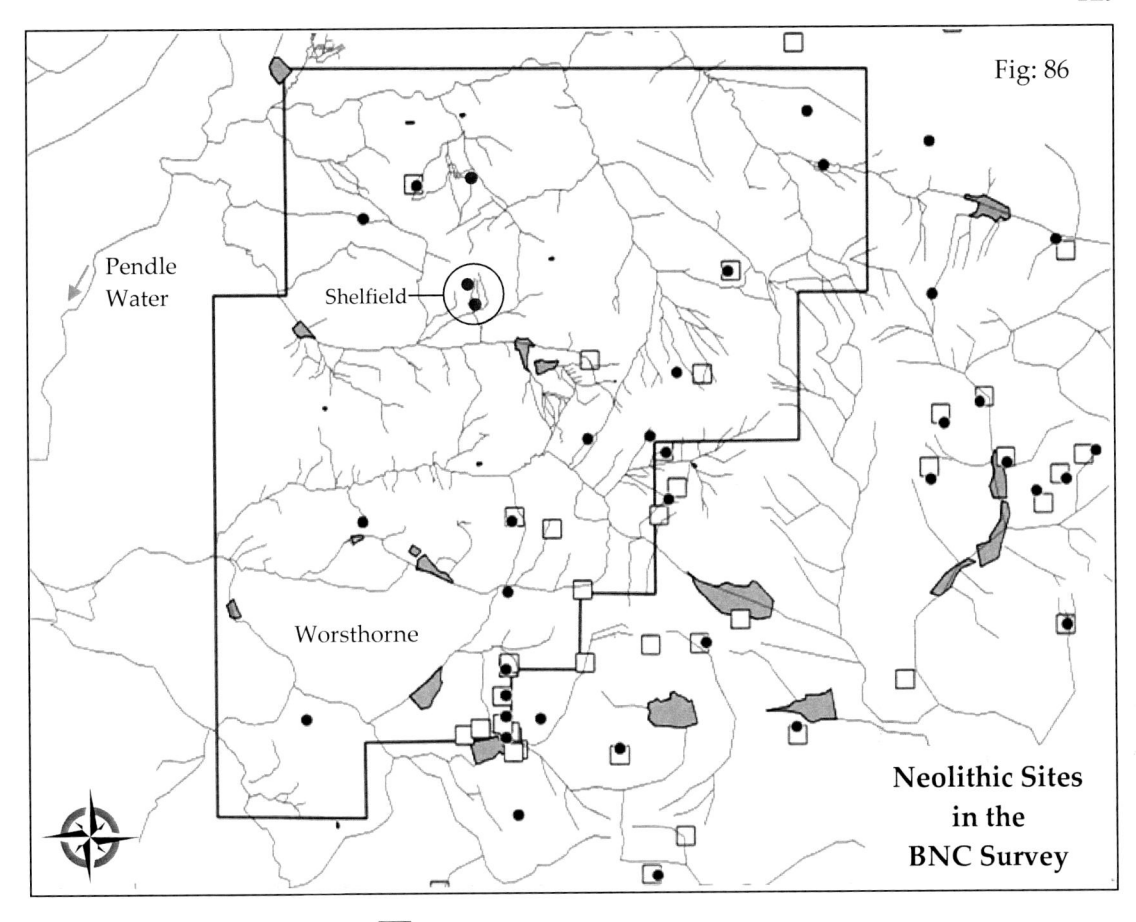

The Neolithic sites represent finds of tools and weapons and a small number of burials. Sixty percent of the Neolithic sites correspond with Mesolithic sites

Fig: 87

Neolithic sites appear within the Pendle district (north of Pendle Water) suggesting that this area was beginning to be occupied in this period. This linear corridor of sites follows the Pendle ridgeway and suggests that this was increasing in importance as an east-west communication route

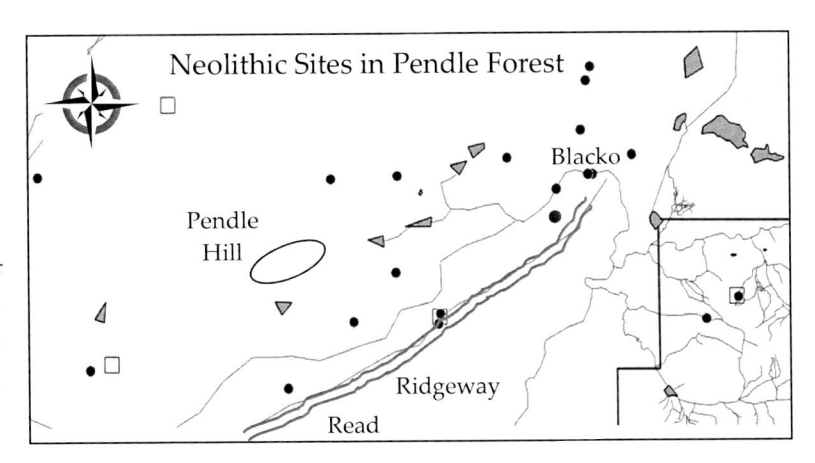

Neolithic Sites in Pendle Forest

© Environment Agency Copyright 2013. All rights reserved

Fig: P88

SD 89

Tile C3

Knave Hill Mounds

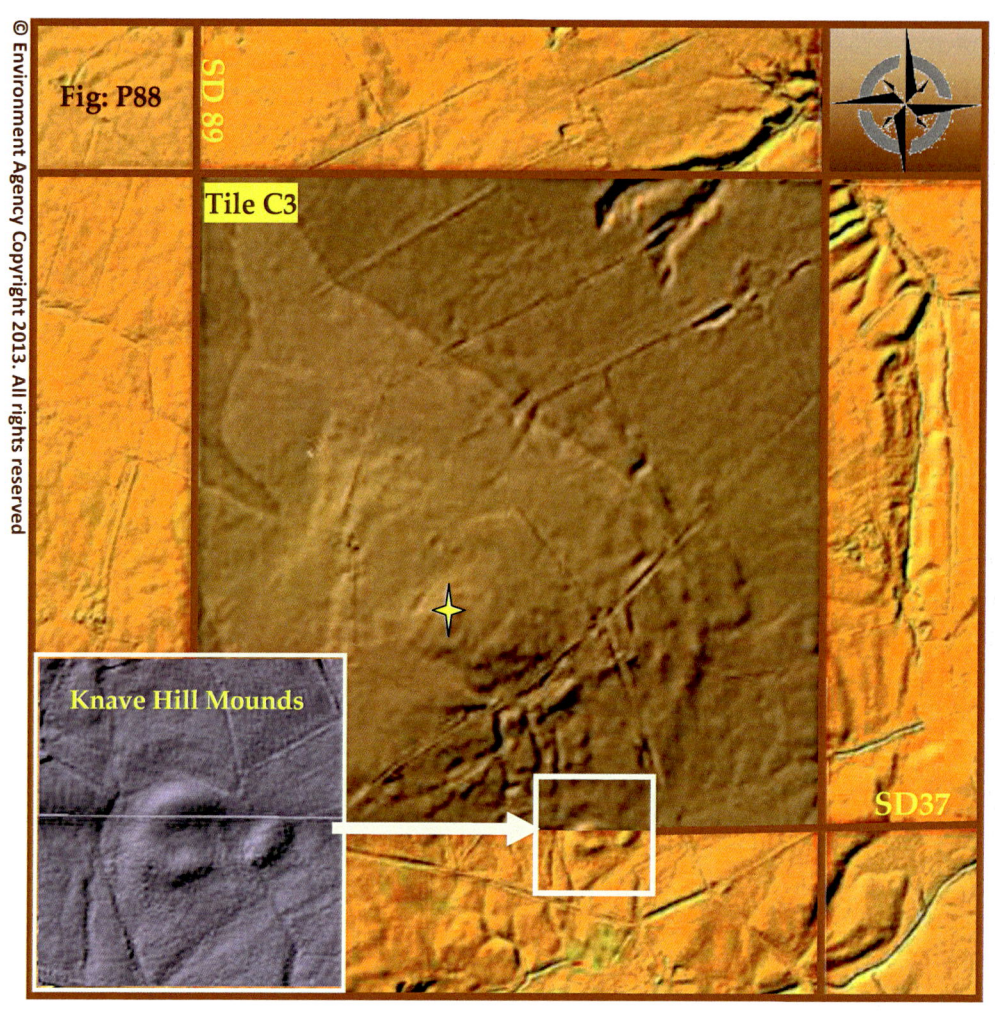

SD37

NW to SE

Fig: P88
Shelfield Hill, Nelson
1m LiDAR

✦ Walton Spire

Inset: Knave Hill

Fig: P89
Knave Hill mounds with Boulsworth Hill in the background

SHELFIELD HILL (WALTON SPIRE), NELSON

Location: SD 89419 37326 **X** 389419 **Y** 437326
Lat: 53.832087 **Long:** -2.1622554 n

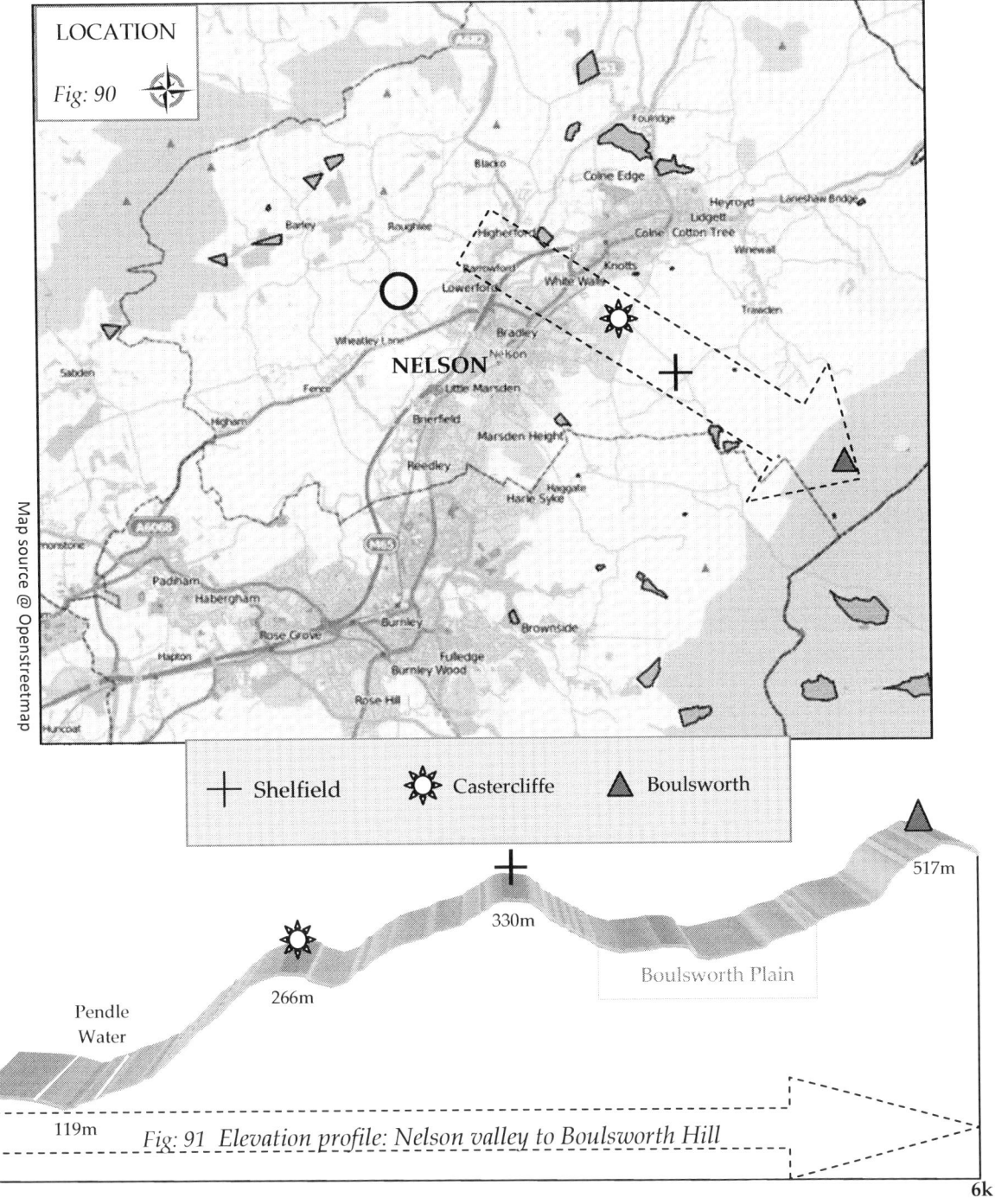

LOCATION

Fig: 90

Map source @ Openstreetmap

+ Shelfield   ☼ Castercliffe   ▲ Boulsworth

517m
330m
266m
Pendle Water
119m
Boulsworth Plain

Fig: 91 Elevation profile: Nelson valley to Boulsworth Hill

0k 6k

Shelfield Hill is described in the English Heritage National Monuments Record as a *'Circular enclosure, of uncertain date or function, recorded on the summit of Shelfield in 1856.'* The writer clearly recognised that an archaeological feature was present on the hill and this is furthered by the statement of a local historian (Wilkinson in Carr, J. *Annals of Colne* 1878) that; *'Shelfield is a large circular encampment of Danish origin, of which some portion of the ditch is indicated by the undulations of the surface, and by a swampy part of the ground on the western slope.'*

In subsequent years lip-service has been afforded to Shelfield by local historians, most of whom take up Wilkinson's opinion that Shelfield was 'of Danish origin.' This has been absorbed into local folklore to the extent that it is generally taken that Shelfield was a 'Viking' camp built during a major battle that took place in the locality. It is natural, then, that Archaeological features within the Shelfield area (stones and mounds) have also been widely attributed to the Scandiwegians.

Given the fact that excavation has always been expensive the lack of archaeological assessment of the area is understandable. Few local antiquarians have possessed either the skill, the will, or deep enough pockets to carry out any serious work in what was commonly viewed as a soggy backwater. Fortunately, we are now able to consult LiDAR technology in order to appreciate the archaeological potential of sites such as Shelfield. While only limited ground survey has been carried out on the site the BNC Survey aerial data results strongly suggest that the Shelfield Hill area has the potential to be one of the most important prehistoric sites within Lancashire.

It can be seen in *Fig: 91* that the landscape between the river valley of Nelson and Colne, and the Boulsworth Hill summit, rises 398 metres over six kilometres. This elevation takes place in a series of 'steps' where two ridges, running NE-SW, break up the long slope. The Castercliffe hillfort sits on a ridge stretching from Waterside (Colne) to Walverden Water (Catlow) while Shelfield Hill occupies a ridge running from Trawden to Float Bridge. It is clear to see why the hillfort at Castercliffe was built on the two hills surmounting the ridge - the commanding view from here is both extensive and stunning. However, this is surpassed by the sight-range from Shelfield Hill; in fact the 64 metre height advantage enjoyed by the hill ensures that it actually overlooks, in fact dominates, the hillfort 900 metres down the valley slope. Given this, it seems apposite to ask why the less obvious site was chosen to be developed as a hillfort? Why was Shelfield not considered to be worthy of performing such a role? Well, the answer appears to be that it was.

However, I am getting ahead of myself here, the Iron Age function of the site must wait for the hillfort section in *Burnley and Pendle Archaeology - Part Two*. The essence of Shelfield Hill, and its relationship with the landscape, can be summed up in three words - prominence, locality and centrality. The focal point of the site takes the form of a circular prominence rising sharply from the head of a triangular plateau based on a roughly conical eminence.

Fig: P92 - 2 metre LiDAR

Shelfield Hill is a conical prominence comprising three distinct landscape elements. The circle is the natural hill measuring 1.4 kilometres in diameter. The inner area is triangular, defined by ditch-work 650 metres from the southern apex to base. The central site is a level, formerly defensive enclosure measuring 150 metres in diameter.

The broken circle is the Castercliffe hillfort enclosure

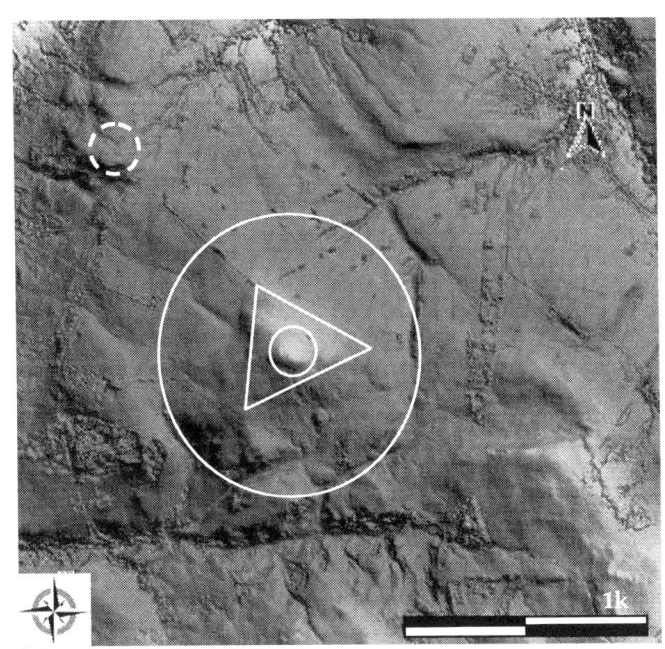

© Environment Agency Copyright 2013 All Rights Reserved

The summit of Shelfield Hill is formed by a raised circular prominence surmounted by the stone monument known as Walton Spire. The photograph shows two distinct terraces running left to right across the image. These are the remnants of defensive revetment earthworks.

Fig: P93

We saw in *Fig: P74* that a number of Neolithic flint weapons and tools were discovered on Shelfield Hill in the early twentieth century and this strongly suggests occupation of the site for at least some part of this period. In fact it would be unthinkable that this landscape feature would not have been utilised for occupation and/or defence within each successive period of prehistory.

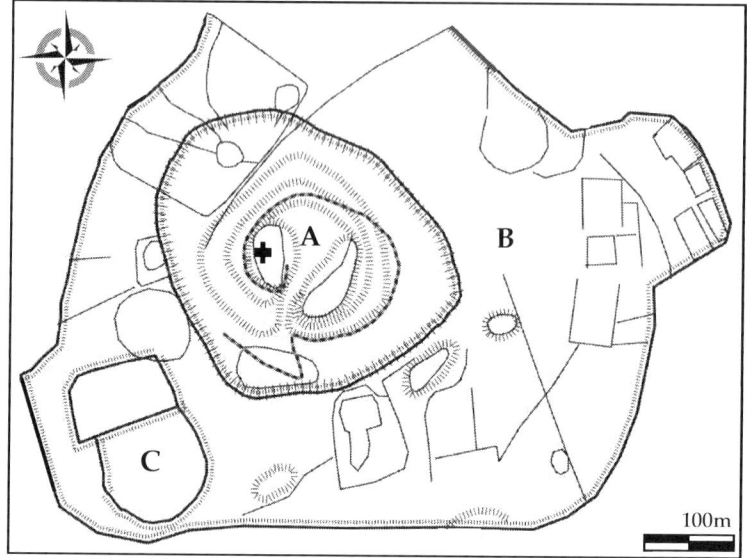

Fig: 94

*Shelfield Hill - **A** indicates the primary enclosure: **B** the outer enclosure: **C** a sub-enclosure*

The hill displays evidence of a great deal of earthwork activity in the form of levelled areas, ditches, banks and stone revetments

✚ *Walton Spire*

On the very highest point of the hill stands a monument that can be seen from the distant Three Peaks of Yorkshire. Known locally as Walton Spire this menhir has possibly been standing sentinel over the surrounding countryside for over five millennia - the history that it has witnessed locked forever within five tons of gritstone.

Fig: P95

Walton Spire with Pendle Hill in the background. The spire is actually a monument of two halves - the base is a massive gritstone menhir while the top half is a sandstone cross erected in the reign of William IV

Fig: P96

The stone cross carries the date when it was erected on the ancient monalithic base by the Rev. Wroe-Walton (1835). The Walton family, of the neighbouring Townhouse estate, owned the land at Shelfield and the standing stone on the hill offered too great a temptation to the good Reverend to leave his mark for posterity

Fig: P97- Reconstruction of the spire stone

Before the menhir was trimmed down to take the new monumental stonework it would have stood around four metres in height

The image has been enhanced in order to show how the stone might have appeared in its original state: (the Viking warrior just happened to be passing by)

The stone on Shelfield Hill would have dominated the landscape and was obviously intended to make a powerful statement by the people who erected it. There is, of course, no firm evidence for the date that the stone was hewn from its quarry bed (on the slopes of Boulsworth) and dragged into its present position. We know from Court Roll records that it stood in the Late Medieval period and it appears to have existed in the Early Medieval. The origin of the name of Shelfield could have its root in a number of Old and Middle English words but the OE *seol* means *show, point out, direct* or *guide* - this is an apt description of the way people in the Anglo Saxon era would have viewed the purpose of the stone. They appear, then, to have named the area *Seolfield*, or *The Field of the Mark Stone*. In essence the stone menhir is a typical feature of the Late Neolithic period and it is suggested, therefore, that it was ancient when the Scandinavian newcomers applied a name to it.

The Shelfield menhir is the largest extant example of a free-standing stone (menhir) within a wide area and the fact that it is located on the summit of a hill makes it particularly rare. A massive number of ancient monuments have been lost to agriculture; countless standing stones once stood proud as ambassadors to the culture of their creators until they fell foul of the modern mindset of land expansion at any cost. For 5,000 years these sentinels survived only to be smashed and dragged to an ignominious fate - many now lay broken and forlorn in muddy ditches and streams.

Thankfully, the Shelfield menhir has survived; partly because the hill it surmounts has been subjected only to light ploughing and partly because Reverend Wroe-Walton chose to utilise the stone as a base for his monument.

Due to its elevated position as the highest feature on the highest hill in the area the cross has been struck by lightening on a number of occasions over the past 179 years - it has been repaired each time and now carries a lightening conductor. It must follow, therefore, that the menhir will have been struck by lightening countless times in its long life; this raises the question as to what the people who erected the stone must have thought when they saw their monument being blasted by a powerful bolt from the heavens? Equally, what did their successors make of the fact that a structure, possibly erected to commemorate the ancestors, could be seen to physically interact with the powers of the otherworld?

This, of course, assumes that the stone was put in place by a society operating within a Neolithic cult although it seems highly likely that whoever erected the stone did so through a powerful need to fulfil some cultural rite, belief or need. A structured archaeological assessment over the extended site would hopefully provide evidence for when the stone was erected but it is suggested at this stage that we see on Shelfield Hill a rare and enigmatic symbol of the Neolithic/Early Bronze Age. At this time the ancestors were commemorated and bold physical statements were placed in the landscape to mark tribal territory and as symbols of high status.

The spire menhir is not the only stone to be found around Shelfield Hill. A large block of sandstone sits on the edge of the field 129 metres to the north of the menhir and, in *The Valley of the Drawn Sword* (Barrowford Press 2006), I described this stone as being 'anvil-shaped.' The name was taken up by enthusiasts of the prehistoric period and very soon the *anvil stone* was cropping up in texts, and on internet sites, where it appears to have been accepted as having carried this name since time immemorial.

Fig: P98 - A resident of Shelfield Hill examines the worked 'Anvil Stone'

The photograph *(Fig: P98)* shows why the stone was described as being shaped like a blacksmith's anvil - from this viewpoint the similarity is clear. However, I now realise that I appear to have 'missed a trick' with this stone. Firstly, I think that I was viewing it from the rear and secondly the stone is actually not in situ. As always, local knowledge is an invaluable asset in historical and archaeological research and so it proved in this case.

The Shelfield Hill farmer informs me that the stone was originally buried in the field some 250 metres to the north-west of where it is now located. Around twenty years ago the field was being re-seeded and the shallow plough persistently hit stones beneath the surface. These were dug out and moved up the hill to be piled on the edge of a soakaway - the largest stone was placed separately to this group and this is the reason why the 'anvil' stone is situated where we now see it *(Fig: P99)*.

Fig: P99
The stone may now stand on-end

It further struck me that not only was I possibly viewing the stone from the back, I was also looking from the wrong angle. When the stone is viewed from a ninety-degree angle it strongly resembles a seat or chair. This might sound somewhat far-fetched but, in defence of my sanity, the stone has been heavily worked on all of its faces - the 'front' face in particular having been sculpted into the profile shown in *Fig: P100*.

1.3m

Fig: P100 - The correct position?

From what can be seen of the neighbouring boulders there is no evidence of them having been worked; they appear to be typical of the stones utilised in field boundaries and hut foundations. The size and shape of the massive block clearly lent itself to being shaped into its present form; whether it was intended to function as a seat is, of course, pure speculation and, as we shall see later, there could be other possible contexts here.

Shelfield Hill is a very special landscape feature in a number of ways. Visually, the hill presents differing faces to the cardinal points - from the north (Pendle) it appears to be a sharply conical eminence; from the east and west it presents as a gradual slope with an upturned bowl on the summit while the southern aspect shows a rounded hill with no defined summit.

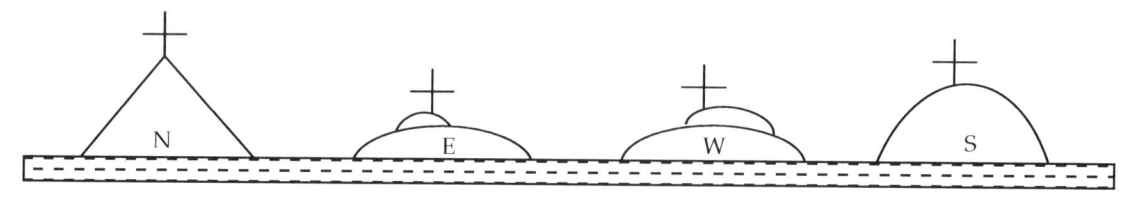

Fig: 101   Aspects of Shelfield Hill from the cardinal points

The shale, sandstone and boulder clay of which the hill is formed means that it retains a large amount of ground water. In the late twentieth century a number of boreholes were drilled with a view to extracting coal from the hill; each test very quickly hit the water table and, for three months, pumps were run night and day in an attempt to drain the water. The shafts could not be drained and the survey was abandoned - this came as no surprise to local people who have long known that Shelfield Hill is a watershed.

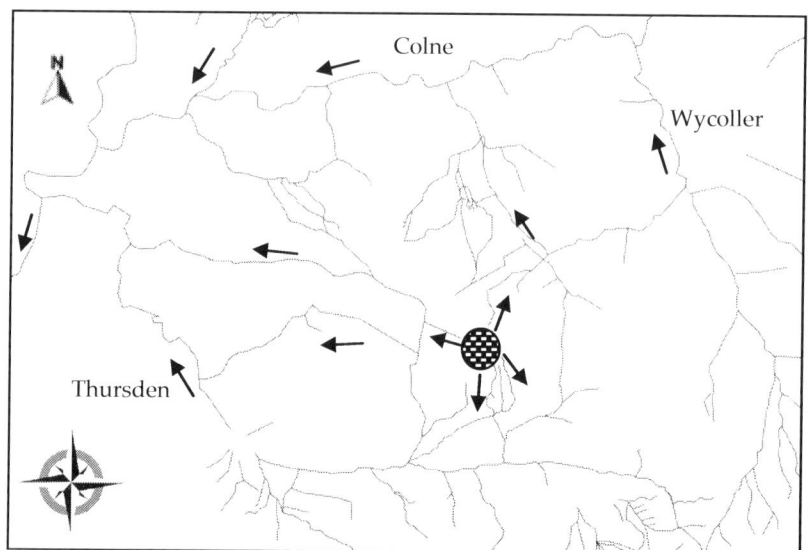

Fig: 102

Water drains from Shelfield Hill to all the major local waterways.

Eventually all the water drains into the River Calder at Burnley

1m LiDAR © Environment Agency Copyright 2013 All Rights Reserved

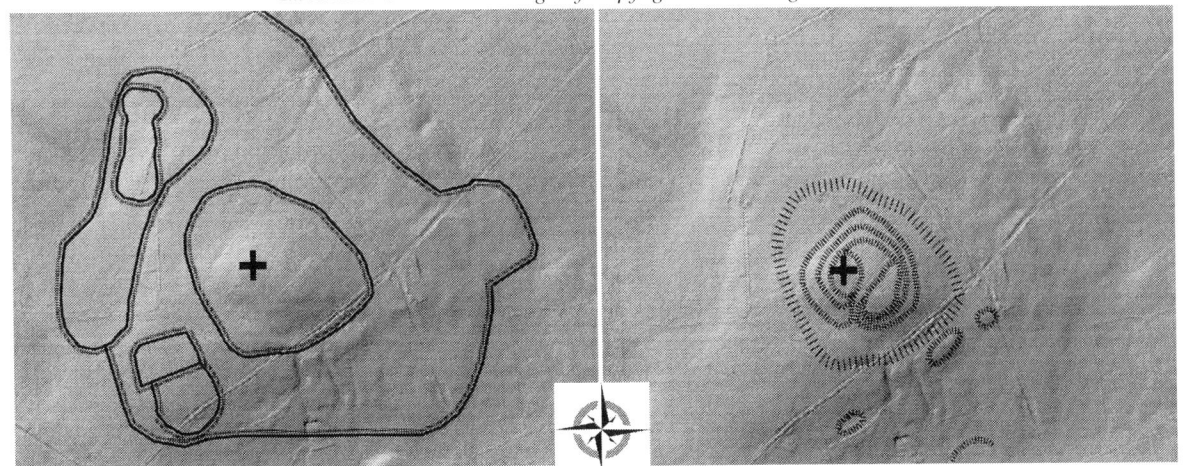

Fig: P103 - The Shelfield outer enclosure   *Fig: P103a - The hill enclosure*

It is becoming clear, then, that Shelfield Hill has special features not apparent in other landscape hill features within the Boulsworth district. The hill forms a watershed and has almost certainly been landscaped at some period into its present distinctive shape Further, the hill is a rare feature, having a menhir dominating the summit of a defended enclosure. The hill also displays a centrality in relation to a district defined by rivers.

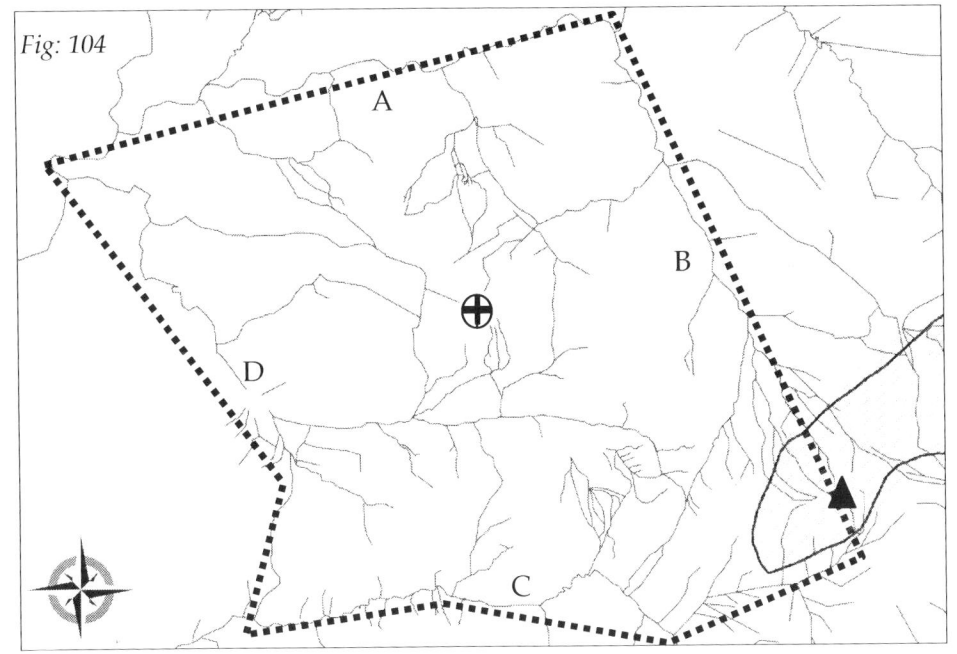

Fig: 104

Shelfield Hill is located at the centre of a district defined by four water courses:

***A)** Colne Water/Pendle Water* ***B)** Trawden Water* ***C)** Don/Thursden Water* ***D)** Walverden Water*

Shelfield sits at the centre of a proposed district/territory delineated by the four waterways into which it drains - this area covers some 28 square kilometres. It is suggested, therefore, that this district was a possible minor kingdom within an extended district stretching from west Calderdale through to south Pendle and east Burnley.

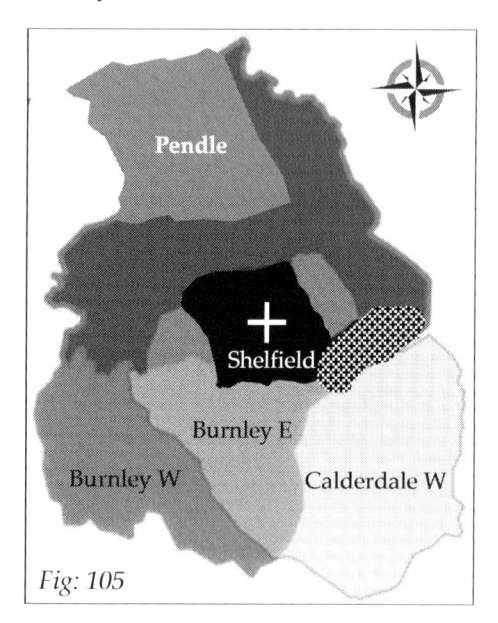

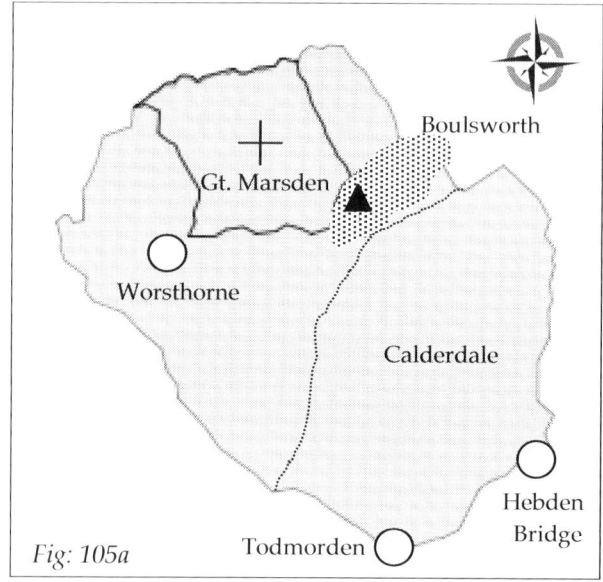

Fig: 105

Fig: 105a

Four rivers form the area around Shelfield suggesting that the hill could have played an important part within a sub-district of an extended ancient territory

It is interesting to note that the Shelfield district *(Fig:105)* covers virtually the same defined area of the Nelson district that was formerly known as Great Marsden. This was the name of the extended Nelson area prior to 1849 when the East Lancashire Railway Company adopted the name of the town centre inn (The Nelson Inn) for its station - the Great Marsden appellation quickly became redundant. The name Marsden was written in a number of ways in late Medieval records: *Marchesdene* (1177), *Merkedenne* (1180), *Merclesdene* (1180), *Merklesdene* (1246), *Marchdene* and *Merchesden* (1258) and *Merclesden* (1311). The word is commonly taken to be the Old English *mercels* (boundary marker) or *merke* (boundary) and *den* (valley) thus giving the meaning of *'boundary valley'*. Given that all the boundaries of the proposed district in *Fig: 105* are delineated by river valleys it is fair to say that Marsden is an apt description for the Shelfield 'territory'. The term was probably first used in the eighth century and, at this time, it was very possibly being applied to a far more ancient district.

The river boundaries of the proposed Shelfield district carry British (Celtic) names: the northern boundary is the continuous waterway of Colne Water and Pendle Water. Colne is thought to be of Celtic origin but the name could also be Latin - *collunio* is a 'lost' Roman station in the Pennines while *colonus* means *tiller of the soil* or *farmer*. Pendle is from the Celtic *pen* for *hill*.

The south and west boundaries are formed by the River Don (the lower part of which is now called Thursden Water); the Don rises on the southern flanks of Boulsworth Hill and it seems fair, therefore, to take the British word *don/dun* (meaning *hill*) as the root although *dun* is a common name applied to places within the vicinity of hillforts. The eastern boundary is a stream rising on the summit of Boulsworth and flowing north past the Abbot Stone (on the higher flanks of the hill) and on to Colne Water as Trawden Water.

Trawden is a possible Celtic name where *treo* means *way* - the English may have appended their *den* (valley) giving *treoden* (the track/way through the valley).

Fig: P106

The Abbot Stone possibly marks the boundary of an ancient territory

The southern boundary of the extended territory of Boulsworth, Burnley and Calderdale is the River Calder - this name is commonly taken to mean *forceful, tumbling, harsh water*. However, there could be an element of the Romans borrowing the Celtic word *caleder* where they referred to the natives of Scotland as *Caled*-onians. Calder is a river name applied only in northern Britain and the Romans were possibly using the Calder name here as a term to describe tribal boundary rivers. The Calder rivers flow into all the major waterways which, in turn, meet the sea at the ancient ports of the Humber, Ribble, Fleetwood and Clyde.

British landscape names do not, of course, provide firm evidence that the Late Neolithic period saw a burgeoning settlement of districts as outlined in *Fig: 105*. However, we do know that boundaries abide in the landscape and that each subsequent generation respected the territorial limits of their forefathers - the alternative often led to warfare.

We also know that the Late Neolithic, and Early Bronze Age, was a time when settlement roots were being planted firmly within the landscape as the practice of agriculture spread northwards through the British Isles. Along with new ideas of settled society came a culture of the individual; this is apparent in burial practice where individuals were placed in single grave sites, or as satellite burials respecting primary burials. The old ways, where the bones of the ancestors were retained by society as part of a communal tradition had gone.

The erection of massive stone and wood monuments at this time has been suggested as being the result of a still-nomadic culture determined to make their mark in the landscape. The burial mounds and cairns scattered along hillsides and ridges were built to provide a visual statement to others that the land was 'occupied'. However, we know that Mesolithic (and almost certainly Palaeolithic) people used wooden stakes to mark out areas of land. Also, particular landscape features (such as the Abbot Stone on Boulsworth Hill) would be utilised as way markers. The massive communal effort required to create some of the Late Neolithic monuments meant that they must surely have been related to settlement - barrows, stone circles and menhirs were making a definite statement among the communities who built them, and also to outsiders.

The very act of building a massive long barrow, or erecting a 120 tonne capstone on flimsy upright dolmens, would have served as an important project to those who had settled in the landscape. In fact, the *act* of monument building could have been the glue that bound a newly settled community and would have been of more importance than the monument itself. A good example here is Silbury Hill, near Avebury in Wiltshire.

Fig: P107

Silbury Hill is a man-made structure reaching 120 feet in height

The latest results of ongoing assessment by English Heritage suggest that Silbury Hill was not actually *designed* to take its present form, rather it 'grew like Topsy' over at least three generations of Bronze Age people between 2,400 BC and 2,300 BC. A study of soil, rocks, gravel and tools within the hill show that it passed through fifteen distinct stages of development. It is possible that over many generations great numbers of people came to a sacred spring, near to the hill site, and each visitor would deposit a basket of stone or gravel as a ritual offering. Eventually the hill took on the shape and size that we see today; the important point here being that the creators were building the mound as part of a *'continuous storytelling ritual' - the final shape of the mound may have been unimportant'* (Dr Jim Leary, English Heritage).

And so we might look upon the stone circles, cairns, barrows and standing stones within the Boulsworth area as having been created by local people who had become firmly rooted to the land. Estate division among each group of settlers became important - an elite emerged among the settlers and the first evidence for 'kingship' becomes apparent in the archaeological record.

The occasional discovery of well preserved Iron Age corpses ('bog bodies') in wetland areas across central Ireland, the Lancashire coast and Denmark shows a defined corridor of cultural commonality. Each of the bodies has been found to have been deliberately killed and placed within a particular peat bog setting in the landscape. In each case there was significant 'overkill' where the injuries were far too numerous to simply kill the person. In the case of the Irish bodies the archaeology can be tied in nicely with history to tell the story of these unfortunates.

In Ireland an ancient oral tradition was chronicled by scribes in the late Medieval and this ensured the survival of early history dating back to the Iron Age (*The Annals of Ireland*). Maps of early Irish kingdom boundaries have been created from the histories and local archaeologists have been able to place each bog body within the context of these districts. Within each kingdom there is a distinctive 'investiture hill' that was utilised to confirm the king of each district. The role of king was something of a poisoned chalice in that each individual was held to be responsible for the well-being of their people - most importantly, they were charged with keeping the relevant deities happy to ensure good weather and healthy harvests.

During the late Bronze Age the climate deteriorated across Europe and this resulted in poor harvests over long periods - this was seen to be the fault of the king and it appears that the tribal chieftains punished those who failed by killing them and placing the body in the wet portal to the underworld as a ritual offering of appeasement to the gods. The kings were, in fact, elected token rulers and could only expect to rule as a figurehead until the next poor harvest, or other natural disaster.

It is interesting to note that the bog bodies were found to have carefully manicured nails and well trimmed hair - they were well nourished and show no signs of ever having carried out any physical work. Furthermore, the deposition of bodies was thought to be limited to the Iron Age but one of the Irish bodies was recently dated to the Late Bronze Age. It would not be unreasonable, then, to assume at least a degree of similarity between the Irish, Lancashire and Danish culture of body deposition. From the Neolithic there was a defined movement of trade between the Irish Atlantic shores, through our Boulsworth district and on to Scandinavia. Fair enough, Boulsworth now has no extensive peat bogs in which to discover the dumped remnants of a rotten king but the notion of territory and kingship would be firmly established here by the early Bronze Age.

Fig: 108

● *Neolithic*

○ *Mesolithic*

✚ *New Neolithic*

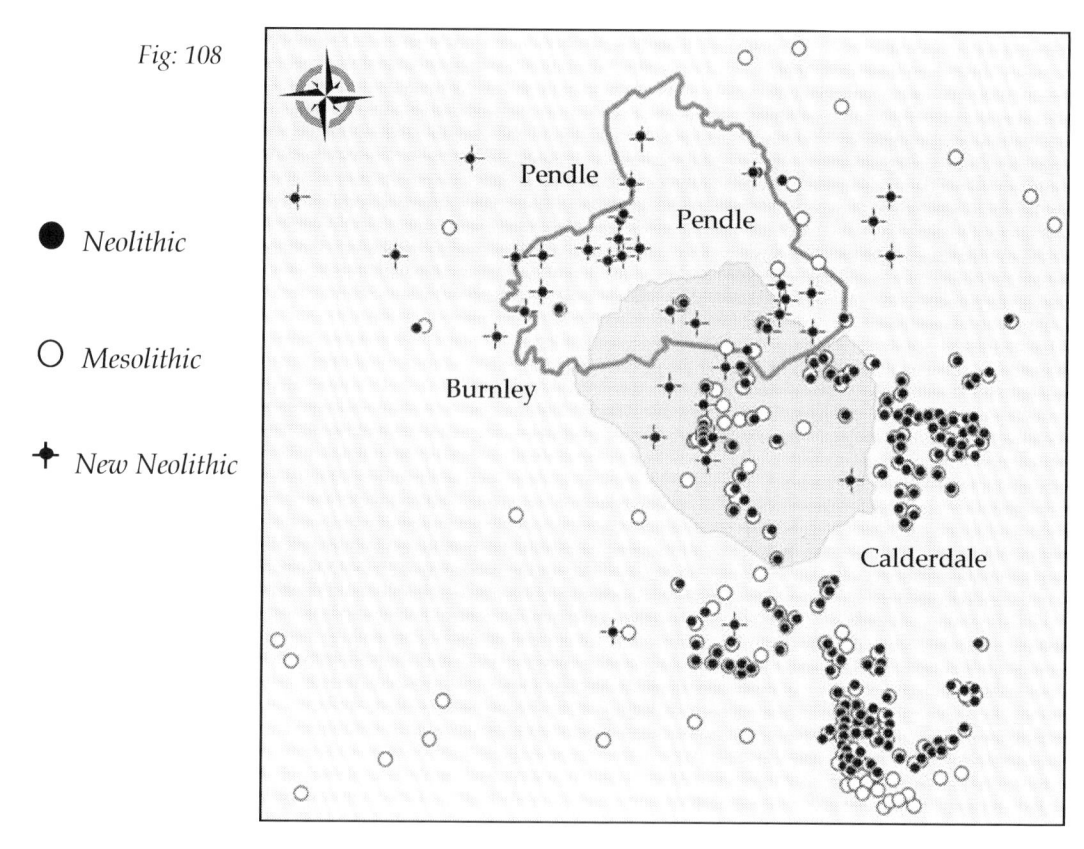

Fig: 108 - A comparison of Neolithic sites against Mesolithic sites: crosses mark Neolithic sites not related to earlier Mesolithic sites. There was a discernible northward movement into the Pendle district during the Neolithic - within the Boulsworth area there were slightly more new Neolithic sites than lost Mesolithic ones indicating that population numbers had possibly increased

145

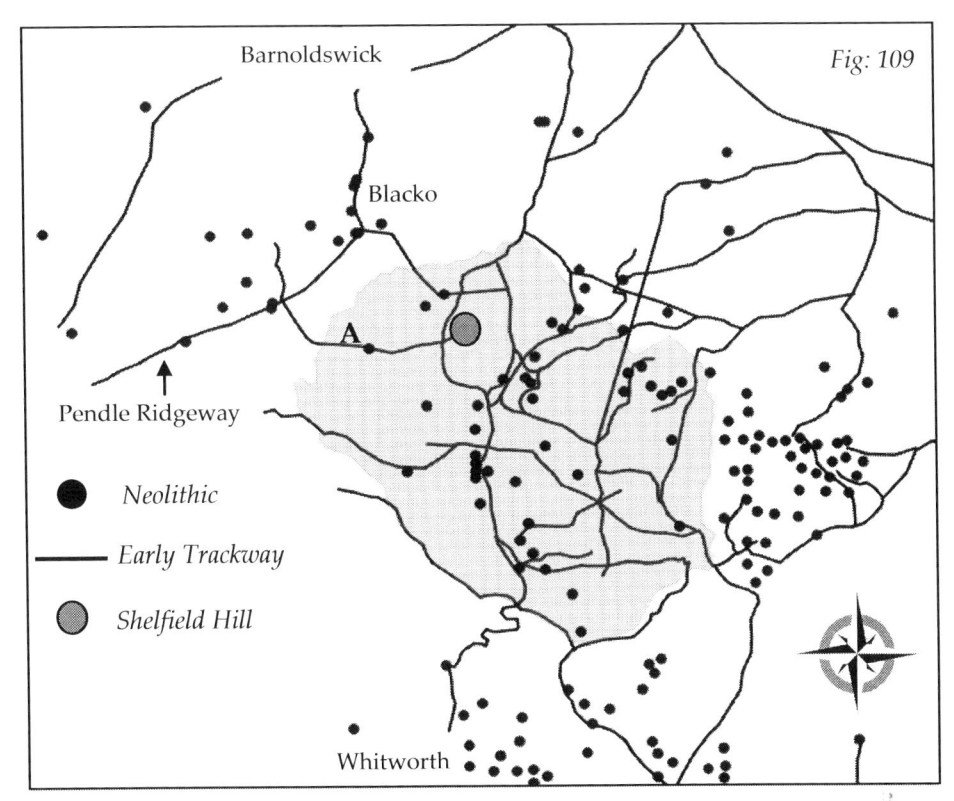

Fig: 109   Neolithic sites in relation to early routes

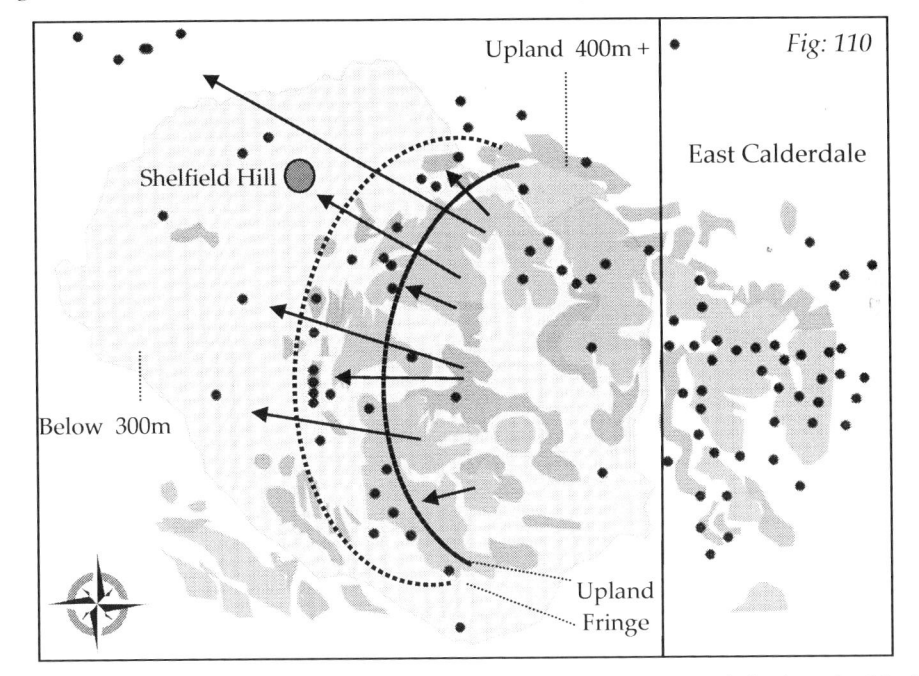

Fig:110 Occupation was shifting to the upland fringe and lower ground during the Neolithic

The evidence of Neolithic and Early Bronze Age burials along Pendle and Boulsworth trackways is an indicator of a degree of settlement. It would appear that the trade of tools and metals (e.g. Irish copper) had increased in volume to a point where the old inter-regional paths had become established trackways. Other tracks also served as communications between scattered farmsteads and settlement foci; a possible example of this being the extant road linking the Pendle site cluster with Shelfield Hill, a stretch of which is called the King's Causeway (marked **A** in *Fig: 109*).

Fig: 110 shows that the area east of the upland fringe contains far more Neolithic sites than the area to the west. The vast majority of these eastern sites are where Neolithic tools have been found in association with earlier Mesolithic sites while the Neolithic sites to the west are largely independent of earlier sites. There is possibly an explanation for this in that the landscape of the eastern area is primarily upland; Neolithic hunter-gatherers were still operating in this environment and were leaving a wide scatter of lithic tools and weapons across the moors. In contrast, the western area is the lower ground of upland fringe plateaux and valley slopes and was, therefore, more suited to agriculture.

In consequence of this we see less sites (arrowhead findspots etc.) in the west but the examples we do see are generally more settlement orientated (burials, enclosures, monuments) than the findspots in the east. This suggests that Neolithic people were moving from the west Calderdale moors northward through Boulsworth and settling on the lower river valley slopes. It also appears from the site pattern in *Fig: 110* that the Mesolithic sites in the uplands of east Calderdale were still being utilised, probably as transient hunting camps, during the Neolithic. However, the trend is for a shifting occupation pattern from the central moors of the Two Metre BNC Survey to the Boulsworth and Burnley plains.

☦ Returning to Shelfield Hill; this area of drained grassland was reclaimed from the Boulsworth plain moor centuries ago but in reality it would have been suitable for stock rearing during the Neolithic. Anyone looking out from Shelfield Hill at this time would have seen that the slopes of Boulsworth Hill were covered in oak forest running up to the summit plateau of birch scrub. On the Boulsworth plain were clusters of alder interspersed with glacial depressions gradually filling with peat. The alder woods carried on down the valley slopes where they met with the boggy reed strips running parallel with the rivers. Among the alder and oak woods they would see plumes of wood smoke rising from the scattered clearings surrounding small farmsteads.

Fig: P111 Looking north: Pendle Hill in the background with Shelfield Hill centre right
Fig: P112 Looking south: View of Boulsworth Hill from the summit of Shelfield Hill

In the Late Neolithic, the bulk of Boulsworth Hill presided over a changing landscape; people moved around in this landscape but not as the fleeting nomadic figures of earlier periods. There was now a sense of permanence and the people who set out in the early morning, perhaps to tend to stock, trap game or gather crops, returned each evening to a family homestead. Members of the extended families would set up their own farmsteads in close proximity to each other and so communities grew into fixed societies - all their energies were expended upon the land and this created a social dynamic where each land 'owner' was prepared to defend their landholding.

A new political elite emerged, possibly from among the best warriors with the backing of the highest priests. Communal projects (building burial mounds and monuments) consolidated the notion of the individual as an integral member of society through a sense of social 'belonging.' Religion and kingship went hand-in-hand and, as long as the ruling elite were able to protect their tribe from the elements (and other tribes) the *status quo* was maintained.

It is possible, then, that as the Late Neolithic merged into the Early Bronze Age (2,100 BC - 1,900 BC) the district of Shelfield presented a landscape of scattered farmsteads with people gradually clearing and draining land within a defined landscape block extending from Trawden to Thursden and Boulsworth to Pendle. Almost at the dead-centre of this district sits Shelfield Hill and it is proposed that this site became an important social and political focus for the surrounding communities.

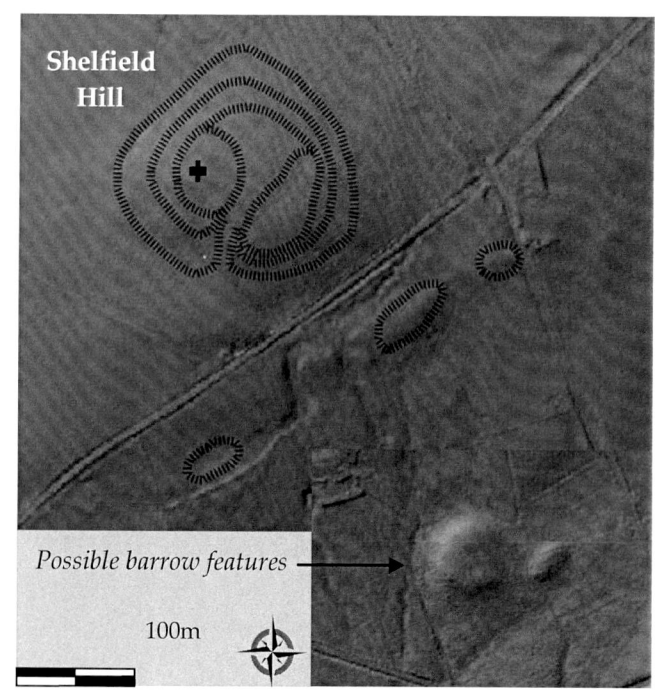

Fig: P113
365 metres to the south of the Shelfield Hill summit are two probable burial mounds. These take the form of a large circular mound 63 metres in diameter and an adjacent feature measuring 36 metres in length and 21 metres in width. At first sight it appears that these features could be a series of Neolithic long barrows and/or a Bronze Age round barrow

Fig: P114

When the mound features in Fig: P113 are enhanced it can be seen that the larger of the two (the 'round barrow') is not a solid mound. It appears there is either a hollow in the centre or the structure is actually a composite of two separate mounds. The broken line indicates the edge of a hollow where material was probably removed to create the mound

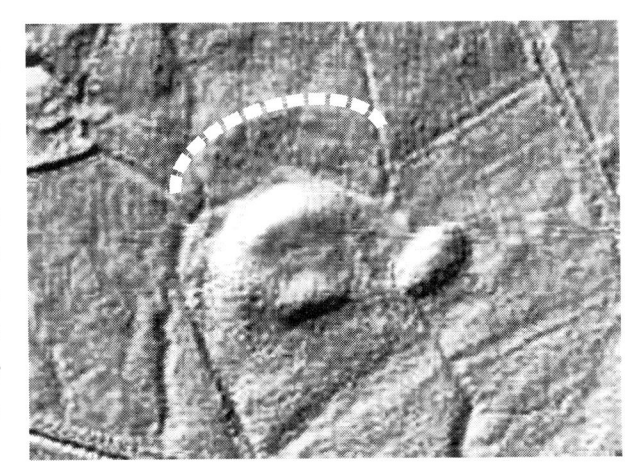

Fig: 115

The illustration shows two possibilities:
1 is a circular mound with material removed and 2 indicates two separate long mounds with an infilled plug of earth at the western end

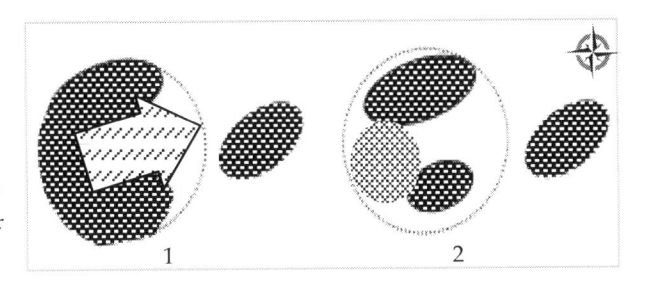

It is very possible, then, that the features illustrated in *Figs: 113-115* are three burial mounds of the Neolithic period or a mixture of Neolithic and Bronze Age mounds. It is difficult to assess these features without excavation but the size, shape and orientation strongly suggest that these features will contain burials of a small number of a community elite who lived and farmed in the Shelfield area. It is further very possible that these are not the only features of their type within the immediate area of the hill.

Fig: 116

A number of well defined and denuded mound features are apparent within an 800 metre radius of Shelfield Hill with a particular cluster occurring on the southern hill slope

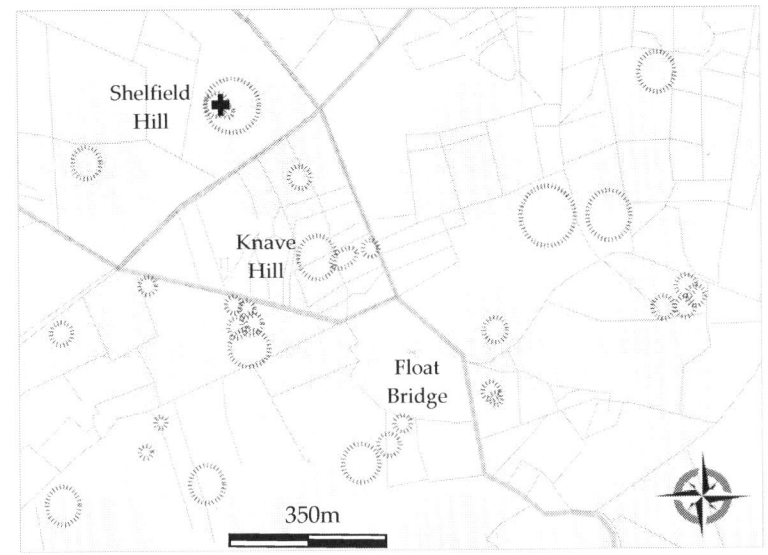

Fig: P117 Taken from Shelfield Hill: the mounds below Shelfield Hill (centre) to the front of Float Bridge Farm. The Ringstone Hill section suggests that the largest mound formed the terminus of a series of five landscape features aligned on a solstice axis

The larger of the two mounds actually carries a name - Knavehill. The *knave* element is shared with Jeppe Knave Grave, a Bronze Age burial cairn on the lower western slopes of Pendle Hill. The modern meaning of *knave* is commonly taken as reference to *wrong-doer* or *rascal* but in the case of Knave Hill this probably does not apply. In the Old English *cnafa* there is an element shared with the Old High German *knabo*, the German *knabe*, the Old Norse *knapi* and the Dutch word *knaap*, all having the same meaning of *boy, youth, servant*. In the Middle High German *knappe* means a *young squire* or *shield-bearer*.

Somewhere within these early Medieval terms may be a description of the purpose of the Knavehill mounds in that a young Scandiwegian prince or warrior was buried here. This would give credence to the local antiquarian notion that Shelfield was a 'Viking' site. However, as always, there is an alternative; the Old English word *nafu* had evolved from the Early German *nabo* meaning *navel* - in turn *nafu* became *nave* describing the notion of circularity/centrality as in *hub of a wheel* or *central place*. It strikes me that this latter description fits the large circular mound of Knave Hill perfectly.

Given that the mound carries its own name it is very possible that the Scandiwegian settlers of this district recognised the former importance of the site and re-used the Knave Hill mound for their own burials.

The menhir on the neighbouring Shelfield Hill would have been the most obvious landmark in this area and, as we saw earlier, the newcomers probably took the menhir to be a landscape marker and named the hill on which it stood *seol field*.

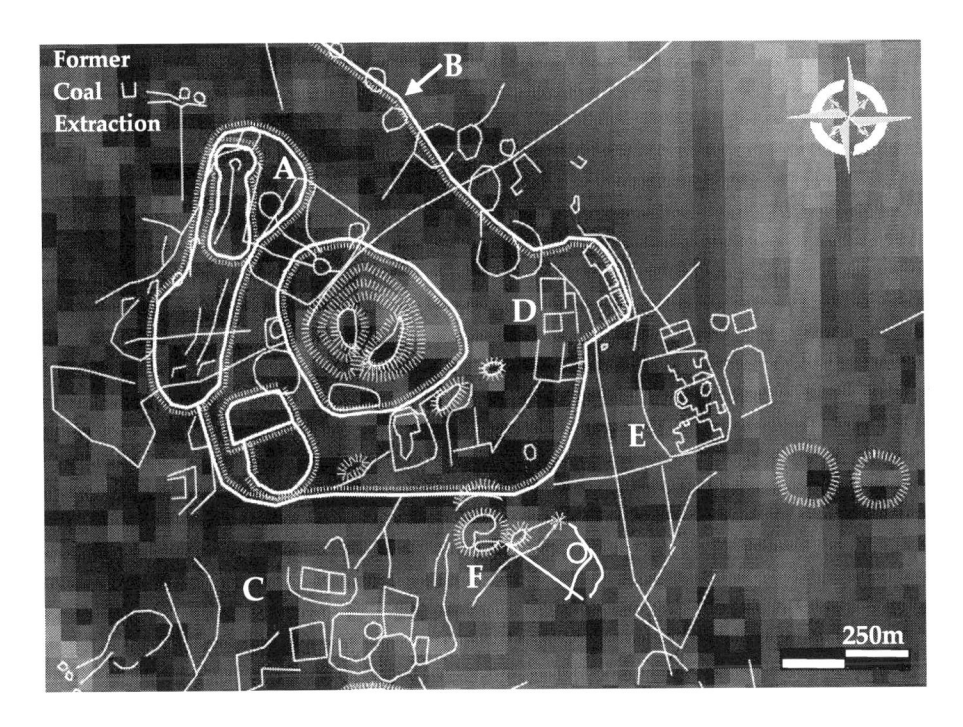

Fig: 118 The extended site of Shelfield Hill displays a complex series of earthworks:

    A)   *Possible occupation enclosure in which the 'Anvil' stone was found*
    B)   *Shelfield outer enclosure*
    C)   *Possible early field enclosures to west of Knave Hill*
    D) E)   *Possible occupation sites*
    F)   *Knave Hill mounds*

Stone: Monuments, Circles and Markers

Fig: P119
The 'anvil' stone (should this be re-named the 'seat' stone?)

Returning to the 'Anvil' stone on Shelfield Hill, it is possible that the story behind this worked boulder ties in with the evidence seen so far to suggest that the hill was an important site during the Late Neolithic and Bronze Age period. The stone was moved from the field some 250 metres north-west of the Walton Spire menhir and placed in its present position around twenty years ago. We saw earlier that the stone has been worked and takes differing forms according to the angle of view - when viewed from a ninety degree angle it appears to have been deliberately sculpted into the form of a seat.

The proposed enclosure **A** in *Fig: 118* occupies the north-western edge of the upper Shelfield Hill slope; from this site northward the land slopes gently down to the Castercliffe hillfort plateau before descending into Colne Water in the valley bottom. The western slopes of Shelfield Hill may well have been chosen as a settlement enclosure site due to the maximum sunlight exposure over each day. Further, site **A** sits alongside an ancient trackway running from the south-west, through Worsthorne and on to Skipton.

In the recent past, surface coal extraction has taken place around Shelfield Farm to the north-west of the hill and this means that care must be taken when assigning archaeological features to this particular area. However, the depression left by the extraction can be discerned in the landscape, its edge is marked by concrete fence-posts a few hundred metres to the west of the proposed enclosure **A**.

If the enclosure **A** does indeed present evidence for early occupation around Shelfield Hill then it is worth postulating that the large worked 'Anvil Stone' that formerly stood within that site could have served a definite purpose within the Shelfield Hill community. In particular the seat shape of the stone suggests that it might have performed as a type of 'throne' on which those of high status would have been seated during important ceremonies. If so then a distinct parallel can be drawn between the 'Anvil Stone' and the Stone of Scone, a block of stone that has been incorporated into the throne of British monarchs for centuries.

Alternatively, if the 'Anvil Stone' did indeed fulfil some ritual purpose it could equally have been utilised by some Dark Age chieftain during local moot gatherings on Shelfield Hill.

*Fig: 120 Aerial images from 1988 show that a feature runs from the direction of enclosure **A** and traverses around the contours of Shelfield Hill, finally making its way into the summit enclosure **C**. It is suggested that this was a trackway used for processional or military access to the summit*

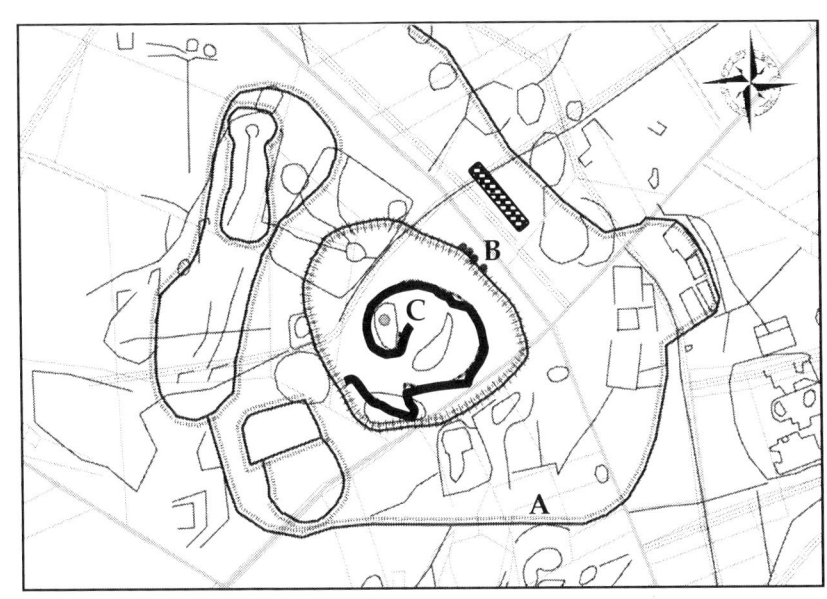

▬ *Trackway traverses the hill and enters the summit enclosure*
A) *Enclosure* **B)** *Row of extant earthbound stones forming revetment* **C)** *Summit enclosure*

Fig: P121 Walton Spire

We have seen that the Walton Spire menhir sits on the highest point of the Shelfield Hill summit enclosure and that the stone base is the largest of its type within the district. The hilltop location makes the stone even more interesting

Most ancient marker stones in the Boulsworth district are distinctive in form and size - commonly around a metre in height and roughly triangular in shape. More often than not these stones mark ancient boundaries and trackways although groupings can indicate the presence of a former burial mound or kerbed cairn

Fig: P122

A typical standing/marker stone at Brinks End

The stone is located within a concentration of Neolithic and Bronze Age sites on the lower slopes of Boulsworth Hill

Figs: P122 & P123 courtesy of Mark Chung

Fig: P123

Another mark stone at Beaver Scar. The crude cross has been added in relatively recent times

Fig: P124

Stones on the Slipper Hill/Hameldon (Worsthorne Moor) burial mound.

Large stones and boulders on mounds such as these can be remnants of antiquarian barrow-digging where stone cists and cairn kerbs have been left on the surface

Fig: P125

A large triangular stone sitting by the trackway on Will Moor. The stone is recumbent, having stood on the flat base marked by the bag. Non-earthbound stones cannot always be taken to have remained in situ as they were often moved during field clearance operations

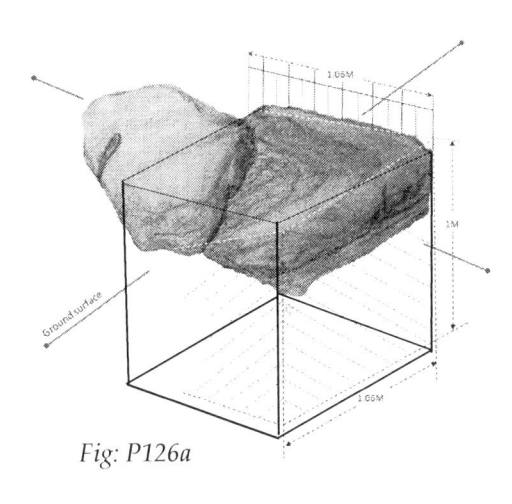

Fig: P126a

P126 - *Sometimes only the tip of a large stone is apparent on the ground. This example on the Pendle Ridgeway was found to be a one metre square block of sandstone (Fig: P126a)*

Fig: P127

Beneath the stone (Fig: P126) a linear group of closely associated bark fragments were recovered. The position of the fragments indicates that they are the vestiges of a post, branch or trunk 13cm in diameter and .3m long - identified as the downey birch species

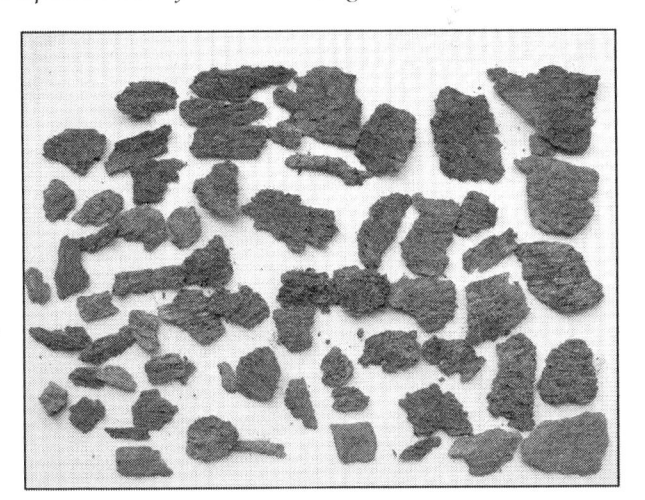

Fig: P128

Another stone from the Pendle Ridgeway. This menhir measures almost two metres in height and sits on a parish boundary. However, the stone does not appear to remain in situ having reportedly been moved by the farmer from its original position near to the stone in Fig: P126

Fig: P129

This massive boulder was recently found buried along with a number of large stones at the bottom of the slope of Ringstone Hill, in Blacko - the name strongly suggests that the stone group was once part of a stone circle

Fig: P130

This stone, part of a linear row of similar stones, sits on the Pendle Water riverbank a few hundred metres upstream from the stone in Fig: P131. The large stone is triangular in shape and is a rare example in that one face carries a number of incised cup marks (inset)

◁ *Fig: P131*   △ *Fig:P131a*

Before and after: *Fig:P131 shows a gritstone orthostat almost 2 metres in length. The stone originally stood upright but river erosion caused partial collapse: heavy rain in 2012 saw it fall and roll over (Fig: P131a)*

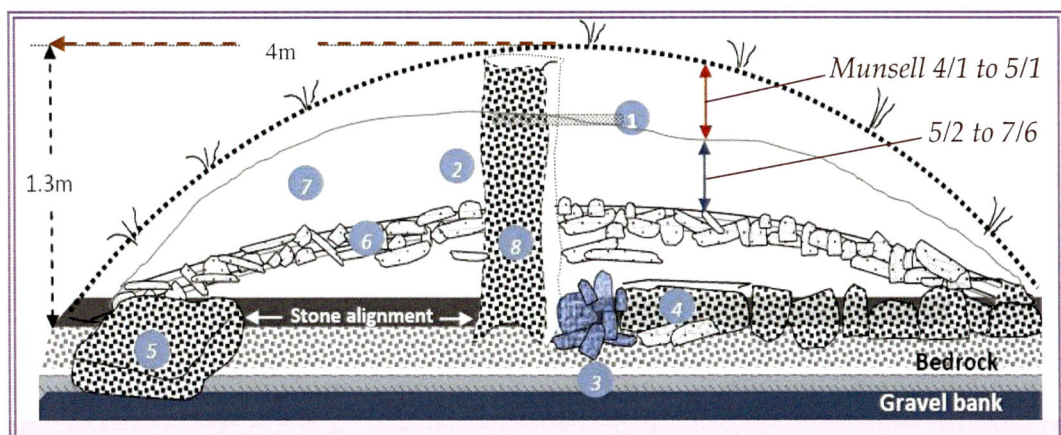

Fig: 132 Section of stone feature at Blacko Watermeetings

1 Charcoal lense between topsoil and fine gravel layer
2 Section face contains river deposited pottery from upstream
3 Small stone cairn set in pit depression cut into bedrock: location of tool *(Fig: P77)*
4 Flat stone - possible capstone: linear row of small boulders aligned east-west
5 Large sandstone recumbent at western edge of feature
6 Layer of sorted stone across feature
7 Chert bar tool within section face *(Fig: P9)*: probable river deposit
8 Original upright position of gritstone orthostat *(Fig: P131)*

Figures *P131* to *132* illustrate a feature on the Pendle Water riverbank that became apparent in 2010 when river action exposed a large semi-upright stone. It was clear that further river-wash would cause the stone to collapse and so a rapid assessment was made of the stone and its river bank setting. The first thing to become apparent is that the stone, being of gritstone composition, is not from the locality. The abandoned Utherstone quarry is situated at the eastern end of the Pendle Ridgeway, a few hundred metres to the south of the site, but the geology here is a distinctive soft red sandstone. The gritstone orthostat, then, was either a glacial erratic dumped in the area or was brought to the site from a distant millstone source.

The exposed river bank section was cleaned up and riverborne gravel was removed from around the stone. It became apparent that a shallow pit 60 centimetres in diameter had been created in the sandstone bedrock and this contained a number of small stones forming a circular cairn around 38 centimetres in height. The cairn was was built with carefully chosen local stones, many of which were of a curved nature, and placed in a tight position between the gritstone orthostat and and a prone flat stone measuring 1.3m in length, .75m in width and 30cm in depth. A charcoal lense was clearly visible in the section, between the topsoil and gravel/subsoil and beneath this latter was a defined layer of sorted stone over the sandy soil covering to the natural bedrock. The whole feature extends to 8m in diameter and 1.3m in height with a defined row of boulders aligned east-west through the centre on the bedrock. The cairn and the gritstone orthostat sat in the centre of this alignment and a large flat stone marks the western end. Poor weather precluded a second visit to the site for over a week and on returning it was found that the orthostat had fallen and tumbled on to its side by the power of the flooded river.

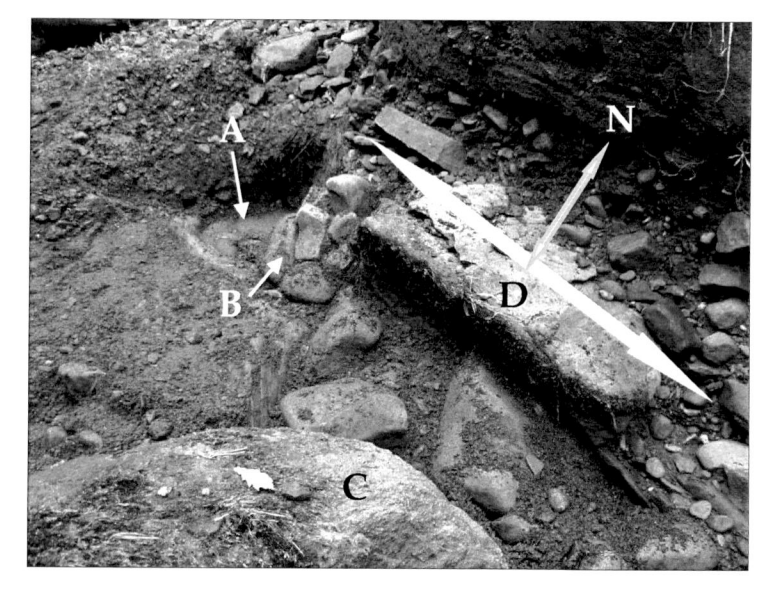

Fig: P133

After the flood: the orthostat lays prone and the river bank has been heavily eroded

A) *Depression in which the orthostat was originally positioned*
B) *Cairn*
C) *Fallen orthostat*
D) *Flat stone*
The white arrow indicates the E-W stone alignment

Following the collapse of the stone the formerly earthbound end was found to have been worked into a concave shape. The reason for this was something of a mystery until a convex, distinctly blue-coloured stone was found in the gravel adjacent to the base. This latter stone fits with the concavity in the orthostat base and it is suggested that the orthostat stood on the blue stone.

Fig: P134   Orthostat concave base   *Fig: P135   Convex blue stone*

The blue stone is clearly not of local origin; blue limestone, and other bluish coloured stone, can be found in Ireland, Wales and the south-eastern coastal districts of England. Whatever the source of this stone it appears that a great deal of effort went into the erection of the orthostat

Fig: P136
Black shale 'blade'

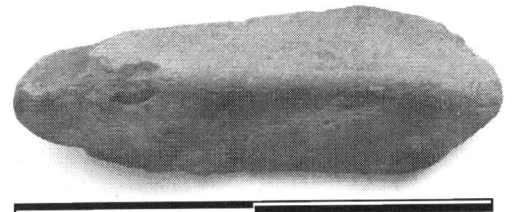

Within the cairn a stone 'chopping' tool had been carefully positioned *(Fig: P77)* and along with this was a black shale object *(Fig: P136)*.

14cm

This took the eye because of the symmetry apparent on the upper surface although it was assigned to the non-artefact box. However, shortly after the item was discovered ™*Current Archaeology* ran a feature relating to the excavation of a Neolithic/Bronze Age burial mound in Southern Ireland. Among the items recovered from the excavation was a polished black shale artefact identical in shape, size and material to that recovered from the Blacko site. The Irish archaeologists described the item as a grave deposition in the form of a shale copy of a contemporary lithic blade. It seems fair to suggest, then, that the Blacko example was such an object but exposure to river action has removed any patina or polish that it might have had. If this is indeed the case then we have evidence for early cross-cultural influence between Lancashire and Ireland.

Fig: P137

Large worked block of sandstone cleared from a field at Ringstone Hill, Blacko. It is probable that this belonged to the group to which the stone in Fig: P129 belonged. Why the stone was worked into a block, or 'squared off' is unclear

Fig: P138

This stone sits in the middle of Pendle Water, is as big as a garden shed and marks the juncture of the Barrowford, Blacko and Roughlee parish boundaries. This was one of a pair known locally known as the Coach and Horses until the smaller of the two was washed downstream in floods of 1966

Fig: P139

A boundary stone marking the western edge of Trawden Forest, possibly dating to the 14th century when a royal edict caused forest areas to be officially bounded. The position of the stone, at Antley Gate on the Will Moor Road, means that it could also have been a post supporting a gate to contain animals within the forest

Fig: P140

Fig: P141

Image courtesy of Ralph Woolnough

Mark stones: the stone in Fig: P140 stood by the roadside in Blacko marking the boundary between Blacko and Admergill. Around the middle of the 20th century a local historian mistakenly decided that the stone was a Medieval cross and duly carved a Maltese cross on it, accompanied by the words 'Black Cross.' Since then the stone has entered the local psyche as Blacko Cross - the stone disappeared around the 1980s. The stone in Fig: P141 is very similar in size and shape to Fig: P140; this example marked a Medieval trackway onto Blacko Hill and was incorporated into the field wall during the local enclosures

Fig: P142

A very interesting group of stones near Shelfield Hill. The group is a field clearance dump from the 20th century when new mole drains were created.

The group consists of large stones and rounded boulders (many of which measure over one metre in length) brought up from around .5 metres below the surface. This suggests that the stones formed part of an early settlement, possibly as associated field walls, structures or even burial monuments

Fig: P143

Menhir on the outskirts of Trawden. The stone is set into the wall along an ancient track running from Winewall to Castercliffe. Other large stones are scattered around the immediate area (Fig: P144)

Fig: P144

The Trawden menhir *(Fig: P143)* stands by the Mire Ridge trackway running from Prospect Farm to the Castercliffe Hillfort via the head of Fox Clough. The stone was probably much larger than it is now - a hole has been drilled two thirds of the way through and the stone appears to have been split lengthways along this line. In the field over the wall there is a drainage hollow into which a number of field drains and small streams empty before heading downhill to Fox Clough. Nearby there was also a natural spring (which now appears to have been covered) and it is possible that this was considered as a sacred place worthy of marking with a stone monument.

CELESTIAL LANDSCAPE

Alternatively, the stone sits on the trackway and this appears to have formed a ditched enclosure boundary at some stage, probably for a settlement on Cow Field, above Beardshaw. The menhir could, then, have served no other purpose than a boundary marker. However, it is worth noting that the stone shows a defined correlation with the mid-winter sunrise. To take this possible astronomical relationship further we must digress somewhat from the world of fully-accepted archaeological evidence and enter the grey realms of cosmological possibilities.

Here we meet the age-old problem of interpretation of the ancient landscape. Speculative interpretation of artefacts and monuments is frequently the cause of sharp division of opinion between those seeking proto-scientific-cum-notational content and those who only see in the same artefact, or monument, abstract symbolism or mundane information. Where some might see a megalithic structure as the ancient equivalent of the modern gravestone (a marker to commemorate a king, a political leader or warlord) others see an astrological implement used by the ancients to 'ground' the stars and planets in order to utilise the rigid universal patterns that they follow.

In this sense some monuments are closely related in a pattern where menhirs and mounds were carefully sited to form small cogs within a large celestial machine. Stone alignments could be used to fix the position of a particular planet and to act as earth-bound representatives of whichever celestial body might be of importance to the monument builders.

To a certain extent the modern science of astro-archaeology has struggled to become fully accepted within the archaeological world. However, experts in their field have now shown that the original purpose of many ancient sites was to relate to the cosmos; for example, one of the primary features of Stonehenge was as a marker of the mid-winter sunset. From the Palaeolithic to the Iron Age our ancestors looked to the skies for their deities and for the more pragmatic purpose of marking the passage of time and agricultural seasons, for navigation and for the prediction of future celestial events.

As the hunter-gatherers settled down to a more settled agrarian existence their attention began to focus more on the orientation of the sun. The beginning and end of each season was connected with the solar movement (or, in some cases, with the heliacal rise of certain bright stars). The people regularly observed the equinoxes (when the length of the day was equal to the length of the night) and the solstices (when a day or night was the longest in the year). In this way they fixed the solar arcs on the horizon and were thus able to predict the annual cycle of the rising and setting of the Sun with great accuracy.

Although the point on the horizon where the sun rose and set is a common orientation found within Neolithic monuments, the other cardinal points were also important. A fixed north point was required for celestial observation and this could be determined in two specific ways. During the day it could track the movement of the sun and its shadow at the equinoxes and in the night sky it could be observed as the spot where the starry sky pivoted around the 'world pillar' that supported the heavens on a vertical axis and linked all the layers of the cosmos. The culture of a 'world pillar', or 'tree of life,' was fundamental to many Palaeolithic and Mesolithic communities around the world who relied upon shamanistic concepts. In this case, the north point represented the spot that assured communication with the afterworld, a task that could only be accomplished by the shaman who assisted the dead in their transition to the otherworld. The shaman could also facilitate communication with those who were already in that world in order to ensure a safe journey for the departed.

Along with the North-Eurasian concept of the world pillar came the belief that the edge of the sky could move up and down in the horizon. This movement allowed people, both alive and dead, to pass into the otherworld. In Northern Europe, the late autumn and winter were seen as the *dark time* related to the dead and the netherworld. The Neolithic shift towards settlement increasingly favoured a culture based on the passage of the sun but old habits die hard and we see in many Neolithic and Early Bronze Age monuments the ability to observe the old celestial beliefs along with the relatively new solar cult.

The accurate observation of the northern sky-point, then, was of importance to Neolithic communities; today, north is orientated in the direction of the Polaris star within the Ursa Minor (*Smaller Bear*) constellation. However, over thousands of years the precession of the Earth around its axis causes a shift in the cosmos in relation to the Earth's fixed cardinal points. This means that in the Mesolithic period the polar star was Edasish (*iota Draconis*) and by 3,900 BC the closest star to the North Pole to be seen with the naked eye was Thuban, from the Dragon (*Draconis*) constellation. Situated north from the ecliptic plan, the Dragon is a circumpolar constellation for most of its observers. This constellation is widely distributed, covering 1,083 square degrees of the sky, but it comprises just three shining stars: Thuban (*alfa Draconis*), Etamin (*gamma Draconis*) and Rastaban (*beta Draconis*). In 1,793 BC Thuban was superseded as the north star by Kappa Draconis.

The pole star, or the 'nail star,' being attached to the head of the sky-supporting 'world pillar' (*illustration left*) held a strong position in the ancient beliefs of many North-Eurasian people; the 'nail' was usually described as being made of iron but in the Finnish and Estonian mythology it is also described as 'golden'. Not only the nail, but also the whole pillar was described as being made of iron, gold, or copper by many North-Eurasian peoples. There are historical accounts that the North-European Germanic tribes had, in their houses and shrines, sacred wooden columns with nails attached to the top of them. In Germany,

Scandinavia and Lapland wooden columns in the temples and outdoor shrines represented the world pillar that supports the sky. The nails of the Vikings were called 'the nails of gods' or 'world nails (Ridderstad, M. *Orientation of the Northern Gate of the Goseck Neolithic Rondel* University of Helsinki Observatory Paper 2010)

In the Nordic countries the application of archaeo-astrology has been widely practised for a number of years and this has resulted in a corpus of knowledge; during the Neolithic it has been found that astronomical orientation was applied in most of the cultures. Azimuth (angle or line of stellar observation) distribution was specific to each culture, settlement or community and indicates that each micro-society observed different stellar bodies and events within a wider common belief system. This is comparable to modern religions where factional elements of (say) the Church of England practised under penumbric denominations such as Methodism and Congregationalism.

Returning to the menhirs at Mire Ridge (Trawden) and Shelfield Hill; the Shelfield Hill site was surely of importance to local Neolithic and Early Bronze Age communities and this raises the question as to whether the menhir surmounting the hilltop enclosure might have been erected to serve as an astronomical observation marker?

Fig: 145

Equidistant Sites

Polar or True north (TN)
is -2° 14' (west) of magnetic north (MN)

(A) Castercliffe hillfort enclosure
(B) Trawden menhir
(C) Shelfield Hill menhir

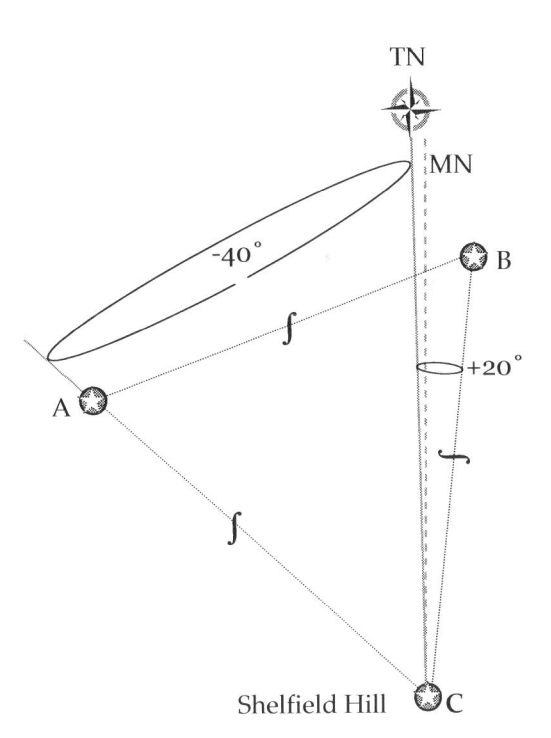

$\int$ = *1,500 metres*

Before presenting the *notion* that the Shelfield menhir may have been erected to serve as an integral part of a local astronomical observatory, any proposition of this kind must be tempered with a word of caution - care must be taken when assigning alignments and spatial relationships to landscape features. While it is true that burial mounds were often deliberately aligned by their builders, the sheer number of stone monuments and markers within the landscape can easily lead to false assumption.

If a handful of dried peas were to be scattered across a square-metre sheet of card then the random pattern generated would allow for a large number of alignments, geometric relationships and numerical coincidence. To be fair, extant ancient standing stones form a less random pattern than a handful of scattered peas; spatial criteria appears to have dictated that stone megaliths, menhirs and orthostats were situated along boundaries, tracks and monumental sites. This can be seen when such stones are plotted on a map as, over an extended area, they tend to coalesce roughly along ancient routes and cluster around settlements. This means that the stones were compressed into linear patterns, sometimes across a distance in excess of five kilometres thus creating an increase in random linear relationships. As a result of this a large number of alignments between extant ancient stones can be observed. To further muddy already unclear waters a number of other landscape features can be thrown into the alignment mix. Mounds and cairns, springs, wayside crosses, crossroads etc. are often counted alongside ancient stones and this greatly increases the number of apparent multi-feature relationships which are often then claimed as proof that their creators had some obscure esoteric reason for criss-crossing their world with linear patterning.

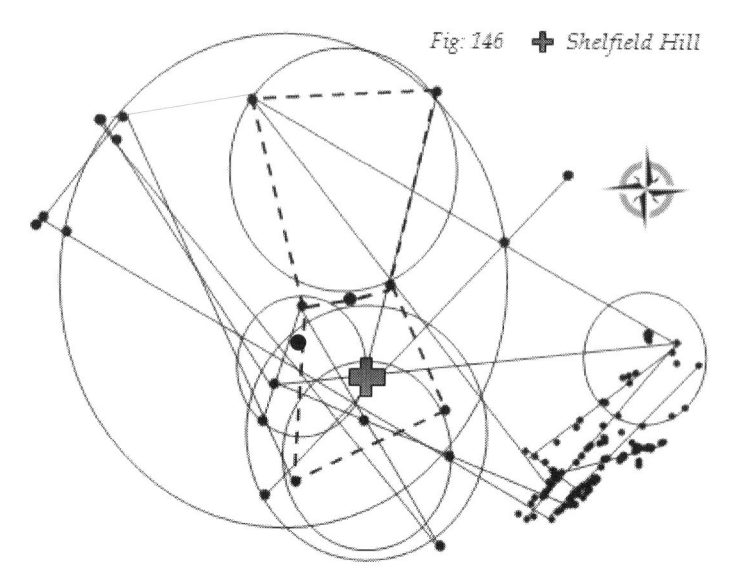

Fig: 146 ✣ *Shelfield Hill*

Extant ancient stones and natural boulder outcrops within a 100 square kilometre area. A mish-mash of linear alignments and geometric patterns emerge when 3 or more sites are plotted. If other feature types were to be added then the pattern incidence would increase dramatically.

A representation of the Orion constellation has been thrown in for good measure (broken line)

Having studied the relationship between extant ancient stones for over forty years I have heard many arguments for their original purpose. These include a 'proven' international network of monumental alignments created by 'power' conducting magnetic lines across the earth's surface (ley-lines). I have been informed on numerous occasions that a friend-of-a-friend had found a once-lost stone circle or alignment of such importance that MI5 agents were dispatched to warn the finder that the site must remain secret. I have seen people rush up to a standing stone and hug it with a passion, only to be apparently 'thrown off' by some hidden force; I have also seen that some people believe that the rock art evident on many moorland stones was symbolic of a lost civilisation whose ancestral roots lay on some distant planet.

An integral part of the archaeologist's work is to interpret hard evidence and build a viable story relating to the culture of the creators of our ancient landscape. This means that there will always be differences of professional opinion in accordance with the viewpoint of the individual; these differences, however, sit within a framework of science-based discovery spanning two centuries. Archaeologists and historians may have their own take on the purpose of certain artefacts, written records or ancient sites but any difference of opinion usually concerns the minutiae of every-day existence - the wider picture concerning ancient cultures, aided by recent advances in scientific methods, is now expanding within a generally accepted framework.

There is, of course, a fly in the archaeological ointment when a purely pragmatic approach is taken in relation to the assessment of sites such as burials, henges, isolated menhirs and stone circles. Where some ethereal monument appears to confound the logic of the modern mind it is commonly assigned to *ritual* - this is followed by the nodding of heads and muttered sage comments without anyone actually having any firm evidence for the original purpose of the site. This being the case, can we be surprised that conspiracy and myth have grown around our ancient sites over thousands of years? Is it fair to summarily dismiss the opinions of those who seek an esoteric explanation for the array of ancient sites scattered across our landscape? The extant evidence relating to the existence of our forebears belongs to us all and, within the confines of reason, we all have the right to an opinion. Those who follow a less scientific approach to the secrets locked within our ancient landscape are often knowledgeable about the location of obscure monuments and do a great deal to bring their existence into the public eye. They usually respect the monuments they visit and, in many cases, advance their interests through like-minded groups who, in turn, raise awareness of the past within our landscape among a public who might not have access to, or indeed an interest in, books on archaeology.

Even in the light of scientific progress we do not have any firm answers to the thorny question of why certain menhirs were erected. Many large standing stones across Britain and France have been proposed by numerous scholars (Lockyer, Hawkins, Newham, Thom, Hoyle *et al*) as integral markers within localised celestial 'engines' or observatories. The notion that Neolithic people were highly skilled in astronomy and numeracy has steadily gained ground within the halls of academia to the point where cosmic influences are now assigned to certain sites as a matter of routine. Standing stones and stone circles might indeed have been designed to fulfil a number of communal requirements such as ceremonial foci, symbols of a phallic (fertility) cult and celestial observatories. In fact this latter can be seen as a largely pragmatic reason for the apparent complexity of some monuments and might provide the most plausible insight into the minds of those who placed their stones in what appear to be random situations.

From personal experience I can say with a degree of conviction that the majority of standing stones within the extended Pendle and Boulsworth district can be assigned to particular categories. Many stones follow routeways and can be seen to mark paths and tracks, especially cross-ridge trackways; other stones mark boundaries and within this category care must be taken to differentiate between ancient stones and the large number of extant Medieval and modern estate markers.

Markers were also set to delineate ecclesiastical boundaries, such as the outlying crosses erected by Whalley Abbey to mark the extent of their lands and the parish boundaries therein. Industrial claim-limits were also set with stones; numerous surface coal mining operations were carried out locally and, in the Boulsworth and Thursden area, there were many lime hushing operations along the streams gushing down from the moorlands - these were apportioned between local landowners who each placed their own stone marker.

Fig: P147
Abel Cross in Calderdale - this monument takes the form of two uprights, each set into its own base. The two bases were formerly a single block (possibly the bottom of a large prehistoric or Roman monument) before they were trimmed and split in order to create a wayside monument. This illustrates the difficulty in dating such stones

Menhirs could be erected to commemorate a person of status, or a particularly important event, and this practice continues to the present day. The assignment of stones to any particular period or purpose is, then, notoriously difficult and, given the fact that we see in our landscape the remnants of some six thousand years of occupation, we must occasionally assume the position of educated guesswork (or in the words of those with a more cynical bent, 'clueless observation').

Perhaps the most enigmatic of all our ancient monuments is the stone circle. These can be the remnants of a stone burial cairn where only the outer rim (kerb) of stones has survived, they can also be what remains of ancient or relatively modern stock enclosures, ancient hut foundations or they can mark flat prehistoric cemetery burials. Where random stones have been cleared from fields they were often piled on the field edges then the smaller ones were used later for modern enclosure walling, thus leaving larger stones in a circular pattern - there is also the consideration that the stone circle has historically been attractive to people and many modern circles can be found adorning the landscape.

The true stone circle, in the Neolithic and Bronze Age sense of the term, ranged in size from the massive site at Avebury, in Wiltshire, to the small circles a few metres across located in many moorland situations.

Fig: P148

Avebury (c. 2,600 BC) is the largest and most impressive henge monument in Britain. The bank and inner ditch is around 1.3 kilometres in circumference and encloses a circle of 98 sarsen stones within which were two smaller circles with a further stone setting near the centre. The picture (Alan Sorrell c.1958) shows a reconstruction of the original site

It was estimated by British archaeologist, Geoffrey Wainright, that the construction of Avebury took 1.5 million man-hours and was created to serve multiple purposes, not least of which was astronomical observation. Avebury is an excellent example of the high degree of energy that Late Neolithic monument builders were prepared to expend - this strongly suggests that the received benefits to the community must have been very high.

Moving from the Neolithic nirvana of Wessex to the northern badlands of Boulsworth, it is quite clear that there is a huge dichotomy of monumental activity between these two districts - if the large number of important sites on the southern downs were taken to be analogous with the modern city of London then Boulsworth would be a tiny hamlet with no pub. That said, we *do* have features handed down to us by our prehistoric forebears, we just have to look harder for them than our southern counterparts.

What, then, are we to make of the enigmatic menhir on Shelfield Hill? In isolation the original purpose of the stone could have been anything from a landscape marker, a fertility symbol or a monument erected to mark some pre-Norman battle or other (Brunanburgh?). However, the Shelfield menhir does not stand in isolation; we are aware of the Mire Ridge menhir, 1,500 metres to the north-west, and the impressive mounds standing less than 400 metres to the south-east. Perhaps, though, the most important site in relation to the Shelfield stone is the Ringstone Hill complex situated 500 metres to the south.

The Lancashire Sites and Monuments Record states that; *On Ring Stone Hill, 3.4km to the south east of the town of Nelson, lay a large stone circle of Bronze Age date (LSMR 1937). Unfortunately, this was destroyed in the first half of the nineteenth century and the stones were used for repairing the local roads.* Ringstone Hill is actually an elevated promontory of land formed on the north side by Pathole Beck and on the south by the Float Bridge and Catlow streams. The seventeenth century Ringstone Hill Farm stands a short distance to the north and took its name from the site. The promontory was almost certainly an enclosed/defended settlement and stands in close proximity to the 'minor hillfort' at Catlow Bottoms. The name of Ringstone Hill obviously describes the promontory as the *'hill by/of the circle of stones'* but it has hitherto been unclear as to the precise location of the destroyed stone circle. However, thanks to the technology of aerial and LiDAR imaging, along with fieldwork, the possibilities can be narrowed down to allow for a case to be made for the circle having been sited within the Ringstone Hill extended enclosure.

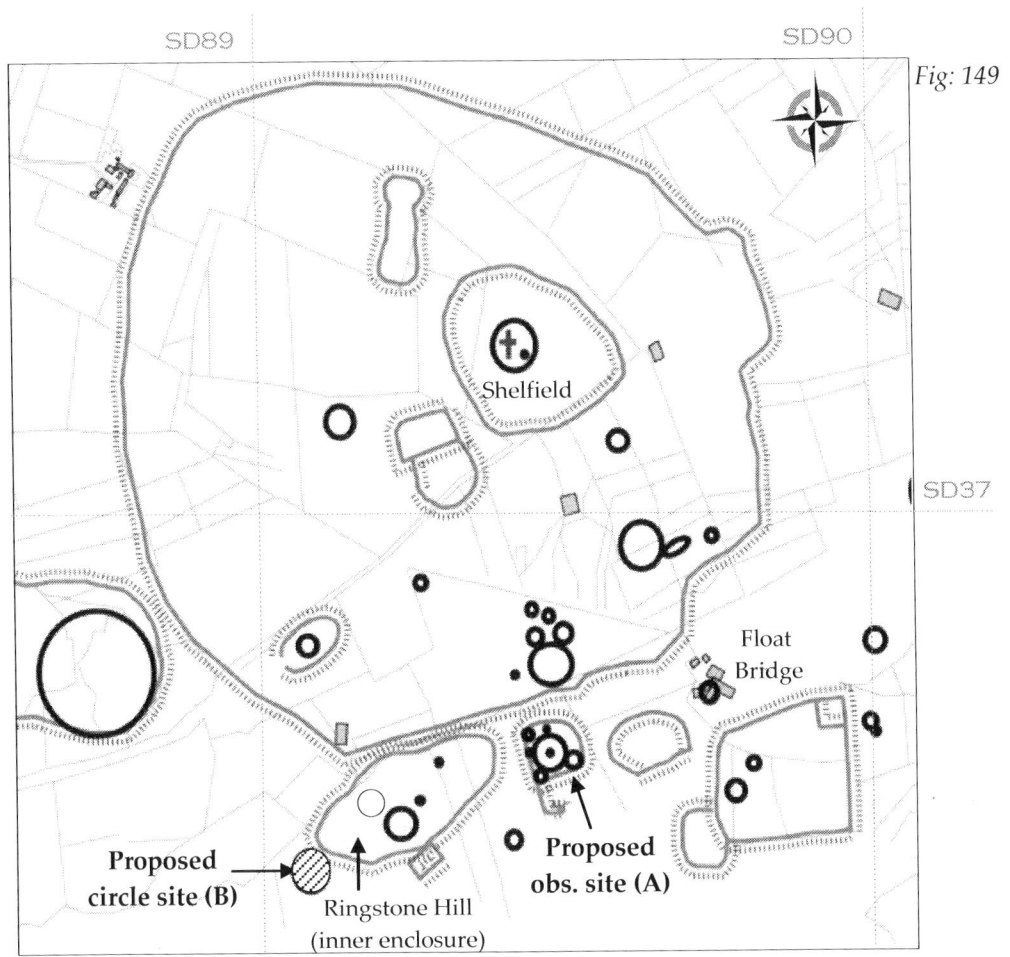

Proposed site of the lost stone circle and possible celestial observation site at Ringstone Hill

⸻⸻ *Ditched enclosure apparent on 1m LiDAR and air images*

○ ● *Circular feature i.e. earthwork enclosure or mound*

⸻⸻ *Wall line and field boundary ditch - extant and removed*

It can be seen in *Fig: 149* that the area to the south of Shelfield Hill contains a number of circular features along with former enclosures. These latter are probably a mixture of stock and settlement enclosures but are difficult to date without field evidence. The Ringstone Hill defended settlement, and the neighbouring defended settlement at Catlow, can be taken alongside the apparent landscape evidence within *Fig: 149* as strongly indicating the presence of a community in this vicinity. The enclosure of possible observation site **A** falls within the extended Ringstone Hill enclosure.

Within the enclosure appear to be a complex of earthworks *(Fig: 150)* with a possible entrance to the west - 1m LiDAR indicates a feature on the inner side of this feature from which point the possible azimuth of a number of astronomical elements can be drawn.

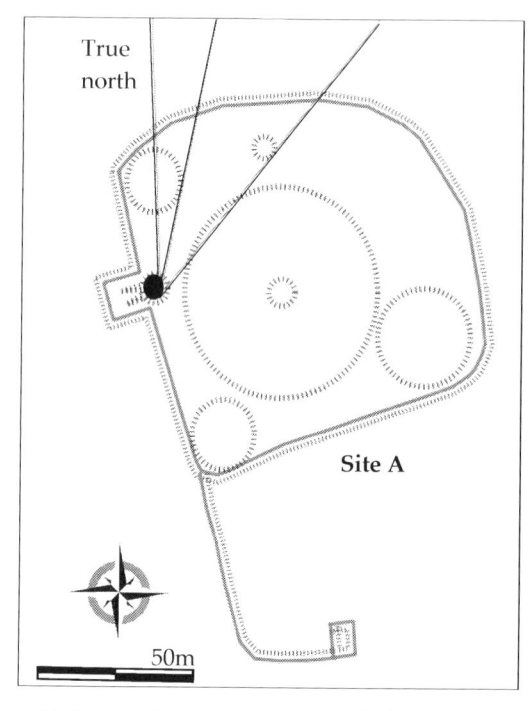

Fig: 150

● *Western point (site A) within a sub-rectangular enclosure - south of Pathole Beck and north of Catlow Brook - south-west of Float Bridge Farm*

SD 89434 36618
X 389434 Y 436618
Lat 53.825717 Long -2.1619958

A number of other circular earthworks and mounds are apparent within the extended Ringstone Hill area. The suggestion that site **A** was a notional celestial observation site is made here to illustrate the possibilities within ancient monumental design and to highlight the celestial association between this site and the Shelfield menhir. When the western point of the circular enclosure of site **A** is taken as a fixed marker *(Fig: 150)* then it becomes apparent that the menhir on Shelfield Hill *could* have been utilised as an outlying celestial marker.

The Shelfield menhir marks the point of true north from site **A** while true south is indicated by sighting along the western periphery of two large mound features on Shuttleworth Pasture (Briercliffe) to the dominant conical Pike Law hill formed by the Monk Hall tumuli. It is interesting to note that the mid-winter sunset can be sighted from the Mire Ridge menhir to the prominent ridge-top hill of Pike Law (another probable tumulus) north of Blacko *(Fig: 153)*. It has been noted in many astro-archaeological studies that burial mounds form landscape markers to facilitate the alignment of monuments to particular cosmic bodies. In many cases the hillside, and ridge-top setting of barrows and cairns provide ideal sighting point on the visible horizon and it is remarkable that a large number of proposed alignments traverse the periphery of these features (rather than following directly through the summit or centre).

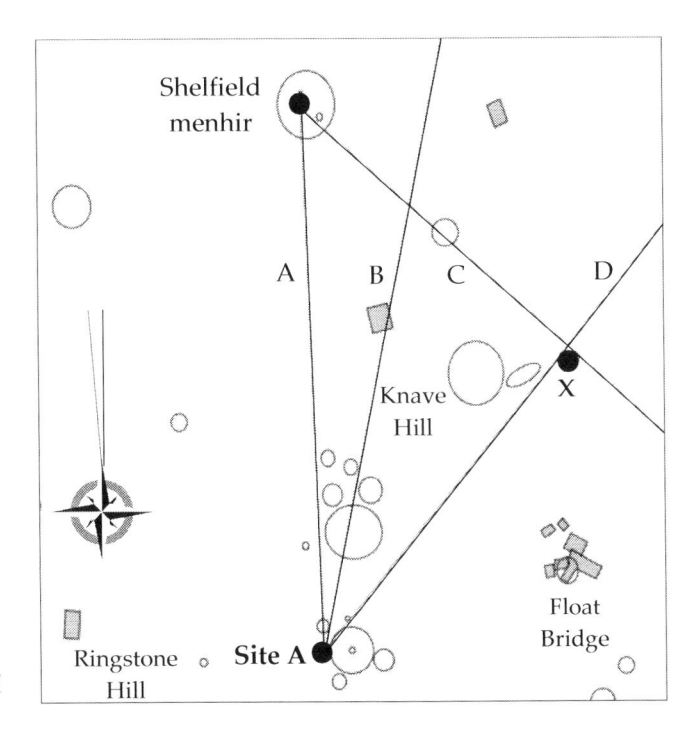

Fig:151

Possible primary astronomical alignments apparent from site A

A) True north from site A to the Shelfield menhir
B) Azimuth to the star Capella (also known as the Goat Star or the Shepherd's Star (Auriga constellation) through the Mire Ridge menhir
C) Mid-winter sunrise from the Shelfield menhir to a notch on Boulsworth Hill
D) Mid-summer sunrise from site A through a now-lost standing stone at Winewall and, reversed, midsummer sunset from the Winewall stone through mound X and site A

X is a low circular mound situated immediately to the east of the Knave Hill mounds thus forming an east-west alignment of three mounds. It can be seen in Fig:151 that sighting from mound X indicates both the annual solstice events of midwinter and midsummer sunrise

When checking the azimuth angle for the midsummer sunrise sight-line of site **A** to mound **X** it was noted that a standing stone marked on the 1848 OS map fell on this alignment. The stone stood on a linear feature (probable boundary) running for over 2.5 kilometres NE from a lost village at Winewall down to the Trawden Forest boundary at Fence Moor. The situation of this former standing stone (Little Thorn Edge, Winewall - SD91704 39411) suggests that it had been a boundary stone but the fact that it appears to be related to a possible observatory function means that the Medieval boundary may have been fixed on the line of an extant ancient stone.

Fig: 152

Solstice sunrise and sunset angles of azimuth (averaged solar standstills) during the Neolithic period

Latitude - 53°
Obliquity - 24.02°
Year - 3000 BC

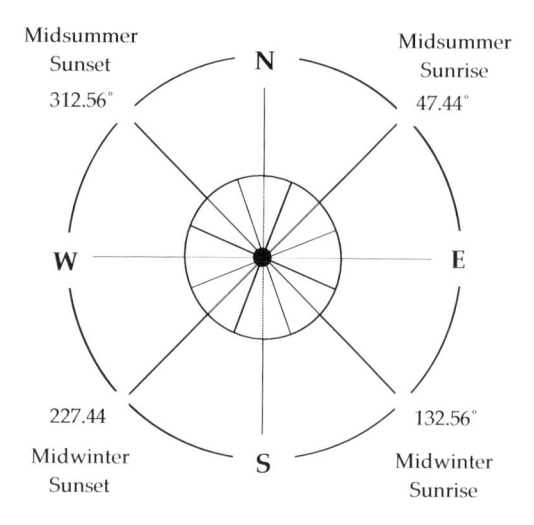

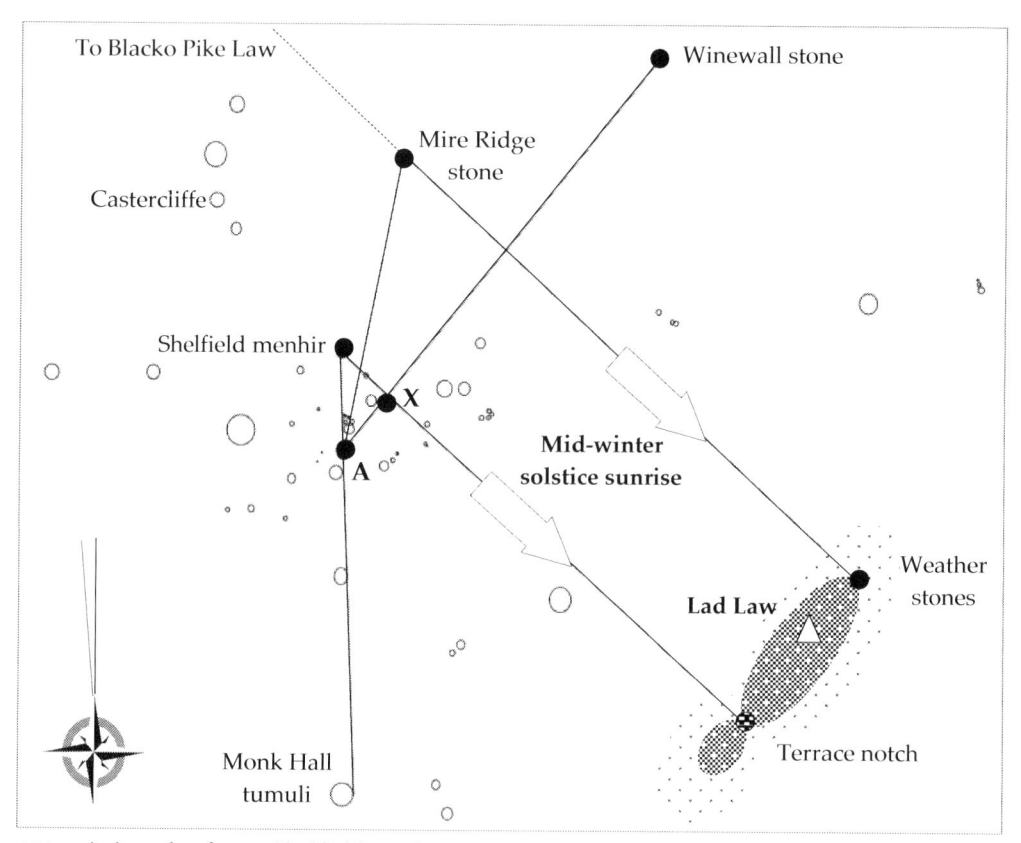

Midsummer Sunset 312.56°
Midsummer Sunrise 47.44°
Midwinter Sunset 227.44°
Midwinter Sunrise 132.56°

Fig: 153 Azimuths from Shelfield and Mire Ridge define the length of Lad Law. The midwinter solstice sunrise corresponds with sight-lines from the Mire Ridge menhir through the Weather Stones on the eastern end of the Lad Law ridge. The line from the Shelfield menhir is marked by a defined 'step' or terracing on the western edge of Lad Law - the line also passes through the Mesolithic flint scatter site, or camp, described earlier

Fig: 153a

Site B: Ringstone Circle

SD 89060 36437
X 389060 Y 436437
Lat 53.824083
Long -2.1676767

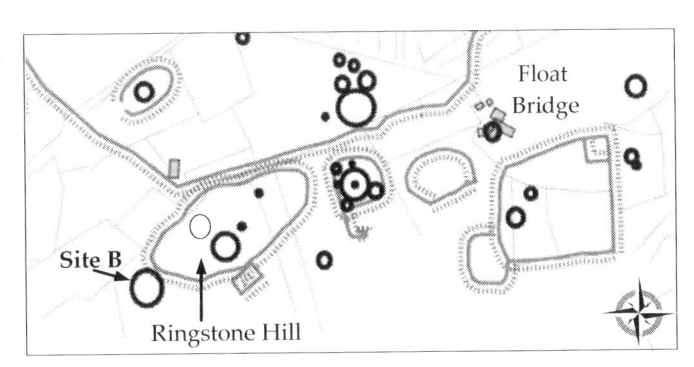

Site **B** is located to the west of the inner enclosure on Ringstone Hill, at the opposite end of the hill to site **A**. A very large recumbent standing stone lies in the reedy grass at this point and this is the reason for the suggestion that this may have been the location of the lost stone circle. Antiquarians reported that the circle was broken up in the early nineteenth century and it is very possible that the heaviest stones were left in situ. Sixty metres distant from the recumbent are two groups of large stones that may also have originally formed part of the lost circle. Care must be exercised here as this area was utilised for a short period (around 1999) for training operators of JCB plant and it is very possible that the large stones within the area were moved around at this time. However, the large recumbent is visible on an aerial image taken in 1988 and this suggests that it may remain in its original position. Other large stones are clearly not in situ but it is very possible that they were removed from the area occupied by the recumbent - in other words they might have been original circle stones.

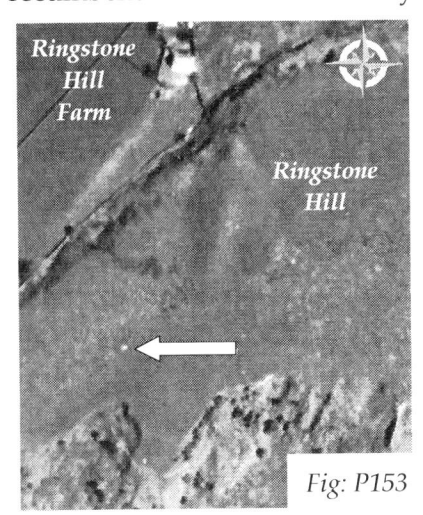

Fig: P153 shows the recumbent stone (arrowed) in an aerial image taken in 1988

Fig: P153a is the recumbent stone - the stone is the central part of a formerly much larger menhir with both ends having been broken off

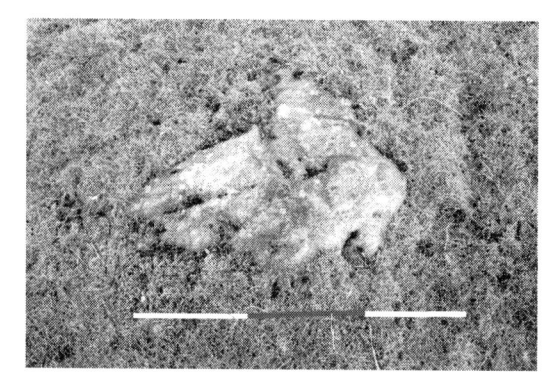

Fig: P153b

One of at least two broken stubs of possible former upright stones remains in the ground near to the recumbent stone. When the circle stones were removed for road repair it appears that the workmen broke them off at surface level rather than taking the trouble to dig them up - the stone displays the resultant chisel marks

Figs: P153c

Two freestanding stones within the recumbent stone locality

Fig: 153d

Stone lying near to the recumbent stone. This example is formed in the shape of an arrowhead trimmed square at one end. However, the square section may have been a supra-surface upright with the heavy end designed to be set in the ground - i.e. a gatepost fashioned from a circle stone?

Fig: 153e

One of two groups of stones 60m from the recumbent stone. Some of these appear to have been broken off larger stones - the example in the foreground in particular could have originally been part of the recumbent stone

Fig: P153f Proposed site of the lost circle at Ringstone Hill (foreground) - looking north with the Crawshaw Hill hilltop enclosure on the horizon. An early trackway led from the proposed circle site directly across the two fields in the middle distance to Crawshaw Hill

Assessment of possible celestial alignments from the proposed lost circle site is interesting in that the Shelfield menhir does not appear to relate with the circle site to any major celestial alignments. However, there appears to be a defined correlation between the proposed circle, Ringstone Hill and the large circular mound of Knavehill.

Fig: 153g

Mound on Ringstone Hill (looking south)

It is very probable that the apex of Ringstone Hill is an artificial mound, possibly a burial feature much like the tumuli at Monk Hall, Briercliffe (see later Hillfort section). The mound could have been sited within the Bronze Age so as to ritually associate with the Neolithic stone circle, some 170 metres to the west, and the possible burial mound(s) located 650 metres to the north-east, on the southern slopes of Shelfield Hill.

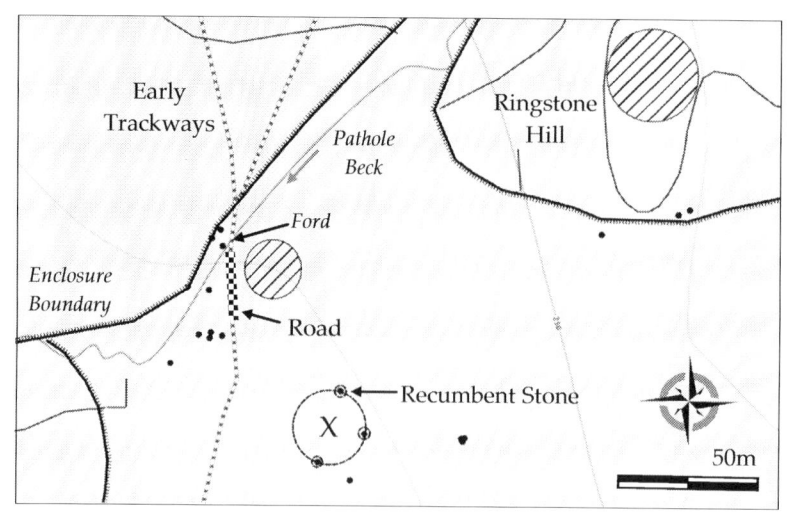

Fig: 153h

*Location of recumbent stone and earthbound remnants of possible circle stones (**X**)*

A cluster of large stones are to be seen along a cambered roadway, from the circle site to a ford over Pathole Beck

● *Surface stones (non-situ)*

Fig: P153i

The disused roadway from the Ringstone enclosure crossed Pathole Beck at the ancient ford (below the gate).

A number of large surface stones are scattered along the sides of the road here (inset - the 'arrowhead stone')

The roadway illustrated in *Fig: P153i* forms a short length of an ancient routeway that ran from the nearby Crawshaw Hill enclosure to the Catlow Bottoms 'hillfort' enclosure via the Ringstone site. The stretch of road in question leads down the scarp of the Ringstone enclosure to a ford in Pathole Beck. It is clear that the road at this point has been upgraded by the use of stone to metal the surface with ditches on either side - a number of large stones lie scattered near to the feature. The ford was also built using stone to afford a dry crossing although it has now become derelict. There is a strong correlation between the design of this cambered/metalled road and the Roman method of road construction but field assessment would be necessary to confirm this.

A more likely scenario regarding this feature is that this was the road said to have been repaired by workmen, using the stone from the Ringstone circle, in the early nineteenth century. In favour of this argument is the fact that this area, around Ringstone and Shelfield, was owned for a long period by the Walton family of Marsden Hall, the neighbouring estate to Townhouse in Nelson. Richard Wroe-Walton owned the Marsden estate in the early nineteenth century and in the 1830s he carried out extensive improvements to it. This involved upgrading Marsden Hall and the estate farms - including Ringstone Hill Farm. The results of his efforts can be seen at Ringstone Hill Farm in the high quality stone gateposts at the entrance to the property; at this time (1835) he erected his cross monument (Walton Spire) on the Shelfield menhir and he also repaired many estate field walls and roads.

The short stretch of road lies 60 metres from the recumbent stone (the suggested site of the Ringstone circle) and a number of large stones are scattered around the road site. It also appears that stone was used to build up the road and to create a camber to facilitate drainage. The Rev. Wroe-Walton would have gained a double benefit from repairing this road in that it was the main access from Ringstone Farm onto the hill and it was also part of an early routeway that would have acted as a short-cut between the Walton seat at Marsden Hall and the road to Halifax in the Thursden Valley.

There is, then, enough evidence to suggest that the Rev. Wroe-Walton's estate workers destroyed the stone circle around 1835 in order to upgrade the Ringstone Hill Farm estate. It is also worth noting that the Reverend was a pious man and the pagan symbols of the Shelfield menhir, and the Ringstone circle, would have offended him. In transforming one, and destroying the other in order to access a free source of stone, he was able to kill two birds with one stone - so to speak.

Fig: P153j

Gateposts in the gateway above the Pathole Beck ford (see image Fig: P153i). These large uprights are not the usual type of gatepost in this area - they are millstone grit and were not, therefore, quarried in the locality. It is interesting that the Shelfield menhir is also millstone grit, as is the recumbent stone. The suggestion is that the two posts were sourced from the nearby lost circle; they may then have been reshaped or split from a single standing stone by Rev. Walton's workmen. The walling here appears to date from the earlier 19th century

It is true to say that the evidence for this being the definite site of the long lost Ringstone circle is somewhat circumstantial at the moment. Due to time constraints it has only been possible to assess the site over a fleeting visit and so it will be necessary to provide more evidence on the ground through a concerted field survey. However, the evidence provided above is the best we have at the time of going to press and so it will be taken that there is a strong possibility of the circle having been at least within a reasonably local area of that suggested above.

Taking this into account those with a penchant for landscape alignments should find interest in the fact that the circle site is one of a series of five probable ancient features that can be seen to align along an axis corresponding to the mid-winter sunset and mid-summer sunrise (see *Fig: 152*).

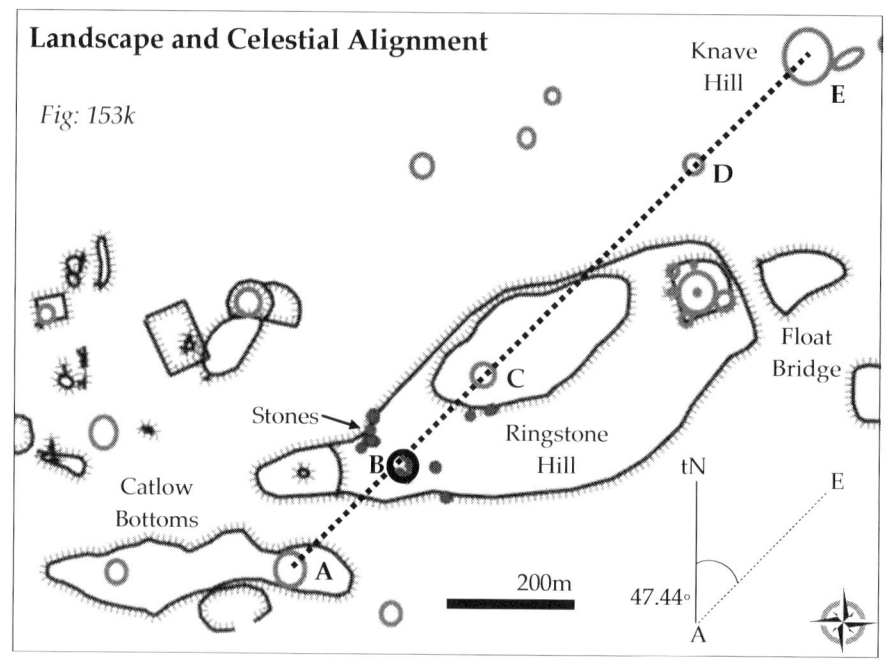

A) Mound within Catlow 'hillfort' enclosure   B) Recumbent stone (circle)   C) Ringstone Hill mound   D) Circular feature or ringwork   E) Knave Hill - circular mound

The argument for the siting of the lost stone circle is perhaps enhanced by the fact that it is located within an alignment of four other sites. Further, the azimuth from **A** to **E** corresponds with the alignment of mid-summer sunrise and, conversely, **E** to **A** is aligned to mid-winter sunset in the Neolithic period (c. 3,000 BC). If these sites were deliberately aligned then we have evidence for continuation between the Neolithic and Bronze Age societies at Shelfield Hill, Ringstone Hill and Catlow.

Ringstone Hill: Postulated Configuration of Stone Circle

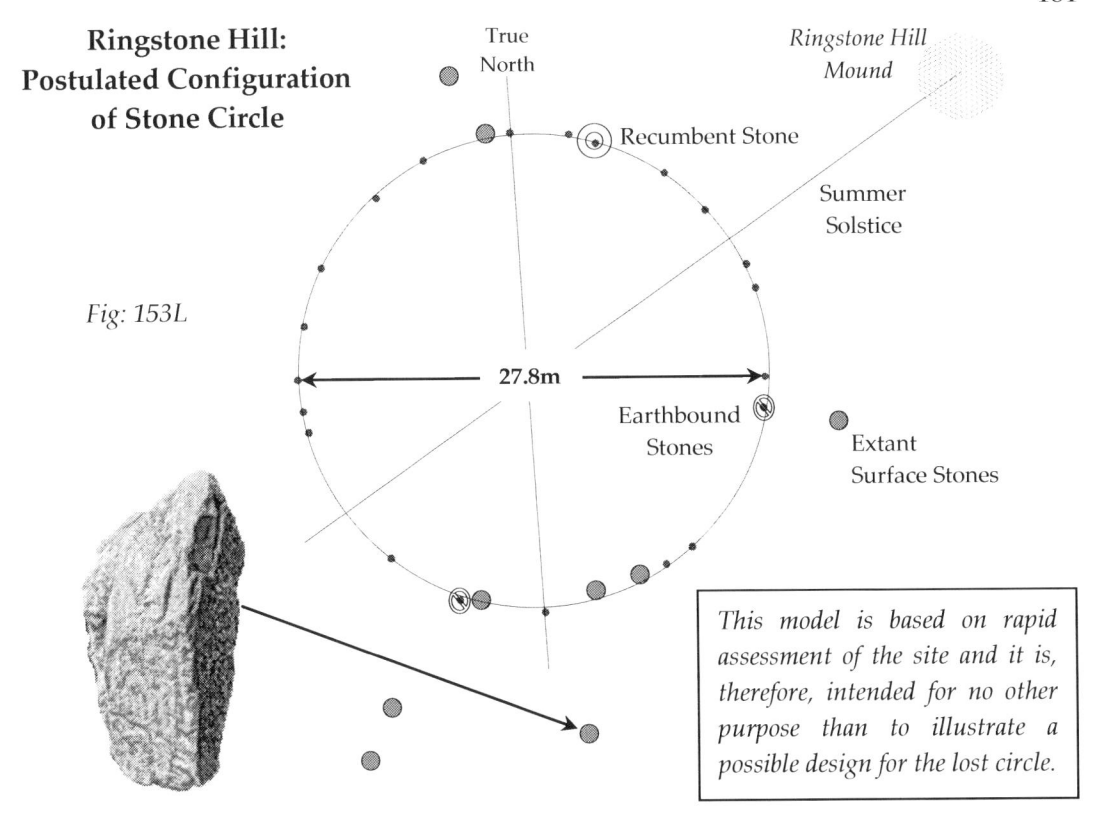

Fig: 153L

True North
Ringstone Hill Mound
Recumbent Stone
Summer Solstice
27.8m
Earthbound Stones
Extant Surface Stones

This model is based on rapid assessment of the site and it is, therefore, intended for no other purpose than to illustrate a possible design for the lost circle.

The distribution of stones within the proposed Ringstone Hill circle is based on the spatial relationship of existing surface stones (including the 'recumbent stone') and the earthbound stubs of probable former uprights. The distance between the extant stones was extrapolated with the resultant distribution illustrated above (*Fig: 153L*).

Four obvious gaps appear in the circumference of the circle, one in each quadrant. This may be a result of the limitations of basing a model on minimum available data - it may also be that the spaces were a deliberate design feature as outlying markers were often utilised to fix celestial alignments. *Fig: 153L* shows the postulated midsummer sunrise in 3,000 BC, based on the azimuth from the centre of the circle, and this falls within a gap in the NE quadrant. However, the mound on Ringstone Hill (150 metres distant) falls directly on this alignment and could easily have been sited to act as an outlier for the circle. It may, or may not, be of significance that this mound also falls directly on a straight line drawn through the Shelfield menhir and the Mire Ridge menhir.

Alignments from the Shelfield menhir, to the eastern and western periphery of the proposed circle, range from 202.8° (west) to 201.2° (east).

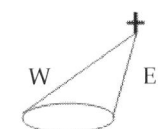

Further Celestial Possibilities: Mire Ridge

Fig: P154
The Weather Stones outcrop lies on the eastern end of the Lad Law ridge and is the most prominent landmark on the hill. The mid-winter sunrise azimuth from the Mire Ridge menhir passes through one particular stone within the group (image-left). A number of the Weather Stones display natural hollows but this stone has a particularly deep depression suggestive of a man-made basin. Given the location of this stone, on the solstice alignment, it is possible that the basin was filled with oil or fat in order to create a beacon. Lighting the beacon before sunrise on the midwinter solstice would indicate to observers (from the Mire Ridge stone) the exact point where the sun would rise on the Lad Law horizon

Hollow stone coordinates:
SD93170 35742
X 393170 Y 435742
Lat 53.817912 Long -2.1052165

Fig: P155
The Mire Ridge menhir

Mire Ridge stone coordinates:
SD89859 38727
X 389859 Y 438727
Lat 53.844685 Long -2.1556153

Taking the mid-winter sunrise counter azimuth from the Mire Ridge stone, the sunset sight-line follows on to the summit of the prominent hill (possibly a tumulus) of Pike Law, above the Blacko/Admergill valley. This does not mean, however, that an observer on Pike Law could utilise a beacon on the Weather Stones as an indicator of the exact winter solstice sunrise - from this elevated viewing position the sun would rise sooner, and eastward of the point observed from the lower ground of Mire Ridge.

Fig: 156

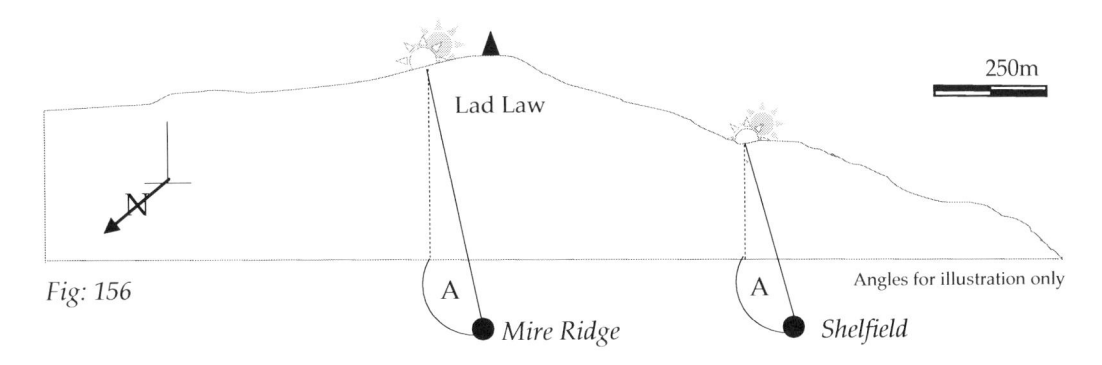

*Fig: 156 Winter solstice sunrise points. The angle at **A** is 133.57° of true north which signifies the point of sunrise in 3,000BC. As a result of the Earth's precession the same point would have been 133.47° in 2,500BC and 133.66° in 3,500BC*

Utilising the natural notch points in the horizon hills, along with man-made markers such as stones and mounds, it was possible to sight from fixed points in order to follow the arc of the stars and planets. This allowed for a surprisingly accurate method of time keeping and seasonal predictions; an example here is that the timing of crop sowing was crucial and it was possible to predict the optimum sowing window for each crop type.

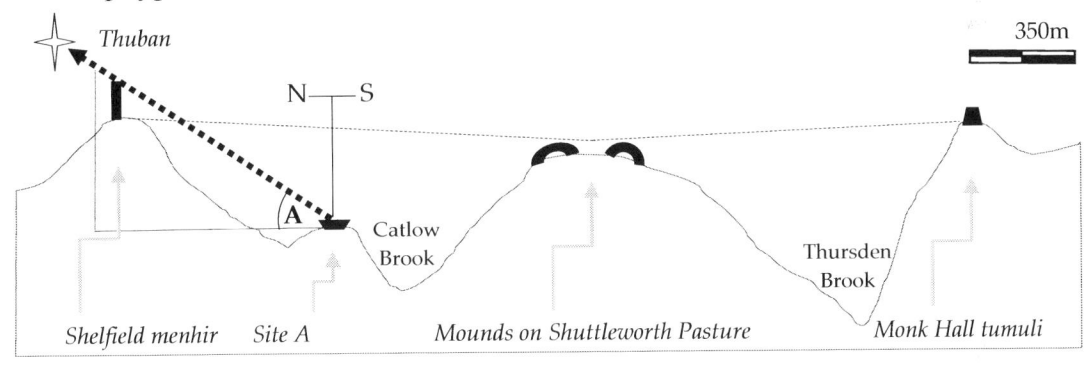

Fig: 157 Contour of the line of true north from the proposed Ringstone Hill stone circle at site A) over the Shelfield menhir and reversed to true south over the Monk Hall tumuli

Taking the elevation of site **A,** and the top of the Shelfield menhir at its probable original height, the angle at **A** *(Fig: 157)* gives an altitude to anything seen immediately above the menhir of 52°. Given that the menhir marks true north from site **A** it is very possible that this alignment was used as an observation marker for the pole star and the northern constellations. Here we have an indication that the large menhir on Shelfield Hill may have been designed to represent the *'world pillar.'*

Fig: 158

Timelapse image of the northern constellations revolving above the pole star with a representation of the Shelfield menhir superimposed

Overnight the stellar sky rotates around the axis of the 'world pillar' which is surmounted by the 'Nail Star' or pole star. In the Neolithic and Bronze Age period the pole star was Thuban. Could it be that a design element of the Shelfield menhir was to act as the 'world pillar' when viewed from the lower vantage point of site A?

Fig: P159

The Orion Constellation is a prominent feature in the southern mid-winter sky. In the Neolithic and Bronze Age periods the 'Hunter' constellation rose much lower on the horizon and dominated a wide sector of the southern sky.

It is, perhaps, worth noting that the alignment from the Winewall stone to site A (Fig: 153) could have been utilised to fix certain stars within the Orion constellation

We have, then, a possible explanation for one of the reasons for the erection of the Shelfield Hill and Mire Ridge menhirs, and the creation of the lost stone circle at Ringstone Hill. It must be borne in mind, of course, that ancient monuments were very unlikely to have been created to serve a single purpose; we see in modern public buildings a variety of uses by numerous factions within society and ancient sites would have been no different to this.

It was suggested earlier that one of the major benefits to the builders of megaliths and barrows would have been the coalescence of community spirit, the firming of a sense of the individual belonging to the wider society. Another factor would have been the effect that each new monument would have had on the landscape - the perception and understanding of a particular landscape is altered by the construction of a monument while the actual physical landscape is also altered. The monument became part of the landscape and the landscape part of the monument - the invisible mortar binding the two elements was the energy of creation expended by the individual and the wider community.

The materials used for the construction of monuments - wood, earth, turf, stone, sand, ash, charcoal, seaweed, beach sand, quartz pebbles, etc. - would have been gathered from specific locations within the landscape and combined in certain ways to create a new monumental structure. This physical construction took place within an atmosphere of ritual cognisance and performance. In Denmark it has been found that some burial mounds incorporated areas of fertile land (the Lusehøj barrow contained seven hectares) and this has been suggested to have been a gift to the deceased as plough land or pasture to be used in the afterlife; in other words, the land was a ritual offering to honour the deceased (Goldhahn. J. *From Monuments to Landscape to Landscapes in Monument* 2006).

The building of earthen barrows, then, had an impact upon the agricultural landscape of a community by removing fertile soil; conversely, the creation of stone burial cairns created new agricultural land through the removal of loose stones from the fields. An average cairn would require hundreds of tons of stone, and a great deal of time and effort in collecting and moving the material; this could possibly have been seen as a prestigious act to honour the dead and to provide useful land for the occupier of the cairn in the afterlife.

Fig: P160

The Lusehøj barrow

The Danish Lusehøj barrow (Funen island) mentioned above is an example of a complexity of monument building that can easily be overlooked. Seen from today's perspective the barrow is a standard mound of grass-covered earth measuring 36m in diameter and 6m in height. Within the mound was found a Bronze Age stone burial cist and a bronze urn containing the Iron Age remains of a wealthy man wrapped in a type of linen cloth woven from stinging nettles.

Excavation of the barrow has shown it to have been constructed of four different sections, each with its own team of builders. Each section was constructed using turf from different parts of the surrounding landscape and each team used a separate ramp to build their particular section. Four stone rows, radiating from the barrow centre, were included in the different layers, each one being covered by turf and then repeated on the next layer. The formation of the barrow stone rows is suggestive of the Danish mythology relating to the birth and re-birth of the sun *(Fig: 161)*.

Fig: 161

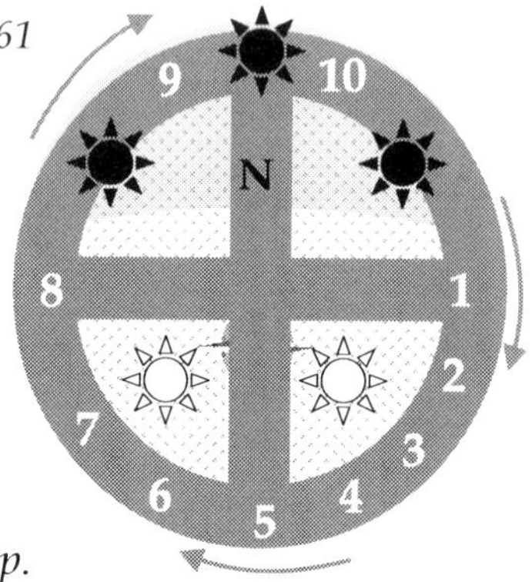

The Solar Myth (Goldhahn, J. 2006)

1) *Position of sunrise where a fish pulls the rising sun from its night ship and puts it in the morning ship.*
2) *The fish is allowed to sail in the morning ship for a while.*
3) *The fish is eaten by a bird of prey while sun-horses ready themselves to fetch the sun.*
4) *Two sun-horses are about to pull the sun from the ship.*
5) *At noon the sun-horses have collected the sun from the morning ship.*
6) *In the afternoon the sun-horse lands with the sun on the afternoon ship.*
7) *After the sun-horse has landed the sun is taken over by a snake from the afternoon ship.*
8) *The snake hides the sun in its spiral curls and will soon lead the sun down below the horizon.*
9) *Two night ships sail towards the newly-set sun. The sun is now extinguished - invisible and dark on its night voyage through the underworld.*
10) *The night ship is followed by a fish ready to fulfil its task at sunrise when the wheel will have come full circle.*

In a number of Danish barrows the radiating stone rows, and outer ring of kerb stones, show signs of having been coloured with red and yellow pigments, according to their position in relation to the sun's cycle (red for setting and yellow for rising). Further, a common form of art occurs where some of the barrow stones are carved with horse motiffes (often in the form of a figure S which represented the sun-horse). The horses are almost always facing in the direction they would take when transporting the sun from east to west.

The creation of Neolithic and Bronze Age monuments by different teams of workers is a common theme, certainly within Northern Europe. Another example of this is to be found in the magnificent stone circle known as the Ring of Brodgar (Orkney). The initial stages of the circle were begun around 2,500 BC with the creation of an outer ditch, or henge, measuring 103.6m in diameter, three metres in depth and five metres in width, with access causeways in the south-west and north-east of the henge. The area of the monument covers 2.1 acres - interestingly, this is exactly the same size as the area covered by the inner stone circles at Avebury *(Fig: 148)*. Within the henge enclosure once stood a circle of 60 standing stones although only 27 survive. There are numerous satellite stones and cairns in the extended area, including a solitary stone known as the Comet Stone, though whether these outliers played an astronomical role in the purpose of the Ring is open to debate. The Brodgar henge is the third largest of its type in the UK after Avebury and Stanton Drew.

Fig: P162

The Ring of Brodgar

Recent archaeological surveys carried out on the Brodgar monument show that each stone was quarried in a different area of the outlying district. It is apparent that the site was chosen to perform a central role within Late Neolithic Orkney society and the act of each satellite community in creating, transporting and erecting their own particular stone, alongside similar stones from neighbouring communities, would have created a strong sense of commonality. In this way a scattered series of small settlements, within a landscape dominated by lochs, rivers, mountains and sea, would have shared common laws, religious beliefs and an ability to combine in times of danger from outside.

On a small loch island, near to the Ring, archaeologists have excavated a village of substantial stone-built houses and, again, it appears that each house was erected by people from different communities. This perhaps suggests that the Ring monument served the purpose of a gathering place at certain times of the year. This function is echoed in all parts of the ancient world where meetings were held to set laws, judge boundary disputes and elect leaders etc. Whether there was an added element of ceremony, ritual and astronomical observation at Brodgar is not presently known.

The massive monumental building programme that took place on the Wiltshire Downs, at the end of the Neolithic and into the Bronze Age, was similar in scope (if not extent) to the roughly contemporary period of monument construction at Brodgar. Over the past decade or so a great deal of archaeological work has been carried out at Stonehenge and the 500m diameter henge at neighbouring Durrington Walls. A large timber circle was erected around 2,600 BC at Durrington; the circle was oriented south-east towards the sunrise on the midwinter solstice and consisted of four large concentric circles of postholes, which would have held extremely large standing timbers. A paved avenue was also constructed on a slightly different alignment (towards the sunset on the summer solstice) that led to the River Avon.

Archaeologist, Mike Parker Pearson, suggests that Durrington Walls was a complementary structure to Stonehenge whereby the timber circle at Durrington Walls represented life and a land of the living, while Stonehenge and its encircling burial mounds, represented a land of the dead. A ceremonial processional route from Durrington, via the Avon, represented the journey taken during the transition from life to death. Other archaeologists believe that Stonehenge was a healing site and not particularly connected to its neghbours.

It seems likely that there was no single purpose for these monuments - rather, they would have been adapted to 'modern' ways of thinking throughout subsequent generations. However, one thing is clear and that is the amount of political will and physical energy invested by each generation over the useful life of the structures. A team led by the University of Sheffield have excavated a very large Neolithic village at Durrington with room for around 2,000 people. This could have been the core workforce (around 200-400 construction workers and their families) responsible for the erection and maintenance of the Stonehenge and Durrington sites but it is thought that the village population might have doubled at certain periods - probably on important feast days.

Artefacts recovered from the site show that people were visiting the village, and attending the feasts, from all across the British Isles. Furthermore, one of the excavated village houses showed evidence of a cobb wall and its own ancillary building; this was remarkably similar in layout to a house at Skara Brae, in Orkney. Here, then, we have the same communal predilection towards centrality as we see at Brodgar, and indeed at many other ancient sites. This implies that the Wiltshire Downs was a highly sacred place drawing 'pilgrims' from across Britain.

It is possible that whole families travelled to Wiltshire, perhaps reviving a folk memory of their nomadic ancestors. Perhaps only certain people of high status would make the journey - or the heads of invited communities wealthy enough to take along a contribution - the equivalent of the 'church roof fund'? It is clear, however, that a surprising amount of trade, and cultural interchange, was taking place at the end of the Neolithic. The meeting of scattered communities at important central monuments provided for a rapid dissemination of ideas into many dark and far-flung corners of the land - perhaps even the Boulsworth district!

It might not be unrealistic, therefore, to suggest that Shelfield and Ringstone fulfilled the role of a central meeting place, ceremonial site and celestial observatory. We know that Bronze Age burials took place at Catlow (a few hundred metres west of Ringstone), there are at least two possible burial mounds at Knave Hill, there appear to have been defined settlements in the immediate Shelfield area, a stone circle stood at Ringstone Hill and an apparently important stone monument surmounts a hilltop enclosure on Shelfield Hill.

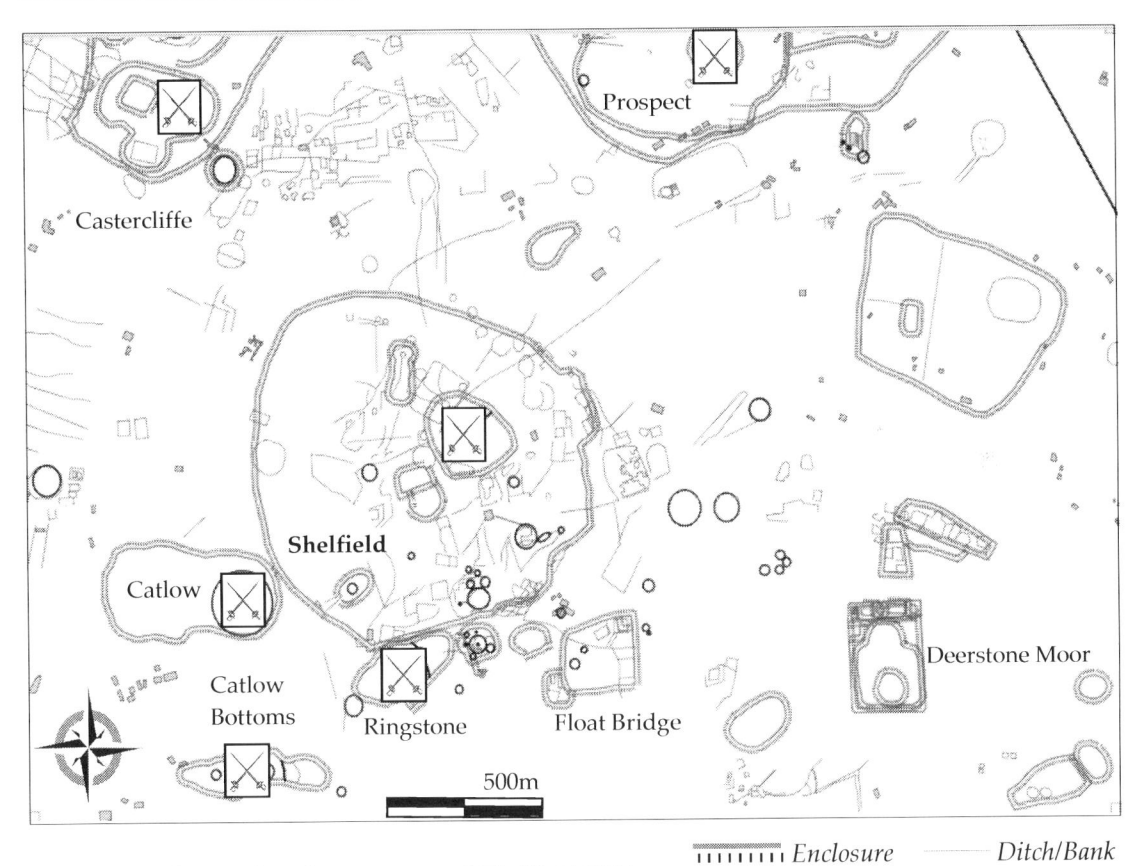

Fig: 163 *Evidence of settlement around Shelfield Hill*

The features illustrated in *Fig: 163* are taken from one and two metre LiDAR, aerial images and field walking. When combined a defined pattern of ditches, mounds and earthwork enclosures emerges around Shelfield Hill. This is not to say that we can take the patterns as firm evidence for stock enclosures, human habitation and early field systems. If all the apparent landscape features were to be assessed by excavation or geophysical survey, it is certain that some will turn out to be relatively modern ditches or lost Medieval wall lines. Some will probably date to different periods ranging from the Neolithic to the Early Modern. Yet others will no doubt prove to be drainage ditches or moorland deer enclosures. In other words, the sources of evidence (LiDAR etc.) cannot differentiate between ancient and modern features - a bank of any age is a bank, a ditch is ditch.

To gain a full picture of the evidence presented by LiDAR the research must be taken into, and below the field. However, where we see structures such as menhirs and stone circles we can be reasonably sure that there would have been settlement(s) nearby. This appears to have been the case with the Shelfield area where, given the large amount of archaeological 'noise' in the landscape *(Fig: 163)*, it would be surprising if there proved to be no Neolithic or Bronze Age settlement evidence on the ground.

Fig: 164

Despite the earlier argument against the acceptance of alignments in the landscape it has to be acknowledged, at times, that some alignments are indeed of interest. The circular path in Fig: 164 is centred on Shelfield Hill and passes through no less than seven farmsteads. It is perhaps significant that the two buildings <u>within</u> the circle are relatively modern

A) Doughty Farm
B) Dry Clough Farm
C) Slitterforth Farm
D) Float Bridge Farm
E) Ringstone Hill Farm
F) Shelfield (Green Midden) Farm
G) Delves (non-extant)

Shelfield Hill

The inference here is one of centrality - is it possible that early farmsteads were located with respect to Shelfield Hill? If this was indeed the case then the farms within our modern landscape could have occupied the same site since the Bronze Age or, at least, the Anglo-Saxon period.
Food for thought, perhaps?

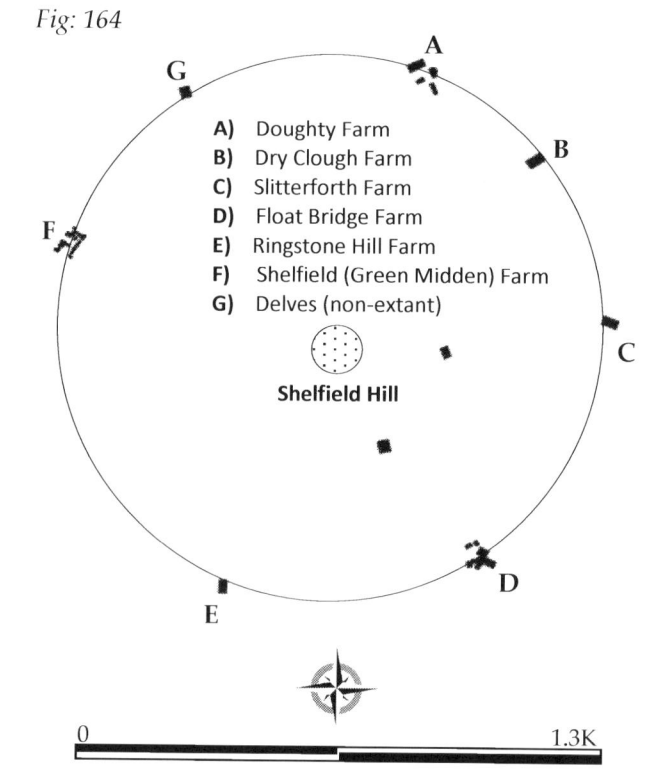

0   1.3K

RINGWORKS AND CIRCULAR MONUMENTS

There are no extant examples of true stone circles in Lancashire (as opposed to circular remnants of cairns, enclosures, huts and barrows) - the nearest ones are to be found in the Pennine Peak District. Within the Burnley, Pendle and Boulsworth Survey area we can, at a push, boast of a small handful of circular stone sites. We have lost circles at Ringstone Hill (Blacko Watermeetings), Ringstone Hill (Shelfield, Nelson) and possibly Ringstones near Worsthorne while a largely extant site still sits on the Pendle ridgeway above Newchurch-in-Pendle (see below). It is likely, of course, that any number of such sites have been destroyed over the past few millennia.

Strictly speaking stone circles fall into the category of 'ringworks' but for our purposes these features will be treated as separate structures. The ringwork has various forms - it can be a banking of earth thrown up into either a complete circle or a circle containing an entrance break or a banked circle containing a central mound. Stones less than one metre in height can be placed around the bankings while many sites have no stones. The circles range in size (average 10.5m diameter) and the large majority contain multiple burials (Barrowclough 2008).

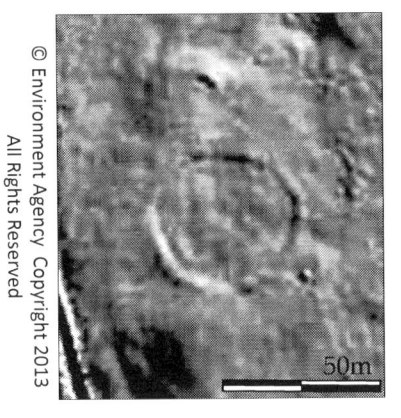

Fig: P165
1m LiDAR extract - Ringwork at Broadbank, Briercliffe SD9024 3522

An earthen bank 45.5m in diameter enclosing an inner ditch. Two excavations in the 1950s and 1960s (University of Liverpool) found a hearth at the eastern end of the enclosure along with flint and chert flakes and a Langdale stone axe. The LiDAR image indicates that the ringwork sits on a raised area of ground and mound features are apparent within the immediate area. Within the enclosure are indications of smaller enclosures indicating that this could have been a small Iron Age farmstead enclosure

Other ringworks within the Survey district are a four metre ring mound with seven stones at Delf Hill (Burnley); a nine metre ring mound at Hell Clough (Burnley); a ring mound with seven stones at Hell Clough (Burnley); a 17m ring mound with seven stones at Hell Clough (Burnley); a 13m earthen embankment at Mosley Height (Burnley); a ring mound at Ringstone Hill (Burnley); a ring mound with stones at Slipper Hill (Worsthorne); an eight metre earthen circle at Twist Hill (Burnley); a 6.5m earthen circle at Wasnop Edge (Burnley); a 10.5m ring of ten stones at Walshaw Dean.

Fig: P166   *The Pendle Ridgeway looking from Sabden Fold*

While fieldwalking on the Pendle Ridgeway in 2010 the author happened to notice a stone in an area of rough ground, around 75m from the ridge trackway. Closer examination showed the stone to be earthbound and a number of similar stones were scattered around the area. With the invaluable aid of interested members of the *Pendle History Society* a rapid survey of the site was carried out.

A one meter cube of gritstone was found to occupy the centre of two concentric rings of stones (*Fig: P126a* and *Fig: P168*) - the inner circle is 14m from the centre with the outer ring at 20m. Six earthbound stones were immediately apparent and ground probes produced another two - it is probable that other stones lay more deeply buried or have been removed at some time.

The Ridgeway site occupies an elevated position commanding wide views of the distant hills and valleys of Burnley, Pendle and the former Craven district of Yorkshire. From the highest point of the extended site a 360° panorama includes the Irish Sea off the Fylde Coast, the major local hills of Hameldon, Boulsworth and Pendle and the rising ground eastwards towards the Yorkshire Pennines. There is a plentiful water supply from streams within the valleys, a short distance to the north and south, along with the natural wells and springs afforded by the ridge-top situation.

Major standstill
Northern moonset?
322° -38°

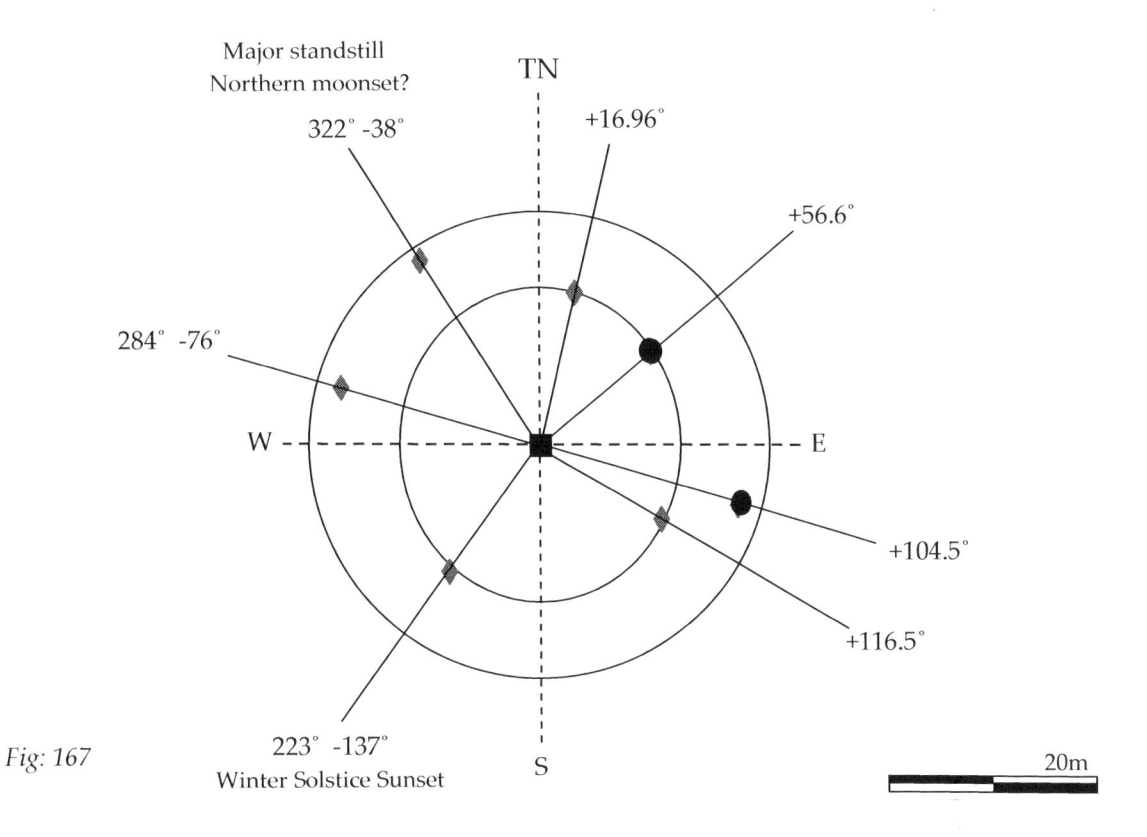

TN

+16.96°

+56.6°

284° -76°

W — — — — — — — E

+104.5°

+116.5°

Fig: 167

223° -137°
Winter Solstice Sunset

S

20m

Configuration of Extant Stones on the Pendle Ridgeway Site

♦ *Buried stones found by probe*

● *Earthbound stones*

■ *One metre square stone block at centre*

Unsure as to whether the stones represented an archaeological monument, as opposed to a field clearance group, it was decided to carry out a rapid assessment of the site. A keyhole trench was opened along the southern edge of the square central block. Beneath the topsoil lies a .3m layer of upper boulder clay displaying both sandstone and limestone colouring. Below this is another .3m layer of somewhat stratified clay, interspersed with dark coloured clay lenses within which occur sporadic samples of crumbling red-yellow grit freestones and layered stone of around 12mm thickness. A heavy blue-grey clay layer of .2m underlies the latter and this reaches a depth of one metre from the surface.

At its full depth the stone extends to one metre with the base resting on a natural layer of unsorted gravel and sand beneath several layers of clay deposit. The deposit lenses were formed in quite separate phases of deposition and represent different periods of change and stability along the ridgeway.

Fig: P168

Nearing the base of the stone block

A flat stone has been placed on top of the block at some time (to the left of the sight-pole)

White lines represent the angle of (glacial?) striation across the face of the block

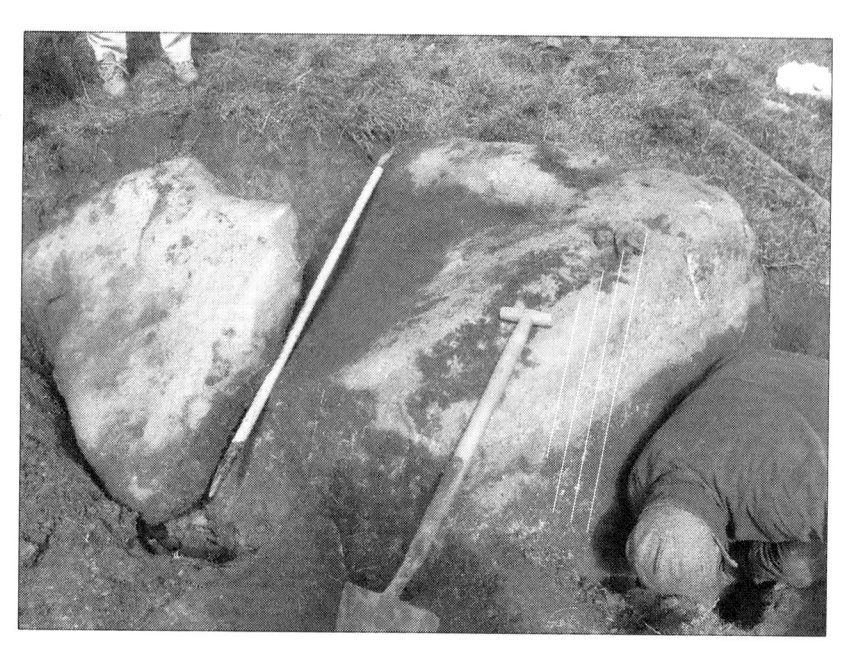

No evidence of stone chipping was found and this leads to the conclusion that, if the stone had been worked square, then this had not been carried out in situ. The evidence from the keyhole trench is that the block sits directly upon the natural gravel surface. This raises the possibility that the stone was deposited by glacial action, perhaps during the Devensian period (18,000 BP to 12,000 BP) and the subsequent depositions of clay were deposited during the later Halocene period, 12,000 BP to 8,000 BP. It is possible, then, that the stone is a glacial erratic.

This raises the matter of the angular nature of the square stone – has it been worked or not? Exposure of the southern face of the stone showed it to carry a number of striations at a roughly 45° angle to the perpendicular edges. This is taken to be evidence of glacial flow across the surface of the stone – the problem here lies within the fact that the striations do not run parallel with the ground *(Fig: P168)*.

There is a suggestion here, then, that the block does not sit in a position corresponding with natural deposition. If the striations are indeed the result of glaciation then the stone must now present on its side. This is not to say that the stone was moved very far, it could have been rolled from one plane to another by the hand of man, or it could have been overturned by glacial action at some period following the creation of the striations.

In the gravel layer directly beneath the stone organic material was found and a good sample of this was extracted intact. The material had the appearance of soggy brown-to-black paper and was taken to be decayed wood. Samples of the material were analysed by a palaeobotanist at *Oxford Archaeology North* (Lancaster) and found to be a species of birch. Given the surface striations on the block, the evidence for birch tree wood (or timber) beneath and a strong suggestion of spatial relationship with a number of other stones within the vicinity, it was taken that the block could form part of an archaeological feature or monument.

Superficial examination of the four stones closest to the block revealed that small boulders of around 30cm were, in fact, earthbound upright stones at least one metre in length and of substantial bulk. The angle within the ground of three of these stones (the fourth stone is a narrow recumbent upright) indicates that they were either deliberately pushed over or that they had fallen naturally over a period of time. These stones do not appear to be random glacial deposits and, furthermore, they appear to correlate very closely with the square stone *(Fig: 167)*.

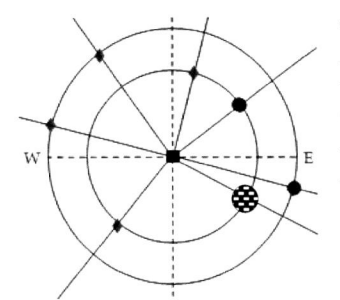

Two other stones within the group were assessed; the first one lying 14m to the south-east of the central block stone *(illustration-left)*. A preliminary dig was carried out to ascertain the extent of the stone which proved to measure 1m in length by .8m in width and .7m in depth.

The topsoil here is the normal depth of 20cm for this site. A .7m test pit showed the ground on the southern edge of the stone to be boulder clay deposition to a depth of 30cm where paler lenses of sand and darker organic matter occur. This appears to be a former ditch and bank composed of inverted turf and material from the natural base layer. Within all strata to 40cm appeared unsorted rounded sandstone pebbles (which appear to belong to the base gravel level) along with larger stones ranging to 27cm x 30cm. Packing stones were found at the base of the stone (indicating that it originally stood upright) along with a core of high quality black chert (not local Pendleside material) which had been placed in the bottom of the ditch adjacent to the stone. A small cairn was also found adjacent to the east side of the former upright - this arrangement is very similar to that we saw earlier at the Blacko Watermeetings *(Fig: 132)*.

Fig: P169

Assessment of the south-east stone (left of picture beneath the pile of small stones)

Dry-sieving produced a green flint micro-flake from the layer that Sylvia is working on

A scatter of 20mm charcoal pieces was found across the the assessment area

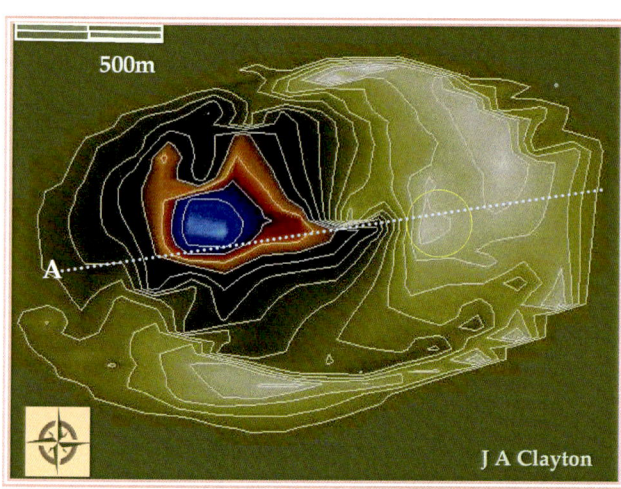

Fig: 170

A digital survey of the extended ridge-top site. Blue indicates a long-mound feature west of the stone group (circled). The original ridgeway track (**A**) follows past the mound and through the stone site

Fig: 171

Another plan of the extended site - created from GPS data

The mound can be seen centre of image with the negative feature of the track (**A**) leading to the stone group (circled).

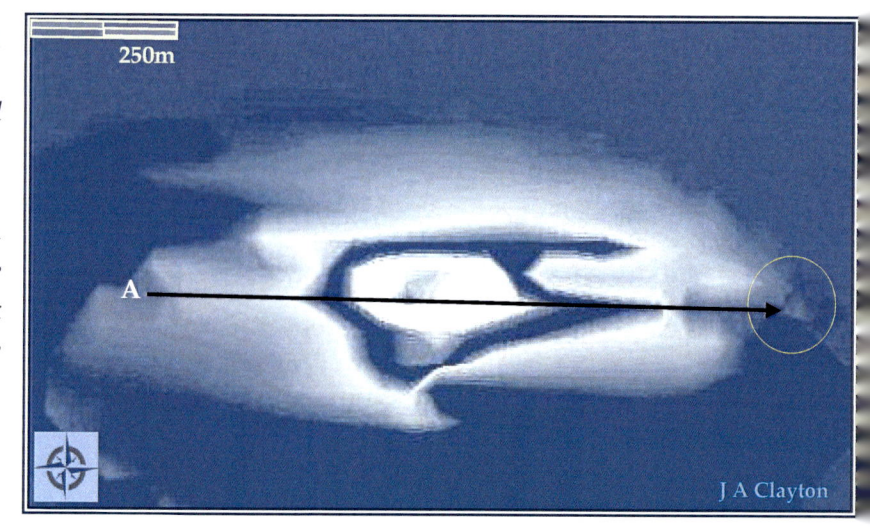

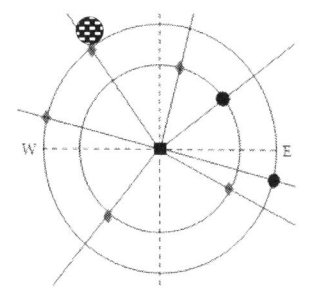

Following completion of the south-east stone assessment the focus of attention then turned to its opposite number in relation to the central block stone *(illustration-left)*. The north-west stone is another earthbound stone situated 20m to the NW of the block stone and, like the others within this group, it displayed distinct iceberg-like qualities in that only 20cm of its bulk protruded above the surface.

A shallow .5 metre wide trench was opened on all four sides – three sides were found to have the typical 20cm layer of topsoil but this layer extended to a depth of at least 50cm on the southern side. Beneath this was the ubiquitous grey and blue-grey boulder clay. Examination of the topsoil layer revealed a number of pot sherds to the west of the stone with a single sherd of a different type beneath the exposed top edge.

The pottery recovered from the western edge amounts to a number of sherds ranging in size from 20mm to 50mm. A fragment of base is evident and the profile of larger sherds allows for an estimate of the type of pot this might have been. The fabric is an oxidised dark-gray core with small flint and silica inclusions. The oxidisation does not appear to have extended across the inside of the body and this suggests that the pot would have taken the form of an enclosed vessel. However, without rim sherds it is difficult to extrapolate either an everted or closed rim. No indication of a spout or handle was found. The dark colour of the fabric might suggest the presence of organic matter within the clay and a low firing temperature (less than 250°) which, in turn, suggests an open-fire method as opposed to the kiln method of firing; the pot is wheel-thrown.

Fig: P171

Pot sherd and reconstruction

No other finds were located in the topsoil layer other than two examples of vitrified local sandstone (15mm across). The clay was removed to a depth of .75m to the south and 1m to the north of the north-west stone. This showed the stone to be buried at an angle of roughly 40° to the surface and to be wedge shaped. The protruding edge is 1m in length and 25cm thick, thickening to a base around 1.2m in length and 50cm thick (the base was not actually excavated). Buried at a depth of .5m another stone, roughly 1m square x 30cm thick (apparently unworked) lies horizontal to the surface (**A** in *Fig: P172*).

On the southern edge of this stone a number of flat sandstones were found along with stones apparently set into a section. At this point the soil is approximately 50cm in depth which suggests that the two large stones were set within a negative feature (ditch or pit?). One stone from the top of the section was removed and this appeared to be a fossilised tree section.

Fig: P172

The protruding top edge was all that could be seen of the north-west stone prior to excavation

Fig: P173

Fossilised fern set within section corner of the north-west stone trench

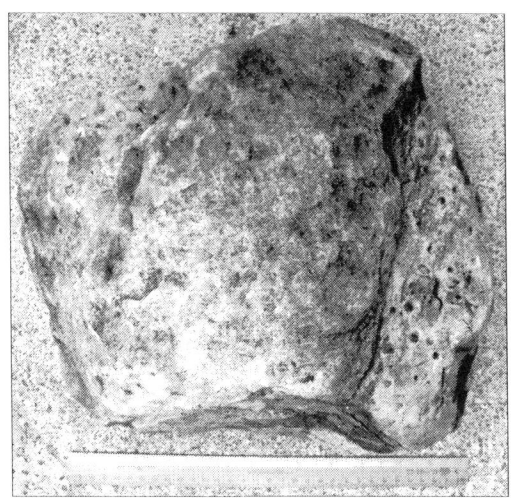

Fig: P174   Tree fern fossil   *Fig: P175   Estuary bed stone*

Beneath the north-west stone, and the adjacent flat stone, were a number of flag stones - at this stage it became apparent that the north-west stone site was a robbed-out burial cist (stone-lined chamber). The large flat stones jumbled within the trench would have formed a chamber that would have been at ground level, or slightly below, with the largest of the stones (the north-west stone) possibly forming a capstone.

It is clear that the two stones in *Fig: P174* and *Fig: P175* are very unusual and would have been chosen by the cist builders for their aesthetic value - the stones were carefully placed in the southern corner of what would have been the cist void. It was decided to leave the stones in situ and not to disturb the site further.

Running alongside the upended north-west stone, and across the extended stone group site, is a ceramic water pipe set within a one metre deep trench backfilled with earth and gravel. Although the pipe trench clipped the north-west stone site it would not have been responsible for the destruction of the cist. It is possible that the proposed tomb was destroyed within antiquity, and that the neighbouring upright stones were pushed over at the same time.

The rapid assessment of the Ridgeway site showed that the stone group is indeed archaeological. Further survey work has been carried out by the *Pendle District Landscape Archaeology Society* and it is clear that the stone group can be viewed as a small sector within a much larger section (1k x .5k) of the ridge-top within which there is evidence for a series of related funerary sites.

The stone group is situated on the immediate southern side of the original ridgeway route and on the side are a number of recumbent and earthbound stones. A Medieval land exchange document shows that this part of the ridge was known as Standing Stone Height. Adjoining this latter group are a series of circular features which, in air images, appear to be the remnants of large pits.

Fig: P176
Markings or carving on one of the stones standing by the original ridgeway track

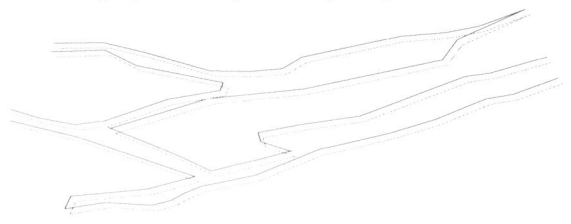

Could this represent a map of local trackways?

In the adjacent field, west of Standing Stone Height, a small stone circle (7m diameter) of five stones can be seen. The two largest stones measure approximately 1m in length by .5m in width and appear to be recumbent uprights. The remaining stones making up the circle are much smaller - all of them are sitting on the ground surface.

Fig: P177

The two largest circle stones probably once stood upright - but did they stand in their present position? Firm evidence is required before this feature can be assigned to any particular period or purpose.

A circular mound of loose stones, around 3m in diameter, is to be found by a stone wall roughly one hundred metres north-west of the small circle - there is the possibility that this is a burial cairn but, again, this requires assessment in order to ensure it is not a field clearance pile.

Fig: 178   PENDLE RIDGEWAY - SECTION

Newchurch-in-Pendle   Sabden Fold

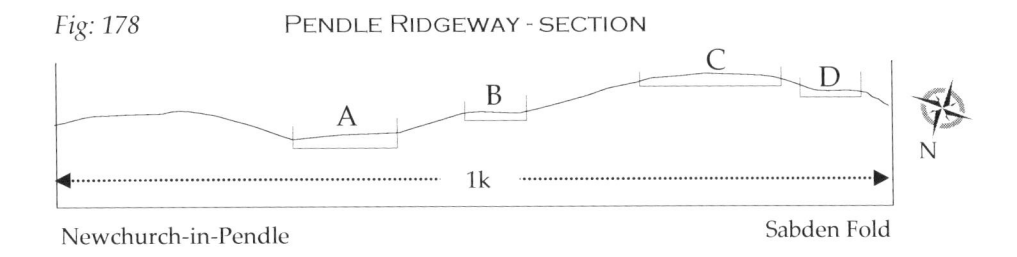

A) Standing Stone Height and large circle group in hollow
B) Small stone circle and possible cairn on level area
C) Possible long-mound on ridge top
D) Stone scatter with earthbound double row leading onto mound **(C)**

Fig: P179 The Ridgeway section from Sabden Fold. The large dyke right of picture runs down to Sabden Old Hall - this is a probable boundary ditch but has not yet been dated

The possible long-mound at **C** *(Fig: P179)* sits on the very top of an elongated elevation of the ridge (from **C** to **D**). The elevation shows evidence for having possibly been enclosed by a ditch and bank and the area is scattered with a large number of surface and earthbound stones. It is possible that the stones were formerly part of enclosure walls or revetments but, among the scatter, it is possible to make out a double linear row running along the ridge top and onto the western end of the possible mound.

A ditch marking the parish boundary runs south from the possible ridge-top at **C** and within 100 metres is a pile of very large stones. The very large upright we saw in *Fig: P128* now stands close to this pile, having been moved by the farmer from its original home a few hundred metres to the east.

Fig: P180

The large upright (see also Fig: P128)

As was the case with the upright in *Fig: P128*, the stones within the pile are field clearance. Within the group is a circular flattish stone that would have originally measured around 1.5 to 2 metres across with a thickness of 30cm. There is also a former 1.5m upright, the broken top of another large stone similar to that in *Fig: P128*, and numerous other large flat and rounded stones. The stones within this collection are very similar in size and form to those found within Neolithic burial mound chambers and it is worth asking the question as to whether they have been moved here from the site of a burial monument?

Fig: P181 ▲ *The field clearance pile* ▶

Above - the broken top from a large upright similar to that in Fig: P180
Right - a mixture of uprights and large flat stones

Fig: P181a

Returning to the possible concentric stone circles centred on the block stone, the group here is set within a hollow on the ridge and there are indications from air imaging that they were set within an enclosure. Among the stones there is a low circular ditched mound (*Fig: P182*).

Fig: P182 A ditched bowl barrow?

Near the centre of the mound a 30cm keyhole test-pit found that a stone flagged surface lay at a depth of 30cm (*Fig: P182 inset*). This was also the case when a second such hole was opened 3m to the east of the initial pit.

In conclusion, although the assessment of the ridgeway site has been limited there appears to be sufficient evidence to show that the one kilometre ridge-top site could prove to be of importance to the archaeology of Lancashire. It is probable that the subject area saw at least a degree of occupation during the Mesolithic period (as evidenced by the discovery of a micro-blade) and it is also very possible that the site contained Neolithic megalithic burial monuments and at least one Bronze Age round barrow.

Furthermore, near Tinedale Farm on the valley floor, directly below Standing Stone Height, is St. Chad's Well - this holy well would almost certainly have been a sacred site in pre-history. In the later twentieth century a small stone bust, possibly of the Romano-British goddess Sulis/Minerva, was discovered near to the well. This, along with Roman pottery recently found by the author in nearby Sabden Fold, strongly suggests that the ridge-top site, sitting as it does on a major ancient trade route, was of importance in the Roman Iron Age.

Fig: P183
Bust found at Tinedale
Image: Moorhouse, C. *Sabden* 1978

It is also probable that the settlement of this area of the Ridgeway carried on unabated following the Roman withdrawal from Britain in 410 AD. In a field at Lowerhouses (Sabden Fold) is a very interesting worked stone - this is generally described as a 'font.' Another 'font' was uncovered at nearby Bullhole Farm in the second half of the twentieth century and this now acts as a flower bowl in St. Mary's Church, Newchurch-in-Pendle. The Bullhole font, however, is cleanly sculpted and the design indicates that it was created as a church font somewhere around the Tudor period - this would suggest that the object was made for the original St. Mary's Church. Following its replacement at some later stage, the font served an ignominious new role at Bullhole Farm where it was used as a water trough for the livestock.

Fig: P184

The Lowerhouses 'font' (elevated image: 5m)

The Lowerhouses 'font', however, differs in design and execution; the body is relatively roughly carved and the bowl has been pecked out in deepening concentric circles with no attempt to smooth the finish. The overall feel of the item is that it belongs to the first millenium AD - whether it was made in the Romano-British, Anglo-Saxon or post-Norman era is open to debate. Further to this, it is interesting to note that a number of clues point towards the neighbouring area of Haddings, Lowerhouses, Sabden Fold and Spen areas (collectively Goldshaw) having functioned as lands attached to a monastic grange.

We know that the well at Tinedale is known as St. Chad's Well, the name is taken from St. Chad who was Archbishop of York in 664 AD and founded the Bishopric of Lichfield in 665 AD. He travelled the northern counties extensively and churches and wells were named in his honour. His influence was felt within our district and Chatburn was possibly named after him (Rev. Father Smith *History of Nelson District 1922*). Although etymology can be a somewhat inexact exercise it is, nevertheless, interesting to see the possibilities in the Old English place-names, and the names of the local farmsteads, in relation to a monastic origin:

- **Haddings**
    Hàdung – consecration or ordination
    Hàd – holy order of office

- **Cappers (Farm)**
    Capellan – chaplain
    Cappa – cæpe – hooded one

- **Saddlers (Farm)**
    Sæd – arable
    Sæt – land holding

- **Tinedale (Farm)**
    After the Tindall family?
    Tinæn – up against (the ridge?)

- **Sabden**
    Scæp – sheep (monastic?)

- **Spen**
    Fibre (wool/cloth)

- **Lowerhouses Farm**
    Formerly had two or three (monastic?) fishponds on the Far Shaw fields

A local farmer reports that he uncovered circular stone foundations in the corner of a field between Bull Hole Farm and Saddlers Farm - a possible Saxon period, or earlier, dwelling? Also, an ancient road known as Watery Lane leads from the hillfort at Portfield (Whalley) through Sabden Fold and on to a river ford at Thorneyholme (Roughlee) known as *Wattlingford* (a name we see in the Roman *Wattling Street*). It has long been considered locally that this roadway acted as a 'coffin route' for carrying the deceased of Pendle Forest directly to Whalley Abbey.

Admittedly, place-name evidence in this case is not strong enough to prove that the was an abbey grange but there is here, at least, a suggestion in favour. Did the font originally reside in a now lost chapel at Sabden Fold - or was it secretly used in the act of Catholic mass at Lowerhouses Farm following the Dissolution? Alternatively, could the object actually be a mortarium from the Romano-British period?

Fig: P185

A Roman stone mortarium of similar size to the Lowerhouses 'font'. This example was used in an Italian olive press

Fig: P185a

The Lowerhouse object: was this a Medieval or Tudor font or did it serve as an earlier mixing bowl (mortarium)?

When looking at the Shelfield Hill area it was suggested that the many of the modern farmsteads we see today are actually located on, or near to, very early farming sites. It seems fair to say that we could also be witnessing the same long continuity of landscape use within the Goldshaw district, alongside the Pendle Ridgeway.

Locally, the Pendle Ridgeway runs from the River Calder, at Read, and through the Forest of Pendle to its terminus at Blacko. We saw that the evidence for Mesolithic movement and settlement within Pendle Forest is minimal but, as the Neolithic period advanced, the area was being increasingly utilised. It was probably during this latter period of population expansion that the former ridge-top hunting track evolved into an internationally important trade route utilised for the movement of goods (and ideas) from the Atlantic seaboard of Ireland across the English mainland and on to the Baltic.

It appears from the evidence of bronze axes found at Read, Blacko and along through the Aire Gap into Yorkshire, that by the Bronze Age there was a well defined trade system operating through our district. Among other materials and goods there was an exchange of metals (gold, copper etc.) from Ireland, and high quality stone axes from Cumbria, across to the east coast ports north of the Humber and onto the Continent. Reverse trade saw the importation of exotics such as Baltic amber, crystal beads and Whitby jet. Goods destined for the east coastal ports south of the Humber were probably taken along the Pendle Ridgeway as far as Padiham where the track branched south-eastward through Burnley, along the Long Causeway into Calderdale.

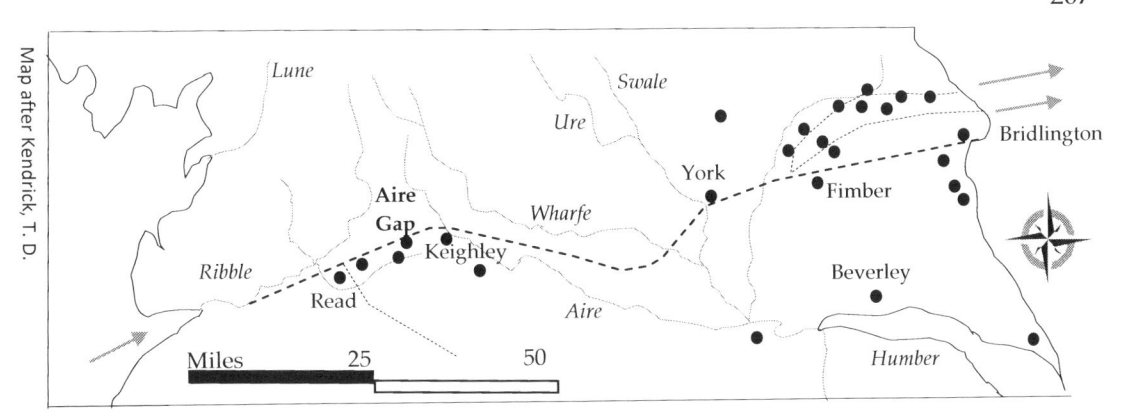

Fig: 186   *Sketch map of trade route between Ireland and Scandinavia*   ● *Flat bronze axes*

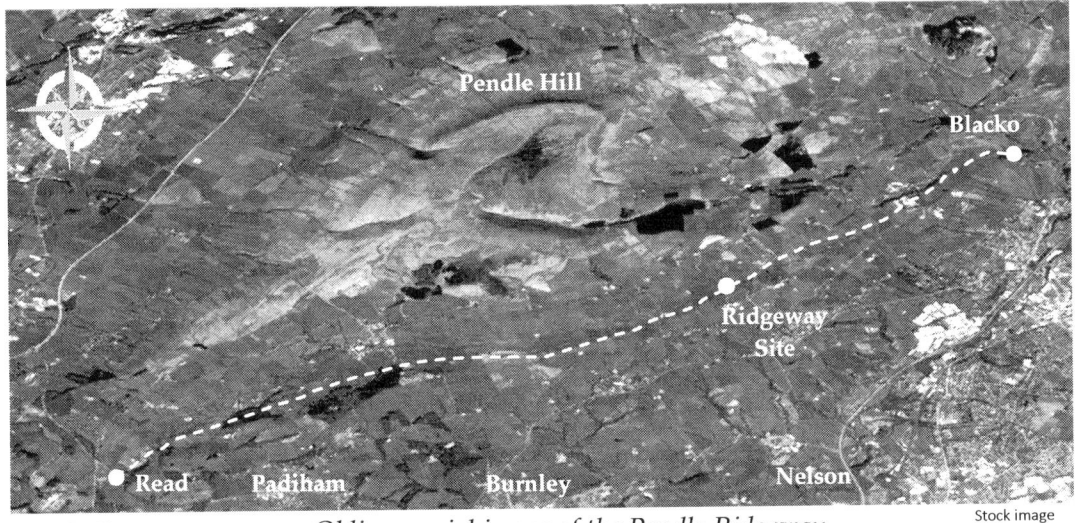

Fig: P187   *Oblique aerial image of the Pendle Ridgeway*

Fig: P188

Lowerhouses, Sabden Fold - a late 16th century building, historically the home of the Nutter family

The house may occupy the site of an earlier monastic grange

Neolithic and Early Bronze Age: Discussion

Although the Neolithic period heralded important changes within the lifestyle of the British populace, the same cannot be said of the dawning of the Bronze Age. The Early Bronze Age was very much a continuation in cultural practice of the Late Neolithic and, for this reason, both periods have been covered together in the text.

The northward spread of Neolithic ideas did not happen overnight, our subject area assimilated the new culture at a later date than did the southern districts. However, by 3,200 BC we see that there were distinct changes in the archaeological record across the whole of the British Isles. Settled farming practice had become firmly embedded in the new lifestyle by this time but a new stability was becoming apparent, probably due to an increasingly developing social hierarchy. Social elites were evident within societies and a new type of ceremonial monument appeared in the landscape. The elongated mounds of the early Neolithic gave way to an expression of circularity; ringworks, in the form of circular ditched henges and stone circles, spread across the land and round barrows were increasingly built to house individual burials.

As the Neolithic advanced the ancient art of stone implement manufacture began to deteriorate. Long distance trade in lithic materials appears to have dwindled, leading to a more localised sourcing of flint and stone - the quality of manufacture also declined and this carried through into the Bronze Age.

The use of metals increased through the Late Neolithic; copper was utilised for tools and weapons across a wide geographic area but, to the majority of people, this would have been a somewhat exotic (and expensive) commodity. Timbers at the Kates Pad trackway, near Pilling, display chopping marks from a form of metal axe and this is evidence for the use of metal woodworking tools having been used in Lancashire around 2,300 BC. Actual evidence for early bronze tools in Lancashire is provided by a few flat axes dated to 1,740-1,640 cal BC (Middleton, R. *The Archaeology of Lancashire* Lancaster University 1996).

Stone cairns and round barrows were being erected across the country from 2,500BC to 1,600 BC. Today, most of the barrows and stone cairns are to be found in the relatively undisturbed upland areas; although a number of lowland barrows can still be recognised the majority have been built over, ploughed level with the ground or bulldozed in the interests of modern farming. Nowhere is this clearer than in our Survey area of Burnley and Boulsworth where we see that evidence for our Stone Age ancestors within the river valleys has, by and large, been destroyed.

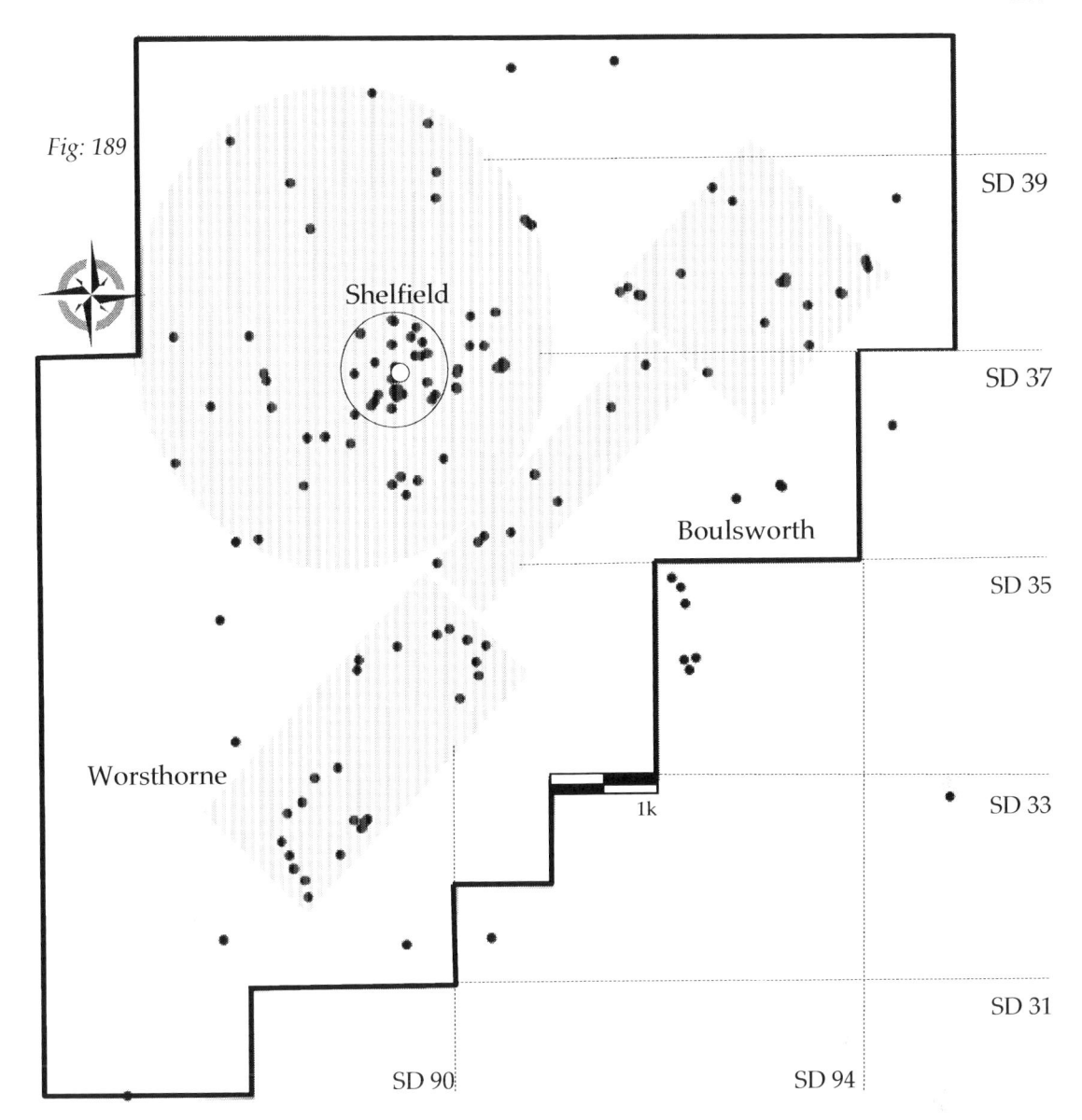

CIRCULAR NEOLITHIC AND BRONZE AGE MOUND AND RINGWORK DISTRIBUTION ACROSS THE BNC SURVEY AREA

Fig: 189 illustrates the distribution of circular mound and ringwork features apparent in 1m LiDAR and aerial images. A dozen of the features are known burial mounds and earthworks but the remainder are elements within the landscape conforming to acceptable archaeological criteria relating to Neolithic and Bronze Age monuments. The shaded areas represent grouping and direction of site clusters while the inner circle defines a circular group of features with the proposed site of the lost Ringstone Hill circle at at its centre.

Circular Feature Distribution with Neolithic Find-sites Overlaid

● *Circular feature* ○ *Neolithic finds*

There are a handful of sites where Late Neolithic finds overlay circular features.

The majority of Neolithic sites halt their northward spread at Boulsworth Hill while the possible Bronze Age mounds and ringworks are scattered across the lower ground and also respect Boulsworth Hill

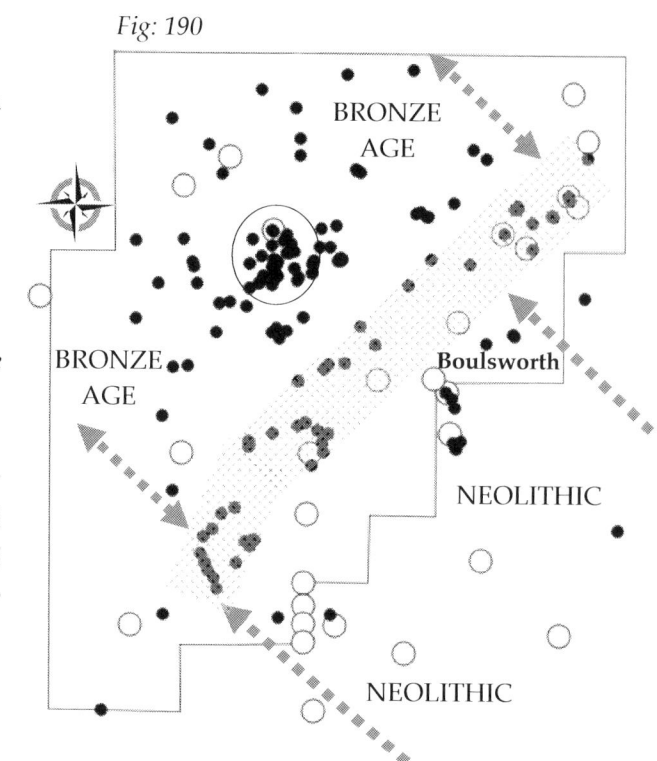

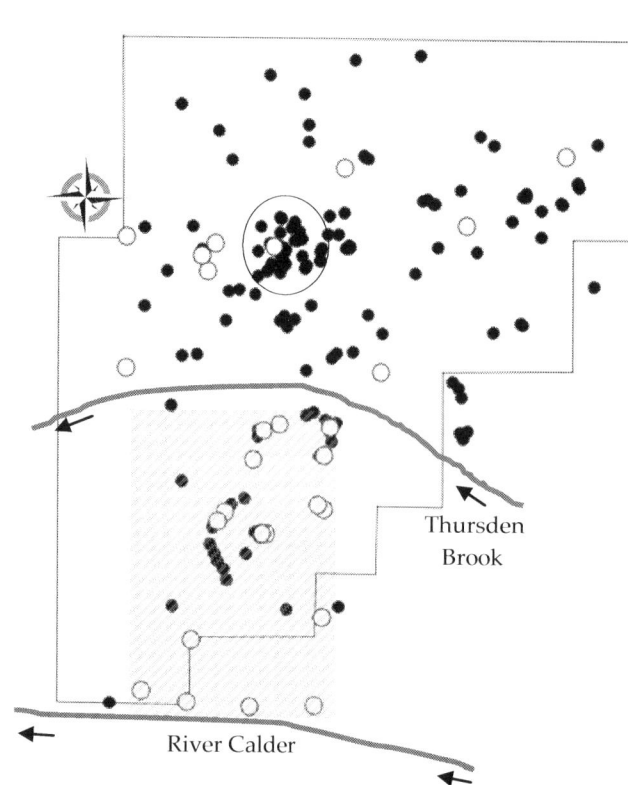

Fig: 190

Fig: 191

Circular feature distribution with Bronze Age find site overlay

● *Mound or ringwork*

○ *Bronze Age site*

Bronze Age find sites form a defined cluster between the River Calder (Cliviger) and the Thursden Valley. There are twice the amount of sites to the south of Thursden Valley as there are to the north.

Conversely there are 75% more circular features to the north than to the south

Fig:192

● Stone   ○ Circular feature

The circular area incorporates the majority of circular features to the north of Thursden. It also contains most of the extant stone monuments within the BCN Survey

It is perhaps of significance that at the centre of this grouping is the Shelfield Hill menhir (arrowed)

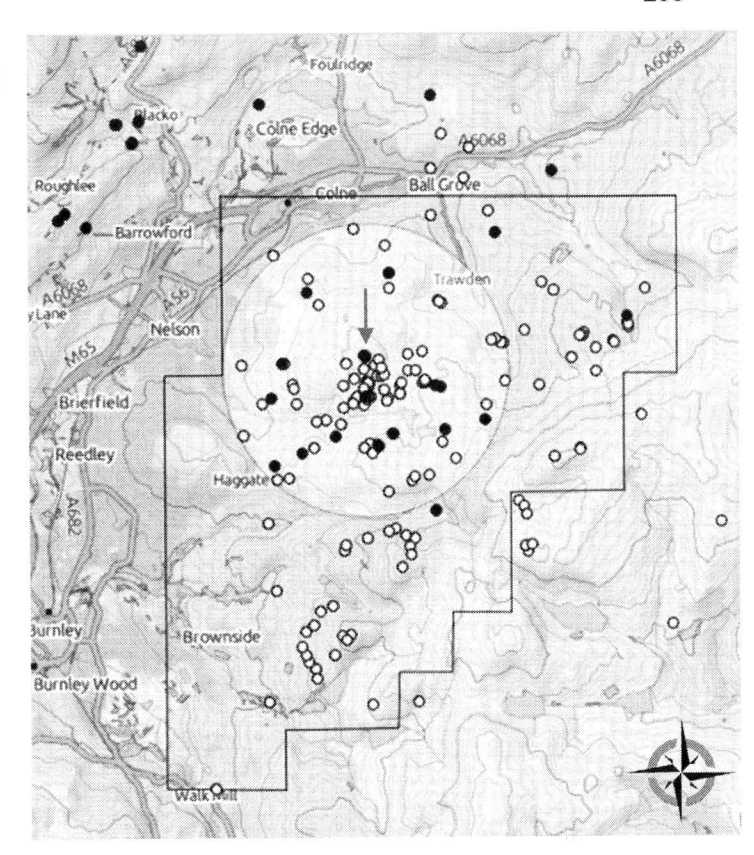

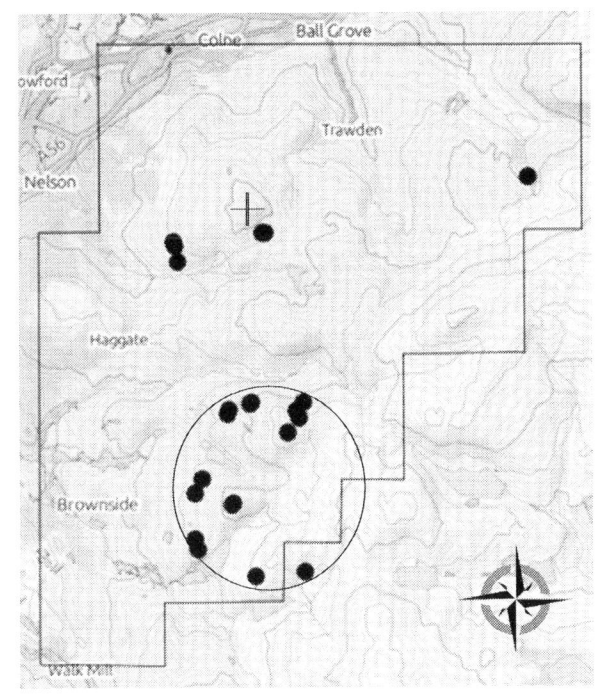

Fig: 193

Burial mounds, ringworks and cairns isolated from the circular feature distribution (Figs: 189-192)

It is clear that the Worsthorne and Extwistle moors contain the majority of <u>known</u> burials within the Survey area (circled)

There is the question, however, as to how many of the other circular features apparent in Figs: 189-192 are actually unrecognised burial monuments?

Palaeolithic to Early Bronze Age Discussion

Of the hundreds of sites recorded in the Lancashire Sites and Monuments Record (LSMR), and the Heritage Environment Record (HER), the Burnley and Pendle district contains only around 3% of sites predating 1,500 AD. This is further reduced when the Roman and Medieval records are taken into account and so we see that the corpus relating to our local prehistory is somewhat scant.

Much of the evidence for the lives of our East Lancashire forebears, in the form of flint tools and weapons, urn burials, coins and metal artefacts were discovered by antiquarians in the eighteenth and nineteenth centuries and this has formed our view of the past ten millennia within the Pendle and Boulsworth districts. However, archaeology has changed a great deal over the past fifty years and, although many of these changes have been slow to arrive in our quiet neck of the woods, we are now making progress.

It is now recognised that the great period of monument construction that lasted through the Neolithic, and into the Bronze Age, left many indelible markers within the landscape and, where we have the wit to understand them, these features have much to relate from the depths of prehistory. In many cases the story that unfolds is one of successive cultures whose outlook on life and death was often far more dynamic than might have been expected when some archaeologists considered them to have been peopled by *'capering ninnies covered in woad.'* Burial monuments were reused over the long periods of the Bronze and Neolithic and this practice was revived when the Anglo-Saxons buried their dead in a secondary context within prehistoric mounds and cemeteries.

The Late Upper Palaeolithic period saw nomadic groups emerging within the British record and this accelerated through the Mesolithic. In many ways the succeeding Neolithic period was a time when huge changes laid down the foundations of our modern world - when humans ceased to be a reactionary force and took control of their environment. The cultural change-over from the Mesolithic to the Neolithic did not happen overnight, nor was there a simple process of neat transition from area to area, south to north. Alison Sheridan argues that Neolithic practice sprang up in sites in the distant north of Britain hundreds of years before the new culture arrived in the south-east of England (Sheridan, A. *The Neolithisation of Britain and Ireland: The Big Picture* in Finlayson, B. & Warren, G. (eds.) *Landscapes in Transition* Oxbow 2010). Sheridan further argues that small pioneering groups of Neolithic farmers travelled to Britain from Brittany, Normandy and Nord-Pas de Calais to establish communities on the west coast of Ireland and on the Lancashire and North Welsh coast in 4,300 and 3,800 BC.

The new settlers erected large rectangular houses (possibly as base settlements) they buried their dead in timber monuments (these were later built of stone) and covered them in long mounds of earth so as to mark their new territorial 'rights.' By 3,800 BC the new farmers had settled the east and northern coasts of Ireland, the Lancashire coast, the south and east coasts of England, the east coast of Scotland and around the Bristol Channel. Slowly but surely the new culture gained a foothold within the indigenous Mesolithic communities and the early Neolithic scatter eventually coalesced into a common agricultural practice across the Isles.

As the Late Neolithic dawned people continued to hone their settled way of life; hunting and gathering still took place (albeit within a decreasing spatial resource) but a settled base, of sorts, meant that roots were being put down and the beginnings of territorial belonging ensued. The dead were increasingly buried within landscape monuments, such as stone cairns, chambered tombs and long barrows. Here we see a commitment of a once-nomadic culture to a new life - the ancestors were now buried in communal features and could be visited all year round, rather than in specific seasons when the hunter gatherer groups were once again in the vicinity of the ancestral grave.

The ritual deposition of metalwork within special areas of the landscape furthered the commitment of the new settlers to their patch of land and this engendered a sense of identity that would become fixed over succeeding generations. The creation of burial monuments, and other ritual 'machines' such as stone circles, provided a fixed sense of 'ownership' of the land - interlopers would be given short shrift when the settlers were able to provide hard evidence, in the form of a cairn or barrow, that their ancestors had been residing on their land for a very long time.

The nomadic lifestyle of the Mesolithic did not require a particular notion of the passing of time, other than on a seasonal basis. However, settled farming practice brought with it a heightened sense of the past. Investment in the land meant that generations of the community became part of the landscape. Also, settled farming required an investment in time in as much as the breeding of suitable livestock took years to accomplish, as did the intake and cultivation of arable land.

Here, then, we see the modern concept of time in that the past is often venerated as 'the good old days.' Especially in times of conflict and uncertainty a settled society finds comfort in looking back over its past successes. Thus the British have traditionally digested the tales of chivalry and courage dished up by Victorian authors - the stories of King Arthur and his retinue of knights remains a firm favourite. Folklore is a good example of this fascination with the 'olden days' from whence an ancient British hero will emerge to save the nation in times of dire threat. Locally, this is illustrated by the story that *'a great king sleeps beneath Boulsworth Hill, ready to emerge when the nation needs him.'* A similar story relates to the Worsthorne area where *'five kings lie buried'* - although this might have a basis in truth if relating to the local Bronze Age burials.

* * * * * *

On a localised level, it is fair to say that the first pioneers who began to explore the post-Devensian Ice Age landscapes of Burnley and Pendle did so in a somewhat transitory manner. The flora and fauna amid the glacier-scrubbed hills and valleys had not yet fully adapted to the new conditions and the small hunter-gathering parties found it necessary to cover large areas in search of food.

Ebbing and flowing across the Doggerland plains, between Britain and the Continent, the Palaeolithic people *reacted* to their environment and, therefore, they left very little trace within the archaeological record. It is probable that transient Palaeolithic camps lay buried deep beneath the peat covering of Boulsworth Hill and from these sites the hunters would have followed the movement of game animals and visited the surrounding rivers of Wycoller Beck, the Calder, the Brun and Colne Water on foraging trips before silently drifting onward to their next day's shelter.

The two thousand year period following the final retreat of the ice-sheets saw a new 'permanence' whereby forest and scrubland colonised the hillsides of Boulsworth and Pendle. Animals, birds and fish proliferated and the hunter-gatherer was able to establish fixed routes between the best hunting grounds. The small nomadic communities were now manipulating the landscape (albeit on a micro level); they cleared the scrub from around their camps in order to attract game and they managed small areas for the growing of certain plants and herbs. More time was being spent in each camp and this allowed for a greater knowledge of local resources such as timber, minerals, tool and weapon manufacturing materials, water sources, plants, animals and birds.

Gradually the British population of the nomadic Palaeolithic culture began to expand through the Isles and separate communities looked upon favoured areas of the lansdcape as having been their 'own.' They would not have considered that they 'owned' the land in the way that modern society recognises the individual ownership of land - rather, the people had invested their sweat, blood and tears into the land, their ancestors lay buried within it and this gave them a sense of belonging.

As the last of the Palaeolithic people succumbed to the fancy new foreign tool making methods of the Mesolithic so the old ways of drifting through the landscape began to change. The Mesolithic people developed the practises of small-scale husbandry and stock-keeping within their encampment areas - a sense of belonging became ever-more fixed within their nomadic psyche. And so we see the evidence for this on the slopes of Boulsworth Hill where flint manufacturing sites indicate the presence of camps that would have been occupied for longer than just a fleeting visit.

Small transient camps have also been found across the Worsthorne moors, on the Boulsworth plain and near to Beaver Farm where Mesolithic people, and their Neolithic successors, were camping on the lower ground near to former routeways. These areas can now be described as the 'back of beyond' but in prehistoric times were populated areas alongside relatively busy roads.

We have seen that the new settlers from the Continent, who arrived in Ireland and on the Lancashire coast around 3,800 BC, began to spread their message of 'modern' agriculture. Eventually the spatially static Neolithic way of life had been absorbed across the Isles and, locally, the upland settlements of Calderdale, Burnley and Pendle were gradually abandoned in favour of the lower lying plains around Worsthorne and to the south of Colne. Before the Neolithic period the district covered by the Medieval Forest of Pendle had contributed very little to the archaeological record. However, a marked upturn of sites becomes apparent within the Early Neolithic, especially along the route of the Pendle Ridgeway. This can be seen as an illustration that the settled Neolithic communities were now trading over long distances - living and working on the line of an important trade route would then have been advantageous.

The Early Bronze Age people expanded the Late Neolithic settlement pattern and we see the resultant increase in their funerary monuments within the landscape of today - indeed, it is certain that we are aware of only a small number of such features. Many have been destroyed by the plough but others, although often greatly denuded by the weight of age, are still awaiting our recognition.

Prehistoric Enclosures within the BNC Survey

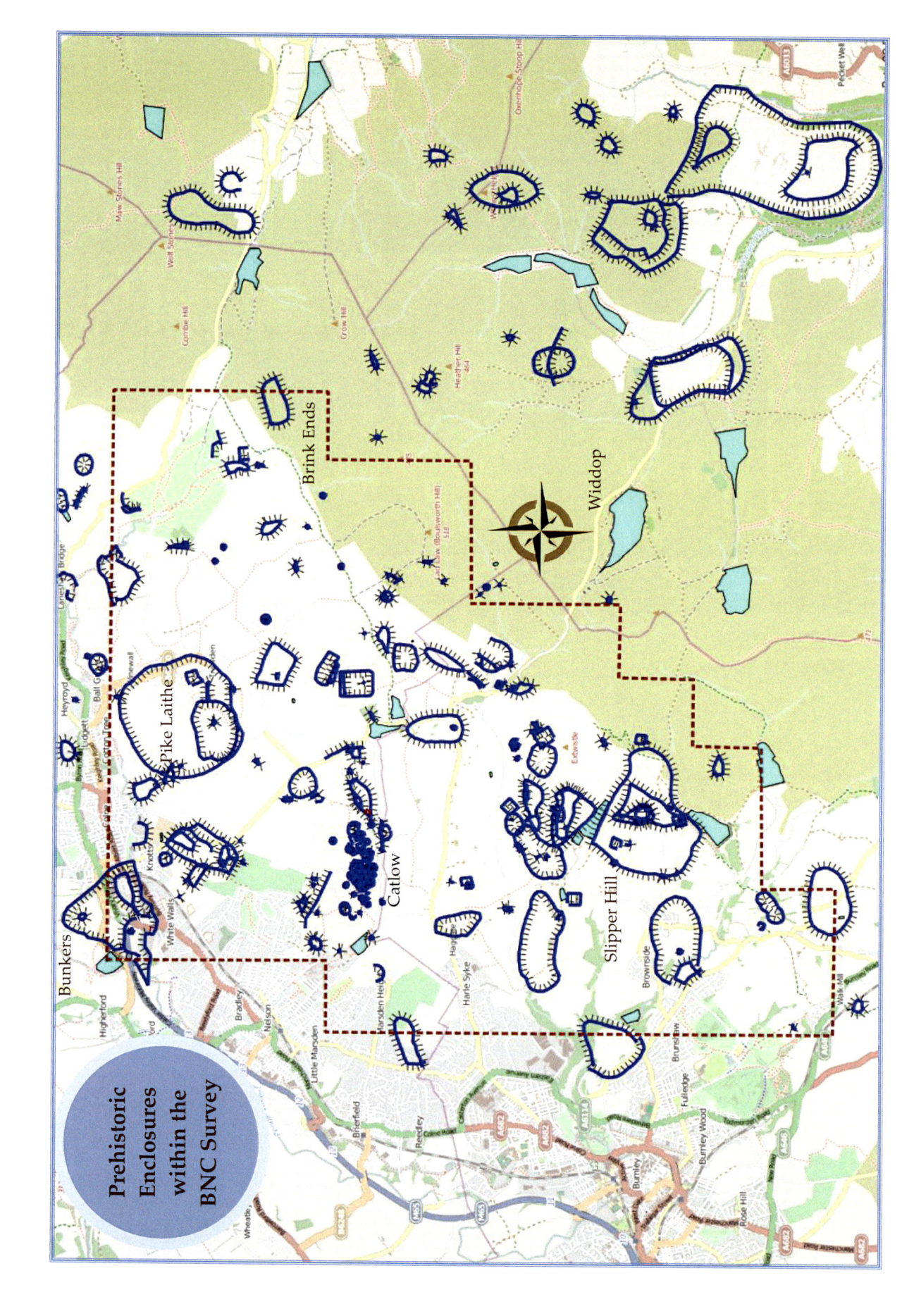

COLNE

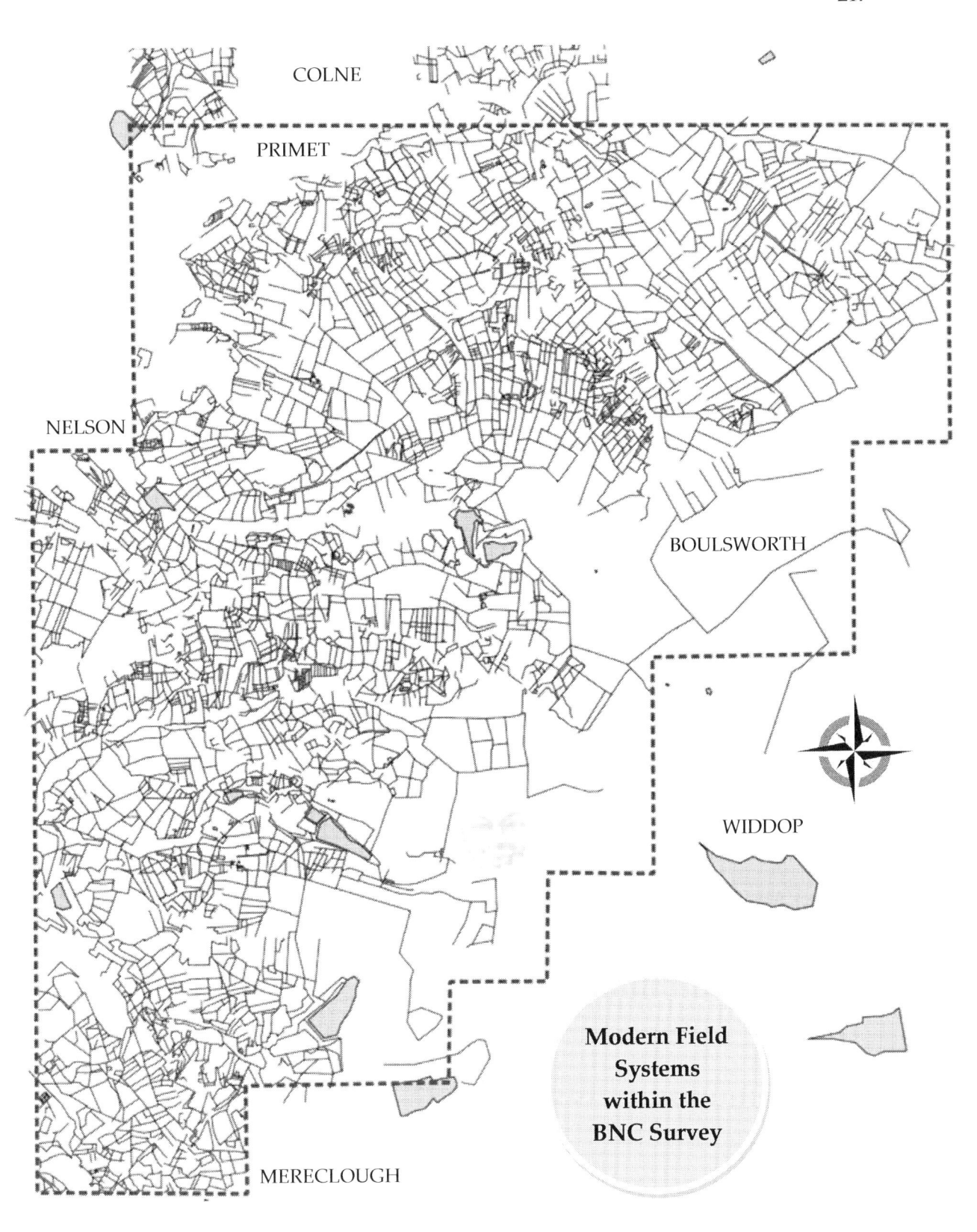

PRIMET

NELSON

BOULSWORTH

WIDDOP

Modern Field Systems within the BNC Survey

MERECLOUGH

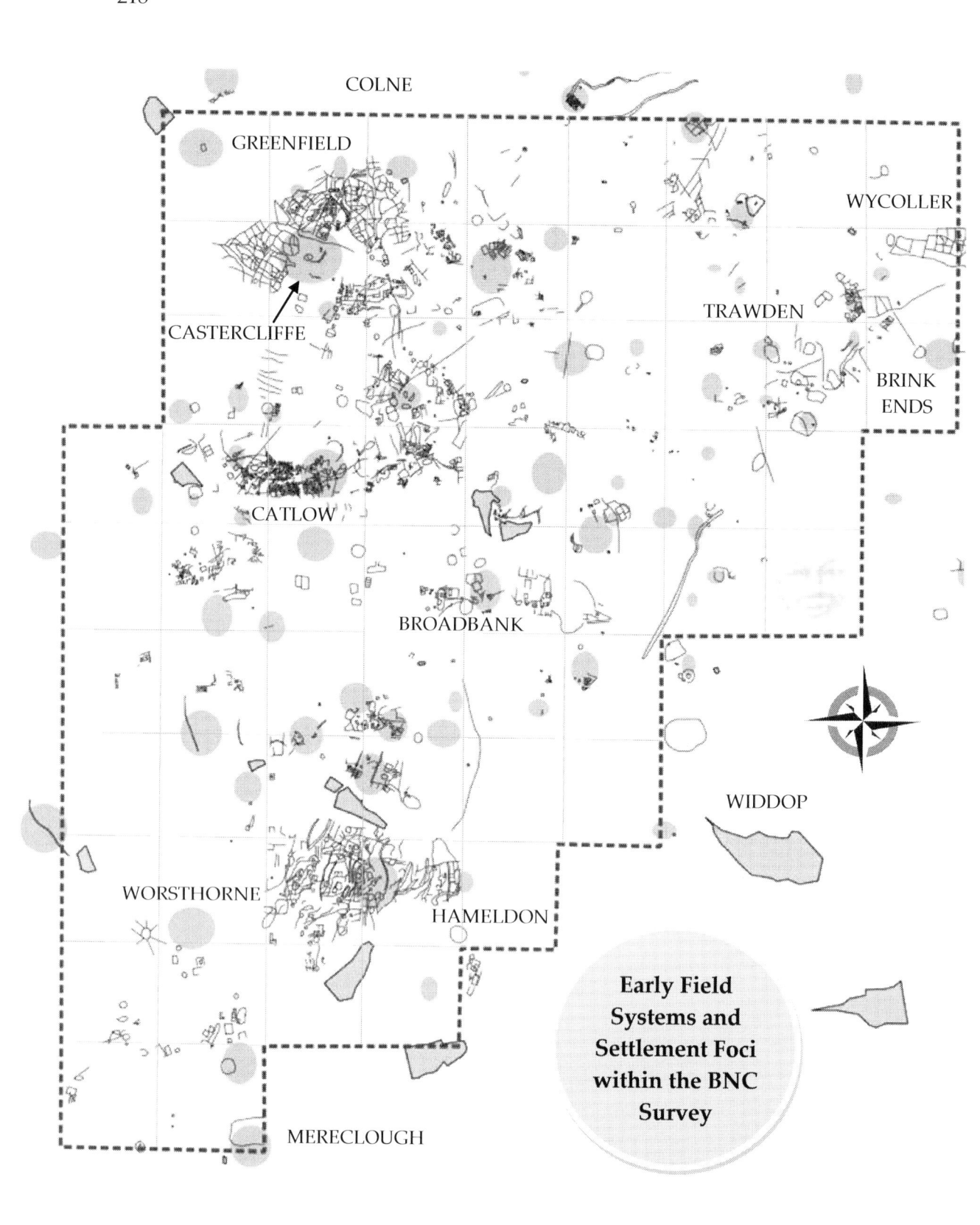

Early Field Systems and Settlement Foci within the BNC Survey

219

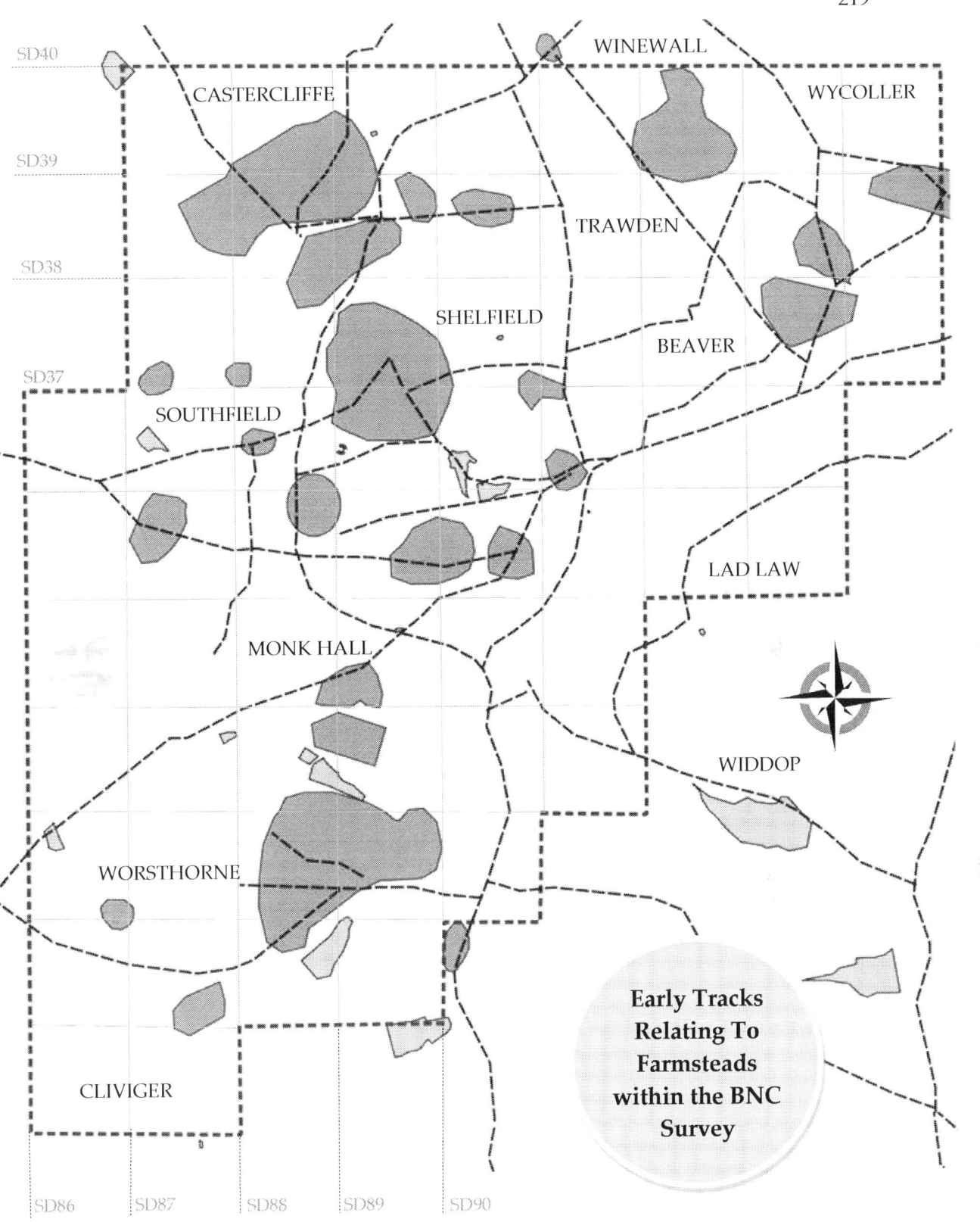

CASTERCLIFFE
WINEWALL
WYCOLLER
TRAWDEN
SHELFIELD
BEAVER
SOUTHFIELD
LAD LAW
MONK HALL
WIDDOP
WORSTHORNE
CLIVIGER

Early Tracks Relating To Farmsteads within the BNC Survey

BIBLIOGRAPHY

Bagley and Hodgkiss *A History of the County Palatine in Early Maps* Richardson 1985
Bailey, G. & Spikins, P. *Mesolithic Europe* Cambridge University Press 2008
Barrett J.C. and Kinnes I.A. eds. *The Archaeology of Context in the Neolithic and Bronze Age: Recent Trends* University of Sheffield 1988
Barrowclough, D. *Prehistoric Lancashire* History Press 2008
Barton, R. & Roberts, A. *The Mesolithic Period in England* 2004
Bell, M. and Walker, M. *Late Quaternary Environmental Change: Physical and Human Perspectives* 2005
Bennett, W. *The History of Burnley* Vol. 1 Burnley Corporation 1946
Bennett, W. *The History of Marsden and Nelson* Nelson Corporation 1957
Bentley, J. *Portrait of Wycoller* Nelson Local History Society 1975
Berger, R. *Radio Carbon Dating* Paper California Press 1979
Blakey, J. *The Annals and Stories of Barrowford* 1929 Reprint - Barrowford Press 2013
Booth, T. *Ancient Grave Mounds on the Slopes of the Pennine Range* Todmorden Advertiser 1899
Bradley, R. *The Social Foundations of Prehistoric Britain: Themes and Variations in the Archaeology of Power* Longman Group 1984
Bradley, R. *The Prehistory of Britain and Ireland* Cambridge University Press 2007
Brown, I. *Beacons in the Landscape* Oxbow 2009
Brown, P. *Megaliths, Myths and Men* 1976

Carr, J. *Annals of Colne* 1878
Carr-Gomm, P. *The Druid Tradition* Element 1991
Chadwick, A. M. *The Iron Age and Romano-British Periods in West Yorkshire* WYAAS 2009
Clayton, J. A. *The Valley of the Drawn Sword* Barrowford Press 2006
Clayton, J. A. *Admergill with Blacko and Brogden* Barrowford Press 2011
Cole A. & Gelling M. *The Landscape of Place-names* Shaun Tyas 2000).
Cookson, S. & Hindle, H. *Wycoller Country Park* Hindle Colne 1985

Dawkins, R. *The Selfish Gene* Harper Collins 1978

Ekwall E. *The Place-Names of Lancashire*, Manchester University Press 1922

Fagan, B. *From Black Land to Fifth Sun* Addison Wesley 1998
Farrar, W. *Clitheroe Court Rolls - Vols 1 / 2 / 3* 1912

Goldhahn. J. *From Monuments to Landscape to Landscapes in Monument* 2006

Hambleton, E. *Animal Husbandry Regimes in Iron Age Britain* Oxford: Archaeopress 1999
Hamilton, S. Manley, J. *Prominent Enclosures in 1st Millennium Sussex* Sussex Archaeological Collections 1997

Harding, A. F. *European Society in the Bronze Age* Cambridge University Press 2000
Harrison, D. ed. *The History of Colne* Pendle Heritage Centre 1988
Hind, D. *Chert Use in the Mesolithic* PaperHodgson, J. & Brennand, M. *Prehistoric Period Resource Assessment* Archaeology North West Vol. 8 Issue 18 2006
Howarth, M. *An Investigation Into the Late Neolithic and Early Bronze Age Round Barrow Monuments in the Wylye Valley* - Thesis - Birmingham University 2009/10
Hutton, R. *The Pagan Religions of the British Isles*. 1991

James, S. and Rigby, V. *Britain and the Celtic Iron Age* British Museum Press 1997
Jones, R. T. Paper Department of Geography, University of Exeter 2009

Kendrick, T. ed. *The Archaeology of Yorkshire* 1932
King, D. J. C *Castellarium Anglicanum* 1983

Levine, P. *The Amateur and the Professional - Antiquarians, Historians and Archaeologists 1838-1886* Cambridge University Press 1986

Masefield R. et al. *A Later Bronze Age Well Complex at Swalecliffe* Antiquaries Journal 83, 47-121
McDevitte, W. A. and Bohn, W. S. *Julius Caesar - The Gallic Wars V*, translation
Middleton, R. *The Archaeology of Lancashire* Lancaster University 1996
Moorhouse, C. *Sabden* 1978

Physical Geography A review of the Mid-Holocene Elm Decline in the British Isles Progress in March 2002 vol. 26 no. 1 1-45
Preston, P. *Mesolithic Central Pennines* Oxford University thesis 2012

Ridderstad, M. *Orientation of the Northern Gate of the Goseck Neolithic Rondel* University of Helsinki Observatory Paper 2010
Schulting, R *What The Bones Say*: Oxford Lecture 2007
Sheridan, A. *The Neolithisation of Britain and Ireland: The Big Picture* in Finlayson, B. & Warren, G. (eds.) *Landscapes in Transition* Oxbow 2010
Smith, C. *Late Stone Age Hunters of the British Isles* Routledge 1992
Smith, Rev. *History of Nelson District* 1922
Spikins, P. *Palaeolithic and Mesolithic West Yorkshire* Paper
Steensberg, A. *Some recent Danish Experiments in Neolithic Agriculture* 1956

Yates, D. *Prehistoric and Roman Landscapes* Windgather Press 2007

Warner, J. H. *The History of Barnoldswick* 1934
Whitaker, T. D. *History of Whalley* 1801

INDEX

Admergill *161,*
Axe (metal) *126, 206, 207, 208, 209*
Axe (stone) *47, 55, 63, 86, 103, 116, 117, 118, 119, 120, 121, 122, 124, 191,*

Barrows *112, 113, 124, 125, 127, 128, 148, 172, 185, 186, 191, 208, 212*
Barrowford *52, 92, 120, 160,*
Beaker People *125, 126, 127, 128,*
Beardshaw *162*
Beaver *89, 93, 95, 154,*
Blacko *92, 129, 145, 157, 158, 159, 160, 161, 172, 191, 206*
Boulsworth (Hill) *12, 13, 15, 16, 19, 20, 21, 22, 31, 32, 47, 49, 50, 53, 55, 56, 57, 58, 59, 62, 64, 66, 83, 84, 85, 86, 87, 88, 93, 96, 120, 130, 131, 132, 141, 142, 146, 147, 148, 150, 154, 173, 209, 210*
Briercliffe *32, 172, 177, 191*
Brink Ends *19, 20, 22, 95,*
Broadbank (Thursden) *191*

Castercliffe *15, 24, 60, 93, 94, 131, 132, 133, 152, 162, 165, 174, 189*
Catlow *16, 132, 170, 171, 172, 178, 180, 183, 189*
Catlow Bottoms *170, 178, 180, 189*
Celts *40, 123*
Colne *15, 19, 20, 30, 31, 32, 84, 85, 88, 94, 103, 124, 132, 138, 141*
Crawshaw Hill *177, 178*

Delf Hill *191,*
Druids *22*

Extwistle (Moor) *22, 64, 97, 115, 122, 211*

Flint (scatter sites) *54, 62, 80, 96, 122, 174*
Float Bridge *132, 149, 170, 171, 172, 173, 175, 180, 189, 190*

Hameldon (Hill & Moor) *22, 50, 154, 192*
Hillfort *15, 25, 39, 60, 94, 115, 132, 133, 141, 152, 162, 165, 170, 177, 178, 180, 205*

Knave Hill *130, 149, 150, 151, 173, 180, 189*

Marsden (Nelson) *140, 141, 179*

Mire Ridge *162, 165, 170, 172, 173, 174, 1801, 182, 184*
Monk Hall *172, 174, 177, 183*

Nelson *15, 19, 20, 24, 30, 32, 84, 88, 94, 109, 123, 130, 131, 132, 140, 170, 179, 191*

Pendle Hill *10, 49, 52, 94, 129, 134, 147, 150, 207*
Pendle Ridgeway *52, 129, 145, 155, 156, 158, 191, 192, 193, 201, 206, 207*

Read *129, 206, 207*
Ribble, River *20, 64, 70, 92, 141, 207*
Ringstone Hill (Nelson) *170, 171, 172, 173, 175, 177, 178, 179, 180, 181, 183, 184, 189, 190, 191, 209*
Ringstone Hill (Blacko) *156, 160, 191*
Ringstones (Worsthorne) *191*
Roman (stations) *141*
Roughlee *120, 160, 205*

Shelfield Hill *109, 130, 131, 132, 133, 134, 135, 136, 137, 138, 139, 145, 146, 147, 148, 149, 150, 151, 152, 153, 161, 165, 170, 171, 172, 177, 180, 183, 184, 189, 190, 206, 211*
Silbury Hill *14, 142*
Slipper Hill (Worsthorne) *154, 191*

Thursden *19, 20, 93, 97, 98, 138, 139, 141, 148, 168, 179, 210, 211*
Todmorden *13, 20, 74, 77, 85, 140*
Townhouse (Nelson) *135, 179*
Trawden *19, 21, 55, 95, 103, 132, 141, 148, 160, 162, 165, 173*
Twist Hill *191*

Walton Spire *15, 130, 131, 133, 134, 152, 153, 179*
Watermeetings (Barrowford/Blacko) *52, 92, 157, 191, 195*
Waterside (Colne) *132*
Wessex *128, 170*
Widdop *20, 22, 30, 32, 62, 63, 75, 87, 93, 98, 122*
Will Moor (and Will O' Moor Road) *21, 22, 62, 89, 93, 95, 96, 155, 160*
Winewall *19, 162, 173, 174, 184*
Worsthorne *15, 22, 30, 32, 55, 64, 74, 75, 87, 88, 93, 97, 115, 122, 123, 127, 129, 140, 152, 154, 191, 209, 211*
Wycoller *16, 19, 20, 21, 32, 85, 88, 89, 93, 138*

OTHER TITLES BY THE SAME AUTHOR

Valley of the Drawn Sword
Early History of Burnley, Pendle and West Craven
ISBN 978-0-9553821-0-9 2006

The Lancashire Witch Conspiracy (1ST and 2nd editions)
A History of Pendle Forest and the Lancashire Witch Trials
ISBN 978-0-9553821-2-3 2007

Rolling Out the Days (editor)
From a Barrowford childhood to wartime Burma
ISBN 978-0-9553821-3-0 2007

Cotton and Cold Blood
A True Story of Victorian Life and Death in East Lancashire
ISBN 978-0-9553821-4-7 2008

Admergill with Blacko and Brogden
History and Archaeology of an Ancient Pennine Estate
ISBN 978-0-9553821-6-1 2009

Lower Barrowford 978-0-9553821-5-4 2009   **Central Barrowford** 978-0-9553821-7-8 2009
Local History Series
Higher Barrowford 978-0-9553821-8-5 2010   **Blacko** 978-0-9570043-0-6 2011

The Pendle Witch Fourth Centenary Handbook
History and Archaeology of a 1612 Landscape
ISBN 978-0-9553821-9-2 2012

The Other Pendle Witches
The Pendle Witch Trials of 1634
ISBN 978-0-9570043-2-0 2012

The Annals and Stories of Barrowford
(Republication of Blakey, J. 1929)
ISBN 978-0-9570043-1-3 2013

Burnley and Pendle Archaeology - Part Two
Middle Bronze Age to the Roman Conquest
ISBN 978-0-9570043-4-4 2014